Andrew Burian

A BOY FROM BUŠTINA
A Son. A Survivor. A Witness.

Andrew Burian

A BOY FROM BUŠTINA

A Son. A Survivor. A Witness.

Yad Vashem ★ Jerusalem
The International Institute for Holocaust Research

Andrew Burian
A Boy from Buština
A Son. A Survivor. A Witness.

Academic Editor: Naama Shick
Language & Production Editor: Gayle Green

ISBN 978-965-308-517-6

Second printing 2017

Typesetting: PageUp
Printed in Israel by Offset Nathan Shlomo Press

This memoir is dedicated to the loving memory of:
my dear mother
Matilda (Bruckstein) Brandstein,
who perished in Auschwitz-Birkenau.
I forever mourn the loss of my mother;
and
my extraordinary father and brother,
Ernest Burian and Tibor Burian,
who survived the Shoah together.
I miss them every day.

Contents

This is what happened to me.
This is what I saw.
There was not one Holocaust.
There were six million Holocausts.
I am witness.

— Andrew Burian

PROLOGUE

I am not a philosopher. I am not a historian. I am not even a writer. What I am, is a witness to the Holocaust. I have witnessed much. I have experienced much.

I was not always a witness. Once, I was even a child, but that did not last very long as I quickly became a subject of hatred and later a prisoner. "They" tried to turn me into an animal. "They" failed with me, but not with everyone. However, in the process, I became an orphan (or so I thought at the time), a killer, a displaced person and an immigrant. Today, I am a husband, brother, father, grandfather, great-grandfather and friend. Yet, people think of me as a "survivor." I am. I did. But for me, it is not enough just to survive. I must bear witness.

In 1948, at the age of seventeen and a half, when I first arrived in this wonderful, compassionate country of America, I encountered attitudes that were typical of the time. For instance, when I tried to speak about the Holocaust with the elderly Jewish couple from whom I rented a room in New York — a subject that I believed would be very near and dear to them — I was shocked at their reaction, "Oh yeah…yeah…we had it tough, too. Do you know that we had to stand in line for sugar? And meat was

9

sometimes scarce and sometimes not even available? We had those coupons you know...." I concluded then, falsely I might add, that there was nobody to talk to; that Americans with all their benevolence and their effort during and immediately following the war, reverted back to a narrow, cocoon-like perspective, busying themselves with the pursuit of their livelihood and the good life that this blessed nation provided. I did not think that anything I would have to say would interest anyone. I began to believe that people cared more about the slightest imposition to themselves and their pocketbooks than about one of the greatest, if not the greatest, catastrophes that had befallen mankind. This conclusion did not necessarily make me bitter, but it made me wary of people and negatively impacted my understanding of their motivations. While I am sure there were additional psychological reasons for my remaining silent, the negative reaction of people certainly was a contributing factor.

I did not speak much about the Holocaust throughout the years to anyone, not even to my children. My dear wife, Ruth, had gleaned bits and pieces of the story, which cumulatively gave her an incomplete understanding of my experiences. However, my children were the ones who made me understand that I had to end my withdrawal, and after fifty-one years of silence, I had to speak out. They argued against my silence by asking why their children should be denied knowing firsthand, from their grandfather, about the catastrophe that befell our dearest.

I gave their argument a great deal of thought and concluded that I did not need to have a special point of view or an astonishing revelation to bestow upon others, Rather, I had to speak out simply to convey my experiences. I had to stand as an eyewitness and give testimony to man's inhumanity to his fellow man. We, the survivors, are dying out and soon there will not be opportunities to hear from an eyewitness.

I have since spoken about my experiences at universities such as Yale, Princeton, Harvard, Liberty and Columbia; at the US Holocaust Memorial Council and Yad Vashem; as well as at many synagogues, schools and organizations. Great efforts are being made to collect eyewitness accounts for posterity and to make them available to all. My video testimony from February 1998 is available in the Fortunoff Video Archive for Holocaust Testimonies at Yale University, Yad Vashem Video Archives and the USC

Shoah Foundation; and an audio interview from July 1983 is available at the Museum of Jewish Heritage.[1]

This is my story. This is what happened to me. It happened to others too, but never in exactly the same way, nor has it affected their lives in the same way. Each experience is as unique as man himself, and because of this, I do not think that it was *a* Holocaust; rather, there were *six million* individual Holocausts. A Holocaust was perpetrated upon me as an individual; I was robbed of my childhood and I was wrenched from my mother's warm embrace. For what reason? What was it that I did? Why? Why?

As a child, I did not understand that which I have later learned to accept, namely that man can be a terrible and cruel being. I did not know to what extent he was capable of such cruelty. I had associated human beings with love, safety, goodness, warmth and understanding; my short, early childhood did not prepare me for the onslaught of bestiality that was in store for me.

At the same time, I wish to emphasize the universal positive lessons that have emerged from my ordeal. I deeply believe in the preciousness and sanctity of life. I believe in the unbreakable bonds of family. I came to learn what the body can endure when the mind has a goal. As you will read, there is always "just one more steeple" for a person to reach. My father, with his parting instructions, gave me a mission to survive. I could not let them make an animal out of me. I had to return home. There was no other choice. I learned that the darkest hours are followed by dawn. Life can be rebuilt. The "American dream" is real. And the Jewish people live on.

The Almighty, in His Torah (the Bible) that was given to the Israelites at Mount Sinai, commands us, *"Zachor et asher asa lecha Amalek..."* — Remember what the Amalekite nation did to us. (They attacked the nation of Israel from the rear, unprovoked, and killed the weak and the young.) We are further commanded, *"Lo tishkach!"* — Do not forget! We are to remember; we are not to forget. Our sages interpret this double,

---

1   To view Andrew Burian speaking at the Liberty University Convocation, 2014, go to: https://www.youtube.com/watch?v=oT7EhixkrUQ; USC Shoah Foundation interview: ps://www.youtube.com/watch?v=gD7fOf1kM1k   and   https://www.youtube.com/watch?v=VXQ3rB_JIXA (accessed, March 17, 2016); Yad Vashem Video Archives: O.93/38143.

seemingly redundant command, as follows: It is for us to remember and we are commanded to see to it that others do not forget. It is for these reasons that I wrench my guts and memory. This is why I bare my soul and deliver but an overview of my story. It is but an outline, considering that any particular day of this conflagration could fill the suffering of a lifetime.

I am what I am. I am an eyewitness. I am a survivor — against all odds. *I am a son, a survivor and a witness.* This, I submit, constitutes my credentials.

* * *

I wish to thank Yad Vashem for providing me with this extraordinary platform from which to share my story. Never in my wildest dreams did I believe that I would one day be published by such a preeminent institution. I wish to thank Judith Kern and Maya Maxym who each assisted on early drafts of the manuscript. Special thanks to Shaya Ben Yehuda (Managing Director of the International Relations Division) and to the Yad Vashem Publications team for their professional and attentive work. I also wish to acknowledge the American Society for Yad Vashem for their fabulous work on behalf of Holocaust remembrance and education under the strong leadership of Lenny Wilf (Chairman), Ron Meier (Executive Director) and Marlene Yahalom (Director of Education). My deepest appreciation goes to Gayle Green, my primary editor, who spent countless hours working with my son, Lawrence, on every aspect of this manuscript. She even helped sort through photographs and old documents and coordinated extensive historical fact-checking. And she did it all with a light touch and with respect for my voice.

I appreciated the suggestions of extended family and friends and for their help in supplying photographs, documents and support. I wish to thank Roberto Bruckstein, Oti Brandstein, Norbert Michael Stern and Juliana Boublil for their assistance in providing helpful information regarding our extended family. Also, Dr. Stanley Weiss for his tireless assistance with our family photos and documents. Thank you to the Allerhand, Boim, Wolf, Thorner, Anhalt, Brenner and Schainker families and my sister-in-law, Therese, for your love, friendship, respect and support. I am a very lucky man to have each of you in my life. I am grateful to my remarkable children, Matilda and Marvin, Saul and Jennifer and Lawrence and Adina who have virtually internalized my suffering, and sustain me with their love and compassion. My grandchildren Arielle and Adam, Daina, Kenny and Yael, Jordan, Atara, Michael, Mathew, Lauren, Jason, Jonah, Ethan, Adam and Erin and my great-granddaughter, Sydney, provide me with love, comfort, strength and confidence in the future.

My son, Lawrence, deserves special acknowledgment. He was relentlessly determined to see this book published and literally made it happen.

And finally, I thank my wife, Ruthie, the love of my life and my best friend. Writing this book took many years. Every time I began describing my last moments with my mother at Auschwitz I would break down and cry. I would stop writing for months. It was Ruthie who had to pick up the pieces. It was Ruthie who built me a home, gave me a family and takes care of my every need. I am eternally grateful.

— Andrew Burian

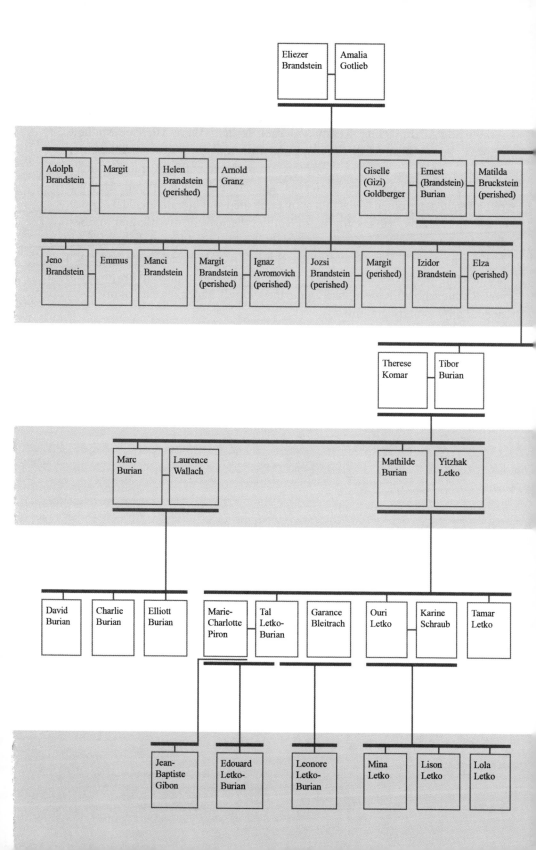

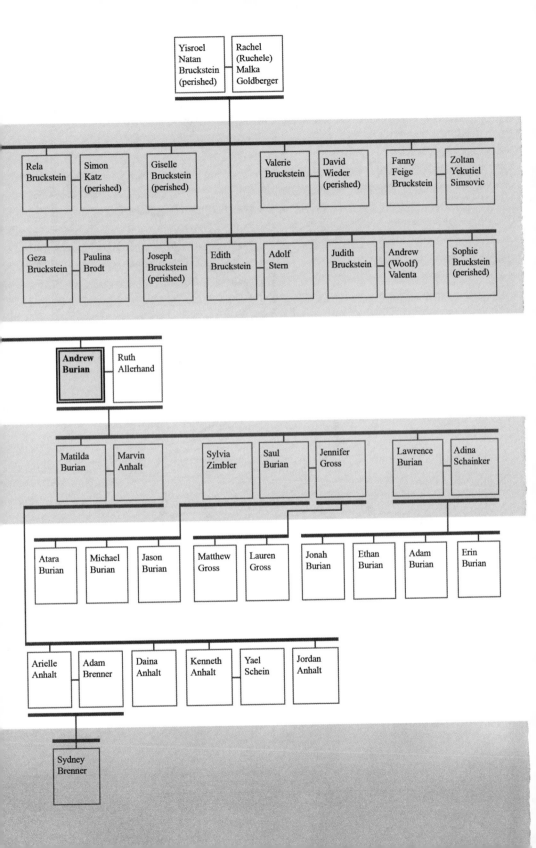

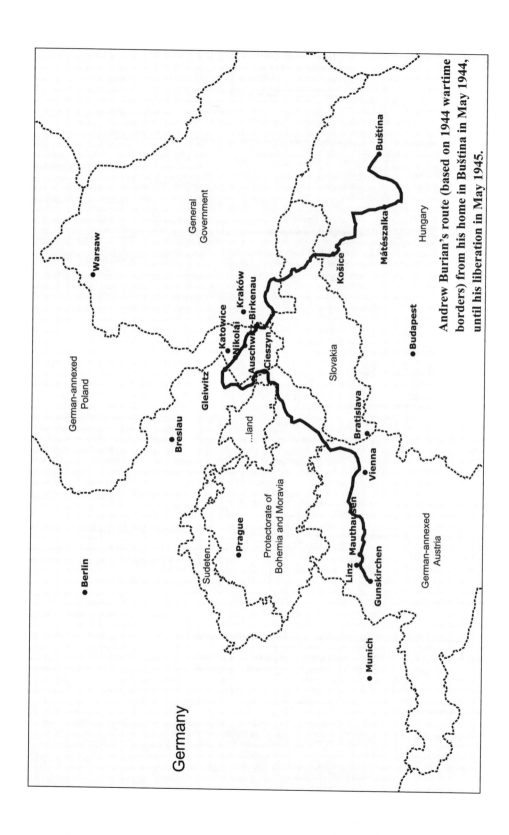

Germany

Berlin

Breslau

German-annexed
Poland

Warsaw

General
Government

Kraków

Katowice
Nikolai
Birkenau
Auschwitz
Cieszyn

Gleiwitz

...land

Sudeten...

Prague

Protectorate of
Bohemia and Moravia

Munich

Linz
Mauthausen
Gunskirchen

German-annexed
Austria

Bratislava

Vienna

Slovakia

Košice

Budapest

Hungary

Mátészalka

Buština

**Andrew Burian's route (based on 1944 wartime
borders) from his home in Buština in May 1944,
until his liberation in May 1945.**

PART I

AN IDYLLIC CHILDHOOD

SCHOOL PLAY

How wonderful it is to be a child, that is, if one is allowed to be one. Yes, once upon a time I was a child, a very happy child — but, alas, for a very short time. Every moment of the day brought new thrills and causes to delight my heart, and I still get a thrill every time a certain pleasant vignette from my childhood comes to mind — a day in school, 1938, when I was not yet eight years old.

The little, cluttered, windowless room behind the stage of our school auditorium was buzzing with the anxiety of the children cramped inside. There was pandemonium of the kind that only seven- to eight-year-old excited children can create and is difficult to imagine unless one has personally experienced it. Nevertheless, the thought of the havoc created when an anthill is kicked over and the ants run in panic, helter-skelter in all directions, would perhaps come as close as any other description.

Our grade of the local Czechoslovak public school was about to perform its school play. My best friend, Pepik, and I were prepping each other and were nervously adjusting and readjusting our uniforms. We went over our coordinated high steps that were befitting soldiers on parade, steps with which we were to enter the stage. Convinced that we would never get it right, we finally gave up and went on to practice the military parade maneuvers with our "weapons," maneuvers that we had been practicing for the last three weeks, but we gave up on that, too. Only our song had some redeeming features, if one discounts our voices and judges kindly from the perspective of a loved one! The rest of the performers were also fidgeting with their costumes and shrieking like geese at no one in particular. The teachers were busy with their futile attempt to make some kind of order of the chaos. The excitement reached a new crescendo when one of the teachers announced a final call for the bathroom. All of a sudden, half of my schoolmates, including Pepik, discovered that they had to go urgently.

Finally, the moment arrived as we heard our school principal announcing to the audience that the play was about to start. A hush like the calm before a storm descended upon the little room as if all the children suddenly became mute and frozen in their places. Pepik and I were the principal performers of the play and were slated to go on first. As the principal finished his opening remarks to the audience and left the stage, he broke our stunned silence by calling Pepik and me to the front of the room. As we attempted to comply with his command, a feeling of great trepidation and anxiety, the feeling of oncoming doom, gripped me. I was convinced that the audience would laugh at us. At this point, my heart began to race as I approached our principal, who nudged us from behind. I told him that I was ashamed, and I wished not to go on because we could not get it right. The principal grabbed us by the scruff of our necks and threw us onto the stage. We could hardly maintain our footing as we stumbled onto the stage, appearing to have fallen off the rafters. "We are forest rangers, state forest rangers, we have rifles and sharp daggers," Pepik and I sang as we proudly marched in military precision across the stage. We sang about the importance of nature and how we protected it. We were properly dressed up as forest rangers in green uniforms with leather straps suspending "daggers" from our belts. We had beautiful hand-carved "rifles" on our shoulders that we threateningly brandished as we sang, describing the duties of the forest rangers to protect the environment.

Thanks to the courtesy of the art classes, the stage was set with replicas of flowers, bushes and other plants, with trees in the background. All the other children in our class were adorably dressed up, with their mothers' creativity, as rabbits and various other animals and birds that one may encounter in the woods. They were hopping around joyfully to the delight of the audience. There was a villain with a mustache and a pipe in his mouth. He had an axe on his shoulder with which he intended to harm the forest by cutting down a tree; he was littering and being careless with his pipe. Pepik and I were the heroes who thwarted the evil intentions of the careless villain and thereby earned the friendship and admiration of "Mother Nature" and the entire animal kingdom. At the end of the play, we received the congratulations of a real forest ranger, who gave both of us medals for our brave and good deeds. The ranger's words accompanying the presentation were drowned out by the ovation of the audience that comprised parents, relatives, teachers, students and friends. As the ovation began to ebb, our teacher signaled for the children to leave the stage. Pepik and I were the last to leave and, as we did, we marched off triumphantly doing our military steps. Our exaggerated march brought on a new vigorous ovation with whistles and shouts of "Bravo."

Following the play, the audience was invited to the gym for a prepared reception. Pepik and I were like celebrities and very much sought after. Parents took turns photographing us with their children. While I relished in the attention, the highlight of this experience was the pleasure of seeing my own mother proud and joyful as the other mothers of my classmates praised her, and her warm embrace and kiss as she congratulated me was my ultimate reward. During the reception, the fathers and brothers of my classmates asked to see our wooden rifles and daggers. They handled them admiringly while complimenting their authentic reproduction. Many stated that they were masterfully made, that they were pieces of art. We told them that Pepik's father, who was the Czech customs duty officer, and therefore could not leave his official duties to be present, had carved and varnished them for us especially for this play. Pepik's mother proudly stood by her son and soaked up the accolades bestowed on her husband's handiwork.

As the day progressed, our not-yet-eight-year-old heads swelled with pride. Pepik, who was a pudgy child, was almost walking on air. He could not wait to tell his father about his triumph and how much his dad's handiwork had been admired. The reception concluded the school day and afterwards, all the children went home with their parents and siblings.

When I got home, I could not concentrate on my homework and solicited Mama's help to a greater extent than usual. I could not wait for Papa to come home so I could tell him about my triumph. Then, at bedtime,

I could not fall asleep. I kept on revisiting the suppertime scene when, with Mother's proud embellishments, I told and retold Papa every little detail of our triumph in the school play. He smiled broadly, as he pulled me closer by my hand. He then hugged me tightly, congratulated me and told me he was proud. He wished he could have been there, but counted on me to understand that he had had to be at work. He kissed me and I kissed his hand in return. My excitement lasted the whole evening and into half the night, when I finally managed to fall asleep with the help of a cup of my mother's delicious hot cocoa, a lingering hug and a goodnight kiss followed by Mama's special tuck-in.

The following day, Pepik and I could hardly wait to go to school. As we hoped, our teacher asked us both to stand up and proceeded to give some very complimentary remarks about our previous day's triumph and shared with us her feelings of pride. Then, proceeding with the day's lesson on nature, she asked the class, "Where does the whale live and what does it eat?" Pepik was keen to answer the question, and to reward him for being one of the previous day's co-triumphants, the teacher picked him. Pepik stood up, squared his ample shoulders, then looked around proudly and mumbled in his usual halting unique style, "The whale...the whale...the whale lives in the forest and eats leaves!" The class descended into an uproar and the teacher called Pepik a dunce and a whale. How fast, within a fleeting moment, fame can evaporate. The epithet stuck and henceforth, Pepik was nicknamed "Whale" by the entire school. I felt bad for him and never called him by that name.

I loved school; there was so much to learn. I was intrigued by science and thrilled by the science experiments. I loved nature and chemistry and physics, which, even at their most basic introductory level, were difficult but seemed to me miraculous. Math was hard and I failed to appreciate, at that young age, its importance. Papa and I spoke about my future profession; he wanted me to be a chemical engineer, claiming that chemistry would be the leading science during my lifetime. I was determined to be a forestry engineer and a gentleman farmer, spending my life with nature and all of our Creator's wonders.

BUŠTINA, MY HOMETOWN[1]

I was born Ondrej Mojzis Brandstein, on December 12, 1930, in the town of Buština (Bustyaháza),[2] located in a section of the Podkarpatská Rus-Máramaros valley in the Carpathian Mountains of Czechoslovakia, which, today, is part of Ukraine. I was named after my great-grandfather Moshe who lived in the same town. The indigenous people of this area are Ruthenians, who adhere to the Russian Orthodox Christian faith. Their native language is a dialect of Ukrainian. The town of Buština is located on the main road, between the city of Chust (twenty-one kilometers to the west) and the town of Tačovo (Técső in Hungarian; seven kilometers to the east).

Originally, Buština's economy depended on timber for which it was ideally located at the junction of the Talabor River and the great Tisza River, which flowed through Hungary and Yugoslavia, into the Danube, just above its capital Belgrade. The Talabor and Tisza transported floats of timber to various lumber mills all along the river. Later, Buština established a more diversified economy in which agriculture and fruit became important commodities, in addition to timber. On the commerce side, Buština was an important center for wholesale goods, supplying the storekeepers of the towns in the entire region.

Our town of Buština comprised six distinctive village sections: *Dorf* (Village), *Central* (Town), *Handal* (Market), *Fenyves* (Pine Woods), *Vasutca*

1   Portions of this chapter have been excerpted from and are based on "The Pledge," from the collection of stories, *The Destiny of Jaacob Maghid* (Romanian) (Tel Aviv: Panopticum, 1975) (Hebrew) (Tel Aviv: Sifriat Hapoalim, 1977; Tel Aviv: Nimrod, 2009). Used by permission of Prof. Alfred M. Bruckstein, Andrew Burian's cousin.
2   The small town of Buština is located in an area that today is Carpatho-Ukraine, but which went through many geo-political changes during the twentieth century. From the tenth century until 1919, it was part of the Kingdom of Hungary. After the Treaty of Trianon in 1920, the area, later referred to as Ruthenia, became part of the newly formed country of Czechoslovakia. The region declared its independence as Carpatho-Ukraine on March 15, 1939, but was actually under Hungarian control. At that time, some 500,000 people lived in the region; about 15 percent were Jews. Once Germany occupied Hungary in 1944, it also regained control of this region. In 1945, most of the region was annexed by the Soviet Union and subsequently incorporated into the independent state of Ukraine. In all, about 80 percent of the Jews in Transcarpathian Ukraine perished during the Holocaust.

(Railroad) and *Benesco* (Over the Talabor). Buština had a long paved main street that was part of the east-west thoroughfare that ran from the *Dorf* section through the *Central* section and over the Talabor River bridge to the *Benesco* part, so that Buština encompassed both sides of the Talabor River. Railroad Street ran north-south, was approximately one and a half kilometers long and ran from the *Fenyves* through the *Handal* section, across Main Street, through the *Vasutca* section to the railroad station and the Jewish cemetery. The crossroads of Main and Railroad Streets was called *"Central."* In addition, Buština had numerous smaller streets, roads and alleys. The *Handal* section was in the southern part of the town, with a main street running its entire length from the *Fenyves* section to the Talabor River, parallel to Main Street, and its own web of smaller streets. The *Fenyves* section boasted the governmental offices as well as the Sokol, the sports center with the town's tennis courts.

Buština was a relatively large, comfortable and economically viable town for some, while for most it was a town like many in the district where poverty for the unskilled and mainly uneducated was rampant among Christians and Jews alike. In 1943, there were approximately 4,000 Jews in Buština out of a total population of about 7,000, with the non-Jewish population comprising Czechs and Ukrainians.

My sainted, beloved mother — of blessed memory — was a Bruckstein and, before we were uprooted from our home, her family had been living in the area for nearly three centuries, with a long sense of tradition. The family stories were retold for each new generation, explaining both the source of our family's wealth and its strong ties to religion and the town.

Sometime in the middle of the nineteenth century, Rabbi Mordechai (Mordchele), son of Rabbi Issachar Dov Ber Leifer of Nadvorna, settled in the town of Buština at the foot of the Carpathian Mountains. He was a charitable and righteous man who had a reputation of being one of the last "wonder-rabbis" on this earth. He modeled his actions on Rabbi Yisroel, the Ba'al Shem Tov and founder of Hasidism. The legend goes that Rabbi Yisroel would give a word of comfort to someone in distress and some sound advice to someone in trouble; heal someone of an unknown disease; give encouraging counsel; help finance the wedding of a poor young woman who had reached marriageable age; and grant funds and good advice to a carter whose horse had died, so that he could purchase a new one and make a living.

About 100 years later, Rabbi Mordechai of Nadvorna would travel the same roads traveled by the Ba'al Shem Tov, accompanied by another fourteen carts, piled high with bread and salt, rolls of shiny white satin for wedding dresses and black silk for bridegrooms' coats, as well as prayer shawls and large festival candles. His entourage also included scribes as well as disciples and companions who had no special skills. In the last carts were housewives and other women who could sew and weave, create a wedding dress for a bride or a fine coat for the bridegroom at the drop of a hat, and cook and bake and light the Sabbath candles. The family story also tells of the righteous rabbi performing miracles in the town of Buština. One of them involved the rabbi's young neighbor, Moshe (my great-grandfather), the son of Yisroel Natan Alter, and his wife (my great-grandmother) Sirka Shapira.

At that time, the inhabitants of Buština were farmers, woodchoppers, foresters, carters and merchants. Buština was situated at the crossroads leading east to Técső, Slatina and Sighet and west to Chust, and from there to the town of Munkács and the city of Pressburg and thence to the capital of the empire, Vienna. Along this busy road came horse-drawn wagons laden with apples, wood and flour from the mill of Buština. The emperor and his entourage, the couriers and other high dignitaries, would return along this road from their bear hunts in the forests of Miramar. It was also the famous "salt road" along which wagons would pass bearing huge blocks of salt hewn from the salt mines. After a journey that lasted days and nights, these wagons were destined for the capital, where His Imperial Highness, the emperor of the Austrians and the king of the Hungarians, Bohemians, Moravians, Bosnians and Herzegovinians, resided. In addition, when His Highness wished to give a rich royal a gift to one or another of the crowned heads of Europe, he would present them with several blocks of pure white salt from the mines of Máramaros.

On the outskirts of the town, beneath a long, high wooden bridge, the waters of the Talabor flowed gently, and rafts made from logs of trees felled in the forests of the region would drift slowly towards the River Tisza, their final destination being the town of Szeged, or even further. On the Jewish New Year, masses of worshippers would gather at the river banks of the Talabor to say the *Tashlich* prayer and fulfill the commandment of casting their sins into the water in the form of pieces of bread for the fish.

Not far from the Talabor, at the edge of the town, stood the Rabbi of Nadvorna's house. It was built of unfired bricks and painted blue, with a roof of wooden beams that had turned black with age and rain. Opposite, in a hut that was also painted blue and covered with wooden tiles, lived Moshe and Sirka, my great-grandparents. The righteous Rabbi Mordechai, who was approaching seventy, a man both uncommonly generous and unimaginably poor, was fond of his neighbors. Moshe was a pale, shy young man, with deep-set gray eyes and a chestnut-colored beard that was just beginning to grow. Together with his wife, who was as young as he was, Moshe had traveled from the distant eastern regions to this remote Carpathian town. The story of how the poor bookkeeper married his wealthy employer's daughter was a family legend.

Already by age sixteen, Moshe was a man with ideas of his own; he was of good stock, being the scion of a famous and learned dynasty; and had excelled in his religious studies. His father, Reb Yisroel Natan Alter, the Rabbi of Pistyn, was the author of the Kabbalistic works *Minhat Yisrael* and *Emunat Yisrael*, and was preceded by generations of learned scholars in the family. Nevertheless, his in-laws were not in favor of the marriage as they were concerned that Moshe was too young to marry. Wounded by the attitude of his in-laws, yet never saying a word, instead of remaining in the home of the bride's parents and being supported by them for the first couple of years, as was the practice then, the young couple left immediately after the wedding in order to go out into the world and be independent. Moshe and his wife, Sirka, crossed the Carpathian Mountains and came to the town of Buština, where they moved into the hut that was painted ultramarine and roofed with rotten beams, right opposite the Rabbi of Nadvorna, Rabbi Mordchele, the miracle worker.

Moshe was a regular visitor at the rabbi's house, never missing a prayer session and often partaking of the Sabbath meal. One Sabbath, Moshe brought a honey cake that Sirka had made for the rabbi's table. According to Hasidic custom, after the rabbi recites the blessing and takes a piece, he cuts a slice and passes the plate along to his disciples, so that everyone can take a slice of what Hasidim call the "leftovers" from the rabbi's plate, a privilege and a joy. This time, by the time the plate reached Moshe, there was nothing left except for a few crumbs. Moshe looked at the empty plate in confusion, not knowing what to do. The rabbi noticed, got up and went over to Moshe's corner. He picked up one crumb after another in his fingers and held them out to Moshe, saying, "Taste, my son; taste your wife's handiwork. What difference does it make that they are only crumbs? Moses was enriched from the fragments of the Tablets, our sages said." Then he smiled and returned to his seat. Moshe knew the saying, but wondered what the rabbi meant by it. However, according to the family legend, from the very next day, Moshe began to prosper, in property, in children and in the esteem of other people.

The "miracle" performed by the Rabbi of Nadvorna, appeared, in fact, as an idea in the quick imaginative mind of Moshe, the son of Yisroel Natan Alter. At that time, Moshe was a subordinate bookkeeper in a plant utilizing wood from the forests of the Carpathian Mountains. He sometimes had to travel far from his home to a part of the forest where timber felling had begun, and took along with him a pack containing food for several days — Sirka's home-baked bread, a few hard-boiled eggs and some apples. In the area of the forest where work was due to begin, Moshe would sit and calculate the number of stumps and trunks that had been felled and the days put in by the loggers and lumbermen as well as the carters, with one horse or two, who transported the logs down to the valley.

In this way, Moshe became well acquainted with the affairs of the forestry administration. He learned the life of the forest into whose thickets and clearings man mercilessly intruded with his axe and pickaxe, his many-teethed saw and his nails of iron in order to trample it and compel it to serve his needs. In the winter, when the snow covered the ground and piled up heavily on the branches of the trees, when everything was frozen and life seemed to have stopped in its tracks, Moshe saw how the foresters came to thin out the trees of the forest and lop off unnecessary branches, weeding out every unnecessary plant and dry branch, so that the other trees and roots could absorb more water in the spring, maintain their freshness and improve their growth. All the logs, branches and twigs that were cut and which the foresters called "dead wood," were left lying where they had fallen, until they rotted away and returned to the earth from which they had come. After all, there was no useful purpose to which they could be put, and it was not anyone's will to collect them and take them down to the valley.

One day, as he took a piece of bread in his hand and recited the appropriate blessing, then sat down on a felled log to eat it with the hard-boiled egg he had just peeled, he looked at the pile of dead wood condemned

to rot in the forest and the verse "Take up your rod in this hand, Moses..."
flashed into his mind. He remembered the Rabbi of Nadvorna expounding
on the verse at one of the Sabbath meals. He looked and trembled. He began
poking around in the piles, selecting, putting aside, and found treasure. It was
not a chest of gold pieces or precious stones for which strangers had labored,
and he would have to work and sweat in order to get it out, but, nevertheless,
it was secret treasure. These abandoned "crumbs" left on the forest floor could
be worth a fortune.

At that time, the fashion of walking sticks or canes had begun to
catch on around the world. No self-respecting person would go out into
the street without one, while men of fashion would have several, whose
color and shape would match their clothes, shoes, shirt collar or tie. At
that moment of inspiration in the forest it occurred to Moshe that the dry
branches or dead wood could, if collected and classified by length, thickness
and type of wood, serve as raw material for the cane industry. Beautiful
canes could be made, with or without curved handles, with ivory or leather
and with pointed steel tips for the winter. The canes could be made of fir or
plum wood and equipped with black-, silver- or copper-knobbed handles.
He could produce walking sticks for older people or mountain climbers,
bent ones for cripples, straight ones for scouts and others for skiers. Not
to mention handles for umbrellas and parasols and any other purpose
imaginable. Anything could be done with the hidden treasure left to rot on
the forest floor.

Soon after, a company for manufacturing and marketing canes was
born, with a tiny office in one of the rooms in the house of unfired bricks,
painted ultramarine and roofed with ancient tiles. The office consisted
of a desk, a chair, headed notepaper, a filing cabinet in one corner and a
hand press in another. The firm thrived and prospered, expanding to many
countries, so that the canes manufactured in a remote town by the name of
Buština were sold to customers far away in Germany, England, Austria,
Switzerland, Sweden and Italy as well as many other countries throughout
the world. Moshe's courtyard also expanded. Warehouses and sheds were
built for storing, sorting and packing the finished product. Furnaces,
stoves and cauldrons were built for boiling the wood prior to peeling and
processing it. Day and night, the courtyard bustled with people. Horses and
wagons brought the dead wood and dry branches from the forest or took

the packed canes to the trains so that they could be dispatched to Moshe's worldwide clientele.

Moshe prospered, as both his business and family grew. He and Sirka had six sons and three daughters. There was Yisroel Natan, the eldest son, named after his father's father, who was the father of my late mother, Matilda Bruckstein; Eliezer Lipa, named after his maternal grandfather who had brought up Moshe until he was thirteen; Haim Yosef, named after Moshe's grandfather on his father's side, the author of *Tosafot Haim* and *Nishmat Haim*; and Zindel, Mordechai and Aharon. The girls were Miriam, Sara and Yocheved. Moshe accommodated his growing sons and daughters one by one in the business, and continued the tradition of charitable deeds. He gave to the needy, fed widows and orphans, helped fund weddings and extended interest-free loans to the poor.

When the Chief Rabbi of Sighet, Rabbi Yekutiel Yehuda Teitelbaum, and the entire Maramureş region heard the rumors of Rabbi Mordechai's miracles and acts of kindness, Rabbi Yekutiel became very curious and was eager to get to know Rabbi Mordechai, but it was difficult as their paths never crossed. He thought about inviting one of the householders of the town of Buština and consulting with him, and if he were to invite someone from Buština, it would undoubtedly be Moshe, the son of Yisroel Natan Alter, who was even related to the Teitelbaum family. Moshe had stayed in their house and eaten at their table when he had been a *yeshiva* student in Sighet, and had even helped to prepare a commentary on the Psalms. Moshe mentioned that Rabbi Mordechai had never yet refused to do something connected with fulfilling a commandment. Therefore, Rabbi Yekutiel Yehuda Teitelbaum invited Rabbi Mordechai to be the godfather at a circumcision ceremony of a fatherless child.

After the moving ceremony and Rabbi Mordechai's departure, Rabbi Yekutiel Yehuda Teitelbaum realized that he had not managed to exchange a single word with Rabbi Mordechai. When Moshe, the intermediary and initiator of the meeting, came over to him and asked what he had thought of the Rabbi of Nadvorna, Rabbi Teitelbaum replied with a smile that was full of meaning, "Never have I heard the godfather's blessing spoken like that!"

Moshe was also privileged to be able to perform a singular task, for he was the first and only person from whom the rabbi himself asked for a loan and, as the rabbi implored him, even received a pledge — the rabbi's prayer shawl. In this way, Moshe was privileged to keep the rabbi's prayer shawl until his dying day. Before his demise, the rabbi instructed his disciples, saying that since he would be "gathered unto his forefathers" and would be buried on the first weekday, it was best that he should be wrapped in his weekday prayer shawl, leaving his Sabbath prayer shawl in the possession of Moshe, to cover a debt he had not managed to repay. Moshe kept the precious pledge for thirty-five years, until his hour came, too. Then he asked to be wrapped in the rabbi's Sabbath prayer shawl when he was buried, probably thinking secretly that up there he would be able to return it to the rabbi, and in return would receive the ordinary weekday prayer shawl. In the year of Rabbi Mordechai's death, late 1895, Sirka and Moshe had a fifth son, whom they named Mordechai, after the Rabbi of Nadvorna. His nickname was also Mordchele.

Winds of change were coming to the Carpathians, including the innovation of people having to take surnames. The authorities began demanding that, in addition to their given names, the Jews should also take surnames. Thus, Moshe, the son of Yisroel Natan Alter, decided to adopt the name Bruckstein, meaning "broken stone," referring to the broken Tablets of the Law shattered by Moses.

THE SABBATH

The Sabbath stands out in my childhood as an unmitigated joy. It was the day of rest and, therefore, Papa was home the entire day and so were all our relatives and friends. There was no work or any kind of business performed on the Sabbath. All Jewish families were in a festive, relaxed mood. As the poet of our Sabbath eve prayer states, the "Sabbath of Peace is welcomed as a groom welcomes his bride and a queen is welcomed by her adoring subjects," or at least as a favorite invited guest. The highlight of the weekly Sabbath was attendance at the inspiring synagogue service that included a topical and scholarly sermon derived from the Torah portion of that week. At the end of the service, families, couples and individuals, dressed in their finest, congregated in front of the synagogue to greet and socialize with family and friends, and then, shortly after, they slowly broke away from the crowd to begin the delightful *shpatzier* (stroll) home. We lived about two kilometers away. At noon, we had the festive Sabbath meal and then the whole afternoon was spent playing with my cousins. There could be NO homework and there were NO "interrogations" by Mama about school. It was the Sabbath! For me, the fact that Papa was home was the paramount embellishment of the day.

In the late Sabbath afternoon, Mother would call us in from the backyard for the traditional *Seudah Shelishit* (third meal) of the Sabbath, eaten before sunset. My cousin Ervin, the eldest and leader of our playgroup, would shout at me with a condescending tone that my mother always called us in too early, just when we were beginning to have fun. It was the usual understanding among the aunts that we were fed in whichever aunt's yard we happened to be playing; everybody fed everybody's children, and if we wanted to, we could stay until bedtime.

I think back to the Sabbath of September 24, 1938, a day before the High Holy Days of that year.[3] It was late in the afternoon, three months shy of my eighth birthday. The day was unusually warm for our town of Buština. The low-lying sun began to cast long shadows as it slowly brought a beautiful day to an end. The descending sun, at a hardly noticeable pace at first, began lowering the curtain on the stage of my world. As the sun reached the top of the surrounding mountains, it began to paint the few clouds in the sky with every conceivable shade of red and purple, illuminating the rest of the sky with an ever-descending intensity. Above the mountains, the clouds swirled slowly, aimlessly, lazily, with a seeming attitude of timelessness, thereby reflecting the rays of the setting sun in an ever-changing kaleidoscopic effect. They reflected unique and fantastic patterns, which were never to be repeated.

An hour before sunset, as the Sabbath was coming to an end, I accompanied the men in the family (my father and my older brother Tibor, whom we called Tibi) next door to Reb Summer's *shtiebel*, the synagogue in his home, for the end of Sabbath evening prayer. Following the service, we returned home to ceremoniously end the Sabbath and welcome the new week

---

3   The author refers here to the High Holy Days of *Rosh Hashanah* (Jewish New Year), *Yom Kippur* (Day of Atonement), the holiest day of the year for the Jewish people, and *Sukkot* (one of the three pilgrimage festivals). These holy days are celebrated in the Hebrew month of Tishrei, the first month of the Jewish civil year and usually in September-October of the Gregorian calendar.

by lighting the multiple-wick candle set aside for this purpose. We, including Mother, gathered around Papa who said the prescribed benediction over a cup of wine and gave each of us a whiff of the ornamental silver box of cloves for the purpose of providing a lingering sweet aroma to the new week. The evening ended in the usual manner, with supper and listening to the radio or to our parents' conversations with visiting family or friends. Bedtime came as the late evening turned to early night. The next day, the High Holy Days were upon us. Beginning with *Rosh Hashanah*, the Jewish New Year, on the Sunday evening of September 25 and continuing for the two following days, Monday and Tuesday, September 26 and 27. This was followed ten days later by *Yom Kippur* (the Day of Atonement), beginning on the Tuesday evening of October 4 and ending on the Wednesday evening of October 5, 1938.

Unbeknownst to us, the innocent children, the British, French and Italians were meeting in Munich to decide our fate. The meeting was held just two days following *Rosh Hashanah*, on Thursday, September 29, 1938.[4] Their signatures on the Munich Agreement sealed our fate. It brought the scourge of World War II, a war that caused the loss of many millions of innocent lives and the countless suffering of innocent people.

THE BRANDSTEINS

My parents, Ernest (Hebrew name: Mordechai, Czech name: Arnost) and Matilda (née Bruckstein) Brandstein and my older brother Tibi and I, made up our immediate family. My mother was one of ten children, eight girls and two boys. My father was one of eight children, three girls and five boys. My parents were the scions of the two most prominent families in the region; they were married in 1927 in the town of Sevluš, now

---

4   The author refers here to the Munich Conference, which convened in Munich on September 29, 1938, between Adolf Hitler (Chancellor of Nazi Germany), Neville Chamberlain (Prime Minister of Britain) Édouard Daladier (Prime Minister of France) and Benito Mussolini (Prime Minister of Fascist Italy). The purpose of the conference was to discuss Hitler's demand to annex the Sudetenland. The Munich Agreement resulted in the German annexation of the Sudetenland in Czechoslovakia. However, the agreement was not signed by any government representatives from Czechoslovakia nor representatives of the Soviet Union, the Czechoslovak ally.

Vinograd. Sevluš, where grapes grew everywhere, including in the front yards, backyards and doorways, is famous for its wine. My Aunt Rela Katz lived there with her husband, Shamu (Simon), and their three children. Uncle Shamu manufactured "Bobby" razor blades in partnership with Uncle David Wieder from Budapest. Uncle Shamu had a lumberyard and a woodturning and processing plant in partnership with my father, where they manufactured products that could be produced on a lathe from wood remnants, such as brush handles, table and chair legs, fancy broom handles, filigrees, chess pieces and more. Papa had wide commercial timber interests in many sections of the Czechoslovak and Romanian parts of the Carpathian Mountains in addition to our lumberyard in town and partnerships in various establishments. Timber and lumber was the traditional Brandstein family business.

While Papa was busy with his timber and lumber business, Mother was the driving force in our family. She was so adamant about the importance of education that it sometimes seemed she was on a single-minded crusade concerning her children acquiring a superior education. No sooner had we arrived home from school, than we were back again in a much stricter and, I venture to add, more productive "school." Mother would sit me down at a table in our foyer, which connected our kitchen to the dining room, and pay attention to me as she went about her chores. Under her supervision, I went over the day's lessons and then the required homework. Mother was an avid reader and she made me read books that I found out later were American novels. By the time we were each twelve years old, Mother had made my brother and me aware of some of the classics.

Although Mother suffered from thrombosis and required many operations throughout her life, she was widely and justly recognized as a beauty and was admired for her various abilities and accomplishments. She excelled in the art of needlepoint and her precision in micro-weaving was envied far and wide. Mother could restore a burn in an expensive cotton shirt or a damask tablecloth by reweaving the damage with its own threads. Her culinary art was extraordinary. Mother had a fantastic personality, was a devoted wife to Papa, an unbelievable self-sacrificing daughter to her parents and a devoted and doting mother. She was born in Romania in the town of Câmpulung la Tisa on May 6, 1906. In 1938, she was thirty-two years old.

For us, life in Buština was ideal. We were, what you could call today, modern Orthodox, and by any standard, well-to-do, living among the upper echelons of society. Almost everybody I knew, and certainly with whom I associated, was a grandparent, an uncle, an aunt or a cousin. Besides the actual family members, I was expected to call all adults "Uncle" or "Aunt," and to show proper courtesy and respect to everyone I encountered. As a child, I was imbued with proper etiquette, which was expected and considered of the utmost importance.

My paternal grandfather's original house, where my father grew up, was across the street from the *Dorf* synagogue in the old section of town. It was a sprawling ranch-type house on a few acres of landscaped lawns with walnut and fruit trees reaching back almost to the cemetery that was more than one kilometer away, near the railroad. The property was surrounded by a fence and protected by a large, ugly and vicious English bulldog, ironically called Pici (Tiny). No one, other than Grandpa or the caretaker, could approach Pici when he was loose on the property. On many a morning, the caretaker would discover someone who, during the night, in an attempt to avail himself of some fruits or nuts, had wound up taking refuge from Pici in a tree.

The new Brandstein house was and still is in the *Central* section of town. It is a prominent and imposing two-story structure located at a commanding location at the crossroads of the two main streets. Being the only two-storied house and located right in the center, today it is the city hall of Buština. Then, it was the showpiece of the Brandstein family's compound and reflected the family's standing in the community. Perhaps the fact that my paternal grandfather, Eliezer (Lazar) Brandstein, had a house complete with a movie theater, illustrates the quality of life we were living. I saw the Disney movie *Mickey Mouse* in 1935 or 1936. We did not see the latest movies and certainly the movie houses of Vienna, Budapest and Prague had nothing to fear in terms of competition; nevertheless, it was fun. In the center of the compound was a deep well that served the whole compound. To the right of the main house was Uncle Izidor's house and behind him was Uncle Adolph's. At the other end of the compound was Uncle Jozsi's house. In fact, three out of the four sons who lived in Buština, built their houses in the compound, except for my father, who built his house across the street from my maternal grandparents. In 1928, when my brother Tibor was born, my parents built and moved into a large solid brick modern house that was second only in stature to his father's house. It still stands on Main Street, approximately one-sixth of a mile east of the Brandstein compound and across the street from my maternal grandparents, the Brucksteins. In addition to the three sons in Buština, my father had another brother, Jeno, who was the eldest. There were altogether five sons, of whom Papa was the youngest, and three daughters, Margit, Helen and Manci.

In 1929, during the Great Depression, the Brandstein family went bankrupt, losing $500,000 in the Wall Street Crash. The family had taken substantial loans from the Živnostenská Banka in Prague to finance their timber operations and had then defaulted on those loans as the demand for timber became virtually nonexistent. The felled timber that the loan financed was left to rot in the forests, for it was not worth the cost to retrieve it. The bank sued the family. Although the timber was fully insured, nevertheless, the insurance company reneged on its responsibilities. The family, in turn, sued the insurance company. Both suits, which were conducted by my father, were still going on more than fourteen years later, when we were deported.

By 1933, the economic conditions began to ease. In order to preserve capital, Father rented out a major portion of our house to the Czech police and we lived in a smaller part of the house. After a while, Mother found this arrangement somewhat tenuous. Therefore, a few years later, my parents built another house next to the now-rented house. It was built on a much more modest scale and we lived in this house until deportation.

At about the same time, in order to generate some income, the ground floor of the showcase Brandstein house, which faced the street and included the theater, was converted into stores, and they fetched a relatively high rent due to their location. Although my mother's culinary abilities were sometimes referred to as magical, nevertheless, we did frequent one particular store for a while to buy their delicious concoctions of herring salads. That is, until Mother was able to substantially improve on them.

Grandpa Lazar, the patriarch of the Brandstein family, was a dignified white-bearded gentleman who dressed in black, wore a hat and sported a silver-headed walking cane or an umbrella, as was customary for an Orthodox Jewish gentleman of his generation and standing. Unfortunately, he passed away in 1937 when I was six and a half years old. Therefore, much to my sorrow, I do not remember much more than seeing him lying in his sickbed propped up on a pillow. Grandma Amalia (Father's mother), who was born in Hungary, was very reserved; she had a "hands-off" attitude concerning her grandchildren who were not very comfortable in her presence, or in her spotless, splendid home. My lack of memory concerning Grandpa Lazar is perhaps due to the fact that neither I, nor any of the other grandchildren, had a very close relationship with Grandma Amalia, so we did not spend much time in the big house. Grandma had a large fenced-off flower garden at the back and adjacent to the house that she tended herself. It was a botanical garden of great repute with exotic plants and flowers, decorated flowerbeds and colored glass globes perched on white poles. It was her pride and joy. Grandma Amalia kept a watchful eye on the garden from her perfect vantage point — the upstairs window overlooking the garden — and any child, including a grandchild, she detected unhooking the latch and laying a foot past the garden gate would invite an admonishing warning from above.

THE BRUCKSTEINS

Across the street from us lived my maternal grandparents, the Brucksteins. They, too, lived in a compound. My grandparents lived in a large farmhouse with a covered porch at the back that ran along the entire length of the house. During the late spring, summer and early fall most family activities took place on that porch. Besides a large country kitchen, it had an elaborate dining room, family room, study and many bedrooms. My mother's immediate family of ten children (8 girls and 2 boys) also included my mother's cousin, Giselle Goldberger, who came from the city of Mukačevo to live with them. Giselle, better known as Gizi, is Grandma Ruchele's niece, her brother's daughter. When Gizi's mother died, she came to live with her aunt. Since there was another Gizi in the family, the older cousin was designated as "Big Gizi," and the other as "Little Gizi." Big Gizi, being the closest to Mother's age, became my mother's best friend. After the war, she became my stepmother.

Grandpa Yisroel Bruckstein was the perennial *Chevra Kadisha Gabai* (chairman of the prestigious Burial Society of Buština) and the de facto *Rosh HaKahal* (head of the Jewish Community) of our town, while his brother-in-law, Uncle Feig, was the titular head of the community in recognition of his renowned Talmudic knowledge. Grandpa Yisroel, too, was a white-bearded gentleman, who dressed in black garb, as was the custom for a man of his position and stature. He was always impeccably dressed and would typically have an elegant umbrella on his arm, which, when not used for rain or as a sunshade, doubled as a walking cane. He traveled on business all over Europe and even owned two apartment buildings in Berlin. He would bring back presents of diamonds, pearls and jewelry for Grandma and his daughters. It was a known fact that the Bruckstein girls were "bedecked" with jewelry. He was a warm person who took great interest in his grandchildren, especially in their learning of the Scripture. On many Sabbath afternoons he would ask me to sit next to him and tell him what I was learning in *cheder* (Hebrew school for religious instruction of young children).

Whenever I thought that my mother was too strict or unfair, as children are bound to think, I threatened to go and tell her mother, my beloved Grandma Ruchele, who lived across the street. This was no idle threat, for I availed myself of this privilege many times. It seemed to me, and rightfully so, that Ruchele sided, at least overtly, with her grandchildren at every opportunity. On one occasion, I threatened to run away, but I must have told my mother one time too many that I was leaving, since Mama's reaction was to call my bluff and proceed to fill a backpack with clothing, some apples and a prayer book. I left the house, but kept lingering within sight. I was surprised that Mother neither ran after me, nor did she forbid me to leave. What's more, she actually encouraged me to go. My pride was hurt to the core while my heart was heavy; nevertheless, with my stubborn streak, I clenched my teeth and fists and braved it. I left home.

So now, where was I to go? That was easy! I went all the way across the street to Grandma Ruchele. Where else was I going to go? I, of course, did not tell Grandma what was going on and proceeded straight to the cookie jar. Unbeknownst to me, my whereabouts and my situation were known to both Mother and Grandmother and a few hours later, Mama came across the street to sit on the porch with Grandma. Knowing that I was hiding within earshot, Mother told Grandma how her dear son Andi had left the house and she did not know where he was, that he must be cold and hungry by now, but maybe he would learn a lesson and would never again be fresh to any adult, especially his mother. In any case, she hoped that he was well and would come home and apologize properly. They went on and on in this vein. After a while, I could no longer take any more of it and came out of hiding, trying to make myself conspicuous. My subtle attempt, while noticed, was completely ignored. They continued to talk about me in the same vein for a few more minutes until I burst into tears and ran to my mother with tears streaking down my cheeks. I was full of apologies. I kissed her hand and begged for forgiveness, which she granted while smothering me with kisses and hugs. I experienced the wonderful feeling of, once again, being part of a very happy family where everything is more than all right — it was perfectly ideal.

Adjacent to Grandpa Bruckstein's home was our lumberyard, which was stacked with freshly cut lumber of various thicknesses and lengths. I loved the smell of the sticky amber sap that oozed out of some of the pine lumber, which was very difficult to wash off my hands and even more difficult to get off my pants. I spent a lot of time *kibitzing* (chatting) with the wood shingle cutters and the crate makers who worked in our sheds. I loved to count the bricks that were being loaded onto wagons and I marveled at how Papa was able to keep track of the entire business in his head. He did not use a calculator although there was a manual Odhner rotating calculator available in his office. He would calculate the cubic feet of the content of a wagon or railcar load the old-fashioned way, using a pencil and paper.

At the back of the Bruckstein house, Grandpa Bruckstein conducted his cane and herb business. Wagonloads of herbs that had been gathered from the nearby mountainsides rolled into the yard where they were dried, purged of dried dirt by being tossed in loosely woven burlap, and finally baled. The bales were tagged and carted off to the rail station to be shipped all over Europe and sometimes beyond. I still love the smell of herbs, especially chamomile. Further back in the yard, wagonloads of sticks, soon to become canes, were unloaded in a shed where they were carefully and skillfully examined for their usefulness and graded for their suitability as canes or umbrella handles. They were then cleaned, their small branches carefully cut without damaging the natural bumps and knots in the stick. Sizing the sticks was a particular skill, for it had to be at a point where one end would remain with a beautiful knob or knot, later to be a handle. After they were cut to size, they were tossed into enormous boiling cauldrons that were fired by dried bark and cuttings. The purpose of boiling the sticks was to facilitate the peeling of the bark and to make the sticks more pliable for bending. The peeled, bare stick revealed a beautiful color that was acquired from the dark syrupy water of the boiling bark. The "good" end of the stick was then inserted into a machine that bent it and secured it with a wire to hold the bend in place; this part became the handle of the cane. The semi-finished canes were then bundled and wrapped in burlap to be shipped off to cane and umbrella manufacturers all over Europe.

The foreman of the cane-boiling and bark-peeling operation was Kiva (I only knew him by his first name), who lived behind the cauldrons and fields with his wife and children in a very modest hut on a small plot of land. Kiva's hands were perpetually stained a deep, dark amber color from the boiled bark of the canes. He was a jovial, God-fearing and independent-minded man, who was fond of children and particularly of me. He let me wander around the yard while keeping an eye on me and shouting to me to be careful. Grandpa considered the work floor with boiling cauldrons to be a dangerous place for children and reprimanded Kiva many times for allowing me to play near and sometimes on the work floor, alas to no avail. Although Kiva had a relatively well paid, steady job, he was nevertheless poor due to the large family he supported. The scourge of poverty was particularly rampant in our Carpathian region. In Buština, perhaps it was not as severe as in other surrounding towns; nonetheless, our town did not escape it.

There were three flagrant examples of poverty of which I, as a child, was aware. One of them was the widow Shaina Rivka and her many children. Shaina Rivka seemed to me an obese old lady with grotesquely swollen legs and feet, who spent her days from sunup until sundown minding her fruit stand that stood diagonally opposite Grandfather Brandstein's mansion in the town center. Selling fruit in a town where it grew in everybody's backyard was not a very lucrative undertaking. She was dependent upon those who were strangers in town and on some folks, including my mother, who purchased from her as an indirect act of charity.

The second was Ruven Chaim who lived with his wife and nine children in the *Dorf* section of town. He was an extremely pious man and for whatever reason, perpetually unemployed. It was said that Ruven Chaim was so poor that, amongst his children, there were only two pairs of shoes, which they all shared in the winter. Only two children at a time could leave the house with shoes, the others had to wait for their turn. Whatever the reason was for Ruven Chaim's severe poverty, it was not because of a lack of ingenuity on his part. In 1941, when the Hungarians deported some Jews to the Ukraine under the pretense that they were not Hungarian citizens, Ruven Chaim, his wife and children were among them.[5] In the spring of 1942, he and his entire family came back on foot across the Carpathian Mountains with his youngest child in the same wooden kneading tub, used as a crib, that he had carried him away in; they survived a treacherous winter in the forests of the Ukraine. The whole town welcomed them and everyone was in awe of his accomplishment. Unfortunately, the family was later deported with us to the ghetto and then to Auschwitz-Birkenau, where they all perished.

The third was the widow Blinde Mima (Blind Aunt) who was totally dependent on charity. My mother had more or less made Blinde Mima's needs her personal responsibility. I was often the messenger of Mother's charity and was always eager to carry cooked and baked goods to her and thereby be the recipient of her blessings. It was said that Blinde Mima's hands had special healing powers, with a specialty for setting broken bones. When I was a toddler, a cow had stepped on my right foot and broken it. I was told that it was Blinde Mima who had set it, although, unfortunately, not all that well. As a child, I had many occasions to feel her wonderfully soothing hands caressing the good limb to compare it with the swollen and perhaps broken one.

The Brucksteins adhered to the Chortkover Hasidic sect. In addition, they were followers of and believers in the sainthood of the Grand *Rebbe* Mordechai Leifer of Nadvorna, of blessed memory, the miracle-working wonder rabbi with whom my great-grandfather, Moshe Bruckstein, had a very close relationship. My great-grandfather built a guesthouse next to his home with all the amenities for the enjoyment of visiting rabbis, and would hire extra servants for his guests. Later, in 1930, when my great-grandfather passed away, I — as the first child born after his death — was named Moshe (Mojzis), after him. His wife, Great-Grandmother Sirka, then moved into the guesthouse and Grandfather Yisroel, being the eldest son, moved into my great-grandfather's house. My father, born on December 17, 1899, just after the Grand *Rebbe* died, had the privilege

5   The author refers here to the forced deportation of Jews to Kamenets-Podolski in the Ukraine. Despite the relative safety of Hungarian Jews at that time, tragedy struck in the summer of 1941. Some 18,000 Jews, randomly designated by the Hungarian authorities as "Jewish foreign nationals," were kicked out of their homes and deported to Kamenets-Podolski, where most were murdered. In early 1942, another 1,000 Jews from the section of Hungary newly acquired from Yugoslavia were murdered by Hungarian soldiers and police in their "pursuit of partisans."

of being named Mordechai, after him. The Bruckstein family maintained their practice of Orthodox Judaism without some of the fanaticism that was prevalent in some quarters.

OUR HOME

Our household was practically self-sustaining; other than the purchase of salt, we were very much independent, as far as staples were concerned. We did, however, augment our stores through purchases at markets. We milled the flour from our grain and pressed oil from sunflower and squash seeds that grew in our fields. Our cow Gyöngyi (Pearly) was like a family member to me. I frequently accompanied our maid, Ilona, to the barn for milking, where she would encourage me to drink the warm, foaming milk right from the milking tub, and I would be happy to oblige. I was so skinny that my mother used to refer to me as her *zhabe* (Yiddish for "frog") because I had blue-green veins running down my temples. When my grandson Kenny was younger, he looked just like that. If he stood sideways, you could miss him! I am convinced that being so skinny and requiring very little nourishment ultimately saved my life in the concentration camps, for I did not need much food to survive. However, prior to that period, my mother used to run after me, trying to get me to take another spoonful of something and she solicited our entire greater family to do so too, as it was well known that I ate next to nothing.

Every weekday morning, a herd of cattle, followed by the herdsman, came down the main street of our town. As the herd made its way to pasture, other cows joined them, including our cow. In the late afternoon, the bells around the necks of the cattle could be heard from far away as the herd made their way home, well fed and with their udders full of milk. I was fascinated by the fact that every cow knew which road to turn off to its home. The herdsman had a long whip, perhaps twenty-five feet long, with a foot-long flax and cotton snapper attached at its end and a short handle with a rope to secure the handle to his wrist. He expertly whirled the whip in great circles a few times around his head and, after giving off a blood-curling shout of "HAYAaaaaaaaACH," he would reverse the direction of the whirling whip with such force that he would nearly fall off his feet, resulting in a loud snap, the sound of which resembled a high-caliber rifle. He then followed it up by repeating his cry. His total repertoire included turning towards anyone within his sight and reveling in his deed while grinning from ear to ear, which revealed his few remaining ugly, rotten teeth. Children often followed him along his route and begged him to snap his whip, an activity that he was very happy to perform. For a few pennies he would include an ever-changing repertoire of some inventive ceremony. I had a particularly good track record of having my performance requests granted because Father rewarded his services handsomely, surely better than many others did.

Our beautifully feathered rooster was my pet and a source of pride; I frequently carried him under my arm to show him off to friends. Sometimes, my cousins and I would set up a cockfight, not realizing that it was inhumane. During these fights, I kept a watchful eye on my rooster and would quickly rescue him if I thought that he was getting hurt, which was seldom, if ever. One day, he went missing from the yard and a new rooster was in his stead. After a careful and devious interrogation, Ilona admitted that since the rooster was getting old he would be served for dinner. I was devastated and cried my eyes out. I decided that henceforth I would sleep with the new rooster to protect him from such a fate. At bedtime, my parents were in a panic looking for me and it took quite a while for them to discover me in the chicken coop. After a bath and much crying and hugging, I extracted a promise from Mother that the new rooster's life would be spared. I am convinced that this episode left a lasting impression on me, since I am a vegetarian today. I loved animals and agriculture and still love anything that has to do with nature.

I also had, for a short while, a little pet dog that was given to me by Pepik's father, whom I named "Kish Pici" (Little Pici), after my grandfather's Bulldog, Pici. The delight I experienced with Little Pici was unfortunately short lived. Little Pici had a habit of digging in gardens for rodents and the like and the police commandant who lived next door took particular pride in his vegetable garden. One day, after repeated warnings to keep my dog out of his garden, he shot the dog.

I had many fascinating diversions that grabbed and held my interest while on the way home from school. One of my most favorite was the artistic work of the blacksmith. The blowing bellows, the white heat of the fire and the white-hot iron that emerged from the fire mesmerized me. The sparks of the heated metal as it was rhythmically hammered into shape on the anvil delighted me. The whoosh of the steam rising from the water as the finished horseshoe was dunked into it for cooling seemed to me like a crescendo of an orchestra announcing that the product was ready. Then the final thrill, the virtuoso blacksmith would shoe the horse with the artistically formed hot horseshoe. He would then proceed to file the hoof for a more perfect contour. I loved horses and thought they were magnificent animals. I constantly inquired of the blacksmith whether the shoeing hurt the horse. He assured me that it did not and was only beneficial for the horse. I would have given anything to be the blacksmith or at least his apprentice; I thought that making something out of a bar of iron was a magical and worthwhile occupation.

Next door to the blacksmith was the barrel maker. He prepared the oak pieces of the barrel with such precision that, when the iron ring that the blacksmith made for him held the pieces together, and after some curing, the barrel would not leak. Whenever I passed the blacksmith's shed, I would stop at the barrel maker's with the intention of watching just for a moment, but would end up staying much too long. Many a day, having lost track of the time, Mother would send Ilona to fetch me, since she knew very well where I could be found.

Each season provided its own unique brand of fun and games. In the spring, I spent countless hours imagining to be the country squire of our estate, watching and "supervising" the plowing and planting of our fields. I loved the smell as the plow turned the earth and was delighted and mesmerized to see the miracle of a budding tree, which I still admire and regard as a miracle; or a leaf making its way out of the ground, which is no less of a marvel, as well as the busy work of a butterfly or a bee. Soon, beautiful swallows that seemed to be dressed in tuxedos began to build their nests, somehow always right under the eaves of our house. They ever so gracefully swooped away and returned with a little mud or straw in their beaks. It took a long time to build the nest and when finished, it was a perfect masterpiece, a work of art. By the middle of the summer we had a family of swallows, and by the end of the summer, it hurt me to see that when the swallows left, other birds occupied their nest, knowing that in the spring the swallows would have to construct new ones all over again. My world was full of fascinating things; wherever I turned I would see the enthralling wonder, the miracles of nature, and the creation of the Almighty.

In the summer, the trees were alive with the buzzing of the powerful deer-horned beetles that were the size of cicadas. The male insect was a favorite playmate of ours. The female of the species had no horns and therefore we, the children (cousins and friends), had no interest in them at all. The male beetle would cling to our clothing with its barbed legs and hold on tight to our fingers with their horns. When strategically placed, they would hopelessly entwine themselves in the hair of girls, whose screeches were a sheer delight to any little boy. A delight, I may add, that I availed myself of often. The birds would have a field day picking the beetles off branches of trees and, when offered from our hands, birds would gracefully swoop down and grab the beetles without touching us.

I ran in the fields among the tall corn and gorgeous sunflowers. I "inspected" our fruit trees and walked and played in the vegetable gardens. I often smelled a fistful of earth with approval, as I saw my father and others do. I preferred to walk through the fields than on the road, picking up an interesting twig or stone along the way. I would stop and admire a beautiful bird, mesmerized by its song. I spent hours watching the river flow and followed with my eyes a fish that was clearly visible in the crystal clear water. I waded in seeking some interestingly marbleized stones, which, if found, I would take home and show to my cousins. As soon as I learned how, I swam in the river by the mill, where it was dammed for the purpose of providing waterpower to the mill and to the turbines that produced the mill's electricity. Swimming in the Talabor River was very dangerous because of the timber floats cascading down the river rapids, over which the float master had very little control. Floats could hit the embankment and break up, causing their loose cargo of timber to float dangerously downriver. In the middle of summer, ice broke away from the mountains and rumbled down to the valley and into the Talabor. By the time the ice reached Buština, it had formed into large sheets with razor-sharp edges. Boys, though not any of my friends or family members, demonstrated their manhood by jumping on the ice and taking a ride, which sometimes resulted in dire, near fatal, consequences.

In the fall, our large yard was full of song and chatter as local men, women and girls were employed to husk the corn and the sunflowers for their seeds, which were put up in the attic of the barn to dry and, later in the year, were taken to my uncle's mill to be pressed for oil. As part of the pressing, the seeds were formed into round cakes that became highly nutritious fodder for our cow.

When the fruits, potatoes and vegetables came in from the gardens, the first wagonloads would go to the rabbi and various poor people. Under Mother's overall supervision, our kitchen was virtually converted into a canning factory for fruit and pickles. We accumulated eggs for Passover and preserved them in barrels of lye, while goose and chicken skins were rendered into fat accumulated in large jars that provided *gribenes* (cracklings), a delicacy eaten with bread or boiled potatoes and fried onions. I loved the smell of the plums as they were made into prune butter in a large copper cauldron that simmered over the fire burning in a pit dug in the yard. The whole house was abuzz; everyone ran to and fro as if aimlessly, but actually with orchestrated precision, carrying out the winter preparations. For more than two weeks our kitchen was as busy as a beehive. This season excited me; nevertheless, with all its hectic activities, I felt neglected by Mother. It just seemed to me that no one, particularly Mother and Ilona, had time for me.

In the fall, there were wagonloads of apples. The mountainous area near our town was world renowned for its apples and mineral water called "Borkut." Wagons full of apples came down the mountain and rolled along our roads to the railroad station for shipment. The smell of the crushed apples in the streets was like perfume. As a matter of fact, Buština had a marmalade and apple cider factory right by the railroad for those apples that didn't make the grade as they were of a lesser quality or were of a shape that was not perfect enough for retail. The apples were naturally beautiful and without pesticides of any kind.

My childhood was simply ideal. Each season had something to look forward to. Although the winters were harsh and long, nevertheless, it was our opportunity for sledding and ice-skating as well as building snowmen, tunnels and igloos. When the sun came out it would melt a thin top layer of the snow. Later, the melted top layer froze, creating a crust that was strong enough to support a man. We walked on the crust with a cane to stabilize ourselves and to provide us with something to break through the sharp-edged crust of ice should we fall through it into the deep snow.

Mondays and Thursdays were partial fast days, as was the religious cutom. Lunch was our main meal and we would have sauerkraut and beans, noodles and beans, or puréed beans with fried onions. Soup was a main staple and among our favorites were string bean that was fortified with sour cream, potato and leek, vegetable, and mushroom and barley. On other occasions, especially in the summer, we would have various fruit, squash or cauliflower soups, or perhaps *borscht* (beet soup), served cold with sour cream and a hot potato. We sometimes had fresh fish that was caught in the Tisza or Talabor Rivers just a few hours before serving. Carp was reserved for the Sabbath. The fish dishes were served with panfried potatoes and steamed or sautéed vegetables. On some Mondays or Thursdays, Mother would serve potato *latkes* (pancakes) or cheese and fruit *blintzes* (crepes) with sour cream or applesauce.

Fresh home-baked sourdough bread was a staple, accompanying every meal. The appropriate type of fresh bread, rolls or muffins accompanied every breakfast, lunch and dinner. Corn muffins with sour cream were and still are my favorite. Papa always reminded us to eat bread; he regularly admonished us with a familiar refrain, "Have some bread, otherwise you will be hungry in a little while." I still love freshly baked bread, especially the crust, and consider a meal incomplete if I do not eat at least one slice of good bread. A choice of bread and butter, warm muffins, cocoa pastry or cheese Danish were the usual breakfast fare, accompanied by coffee with milk and sugar. The coffee beans were mixed with chicory, roasted and then ground.

Pasta was a favored dish, homemade, of course. It was a wonder to see Mother cutting the slices by regulating their thickness, her fingernails serving as a guide for the razor-sharp knife. Many a lunch consisted of pasta lightly tossed in butter with ground walnuts, ground poppy seeds or cottage cheese (made from our cow Gyöngyi's milk) and always garnished with sugar. These pasta dishes were called in Hungarian *diós tészta, makos tészta* and *turos tészta*. Cheese or potato *kreplach* or *pierogen* (dumplings or ravioli) that were served with either sour cream or fried onions were among the favorite meals.

At times, when meat dishes were served, it was often a chicken that was taken from our yard. Turkey was rare, goose meat was served more often, and once in a while, we tasted the delicacy of duck. The preferred beef cut was flanken (short ribs). Chicken and meats, other than liver, were never grilled. Boiled meat was most productive as it also yielded a soup. Veal prepared any which way was a welcome meal, but it became a delicacy when stuffed. Mother created a pocket between the ribs and the veal; she then stuffed the pocket with chopped meat that contained eggs, paprika and herbs. Fried beef called *fasirt* (burgers) were the rage of the family, but the absolute favorite was *lungenwurst* (lung sausage), which was considered a particularly gourmet dish, so much so that when my stepmother Gizi invited my future in-laws for dinner for the first time, she served it. My mouth is watering as I write these lines, even though I am, and have been for some time, a vegetarian.

Thursday was the day for the Sabbath preparations. Whereas the main cooking for the Sabbath was done on Friday, all dairy and fresh-baked goods for the Sabbath, as well as for the rest of the week, were made on Thursday. Seeing that Thursday was a "dairy day," it presented a smaller possibility of conflict regarding the Jewish kosher dietary laws, which forbid the commingling of meat and dairy foods.

One of my fondest memories of my mother consists of the vivid sequences clearly pictured in my mind.

"I am home," I call out, announcing, "I am home from school!"

"I kiss your hand, Mama," I greet Mother as I walk into the foyer of our house. My beautiful Mama enters the foyer from the kitchen with an apron around her waist and a kerchief on her head, and is holding an empty hot baking pan with a dish towel.

"I was just thinking how wonderful it would be if you walked in just now. I have this baking pan encrusted with cacao and sugar, chocolate that oozed out of the *ruggelach* [rolled pastries] and the *kakaos* [Hungarian cake]."

"Mama, I love that," I say.

"Yes, that is why I was hoping that you would walk in. Here, sit down and enjoy it, darling; scrape and eat it with this fork and when you have finished enjoying it, we will look at your homework."

Homework was always the condition!

I feel blessed to be able to conjure up this delightful sequence of events at will, especially when my dear wife, Ruth, bakes or when I see *ruggelach* or *kakaos*. It never fails to delight me; however, it does give me a gentle squeeze of longing in my heart for my dearest mother, followed by a nostalgic sigh for my very short childhood.

The Sabbath meals, beginning on Friday night and continuing on Saturday, always started with the appropriate benedictions that were followed by an appetizer of either *gefilte* (ground and poached) fish or jellied carp. Customarily, fish was always eaten before meat and the two were never cooked, served or eaten together. Since the next course was a plate of chopped grilled liver, eggs, fried onions and seasoning, Papa would take some brandy in order to make the customary Jewish symbolic separation between fish and meat. The serving of the soup signaled the end of the appetizers and the beginning of the main course. Chicken soup with *kneidlach* (*matzoh* balls) or *lukshon* (noodles) was the standard fare. The chicken or meat was served with a salad of cucumbers and onions, and a *kugel* (a potato, carrot, noodle or vegetable pudding) and *tzimmis* (a sweet carrot, honey and raisin stew) would complete our delectable plate. In the winter, it was *chulent* and *kishka* (a casserole that was simmered or baked overnight, containing beef and beef bones, preferably with bone marrow, beans, barley and potatoes, fat and spices and stuffed derma).

It is interesting to note that, if one lived in the upper echelons of society, as our family did, the butcher would give us "nice fat stuff" — "fat" was synonymous with "good" in those days. I recall that if somebody back home said, "Oh, he looks so well," that meant he was fat. People who were scrawny were considered either hungry or sick, or at the very least, as looking unwell. Before condemning that way of life, one must consider the fact that we lived in a harsh, cold climate and the average man worked hard and long hours, burning many calories. It was a different world then.

I was a very skinny child who ate next to nothing. However, when considering my salivating descriptions above it seems that the little I did eat, I enjoyed. My Uncle Izidor nicknamed me *Libamáj* (goose liver paté, in Hungarian). It was his ritual on Sabbath afternoons to sit on his porch facing the big courtyard of my paternal grandfather's compound. Often, especially on Sabbath afternoons, my cousins and I played in the courtyard. When Uncle Izidor was having some goose liver paté as an afternoon snack, he would call out, "Andi, *Libamáj!*" (Andi, Goose Liver!), and I would come running. Every member of my extended family had his or her way to get some nourishment into me and I am still aware of what I eat, and obviously the quality and taste of my mother's food left an indelible impression on me. I am fortunate to be able to conjure up, much to my delight, scenes, tastes, smells or sounds from childhood and thereby re-experience them.

Yiddish was my mother tongue. Prior to the end of World War I, the Carpathian valley was part of the Hungarian section of the Austro-Hungarian Empire under Emperor Franz Joseph of Austria. My parents went to Hungarian and Yiddish schools where German was a required subject; at home they either spoke Yiddish, which was the preferred language, or Hungarian, the official language. The indigenous people spoke Ruthenian, which was their native and unofficial language. After World War I, with the creation of the Republic of Czechoslovakia, our section became part of Czechoslovakia, and Czech became the official language while all the other languages were retained. I spoke Yiddish, Czech or Hungarian at home and Ruthenian to those who spoke no other language. During the war, I, unfortunately, had the opportunity to learn to speak some German. After liberation in 1945, when I returned to Czechoslovakia, I passed the enrollment requirements to the fifth year (equivalent to freshman year of college) of the Real Gymnasium of Liberec (Reichenberg in German) where Russian was mandatory.

The holidays were my favorite days and it seemed to me that we lived from one holiday to another. They measured time as they marked the seasons. Truly, the holidays were an absolute joy. The most favorite of all was *Pesach* (Passover), followed by *Succoth* (Tabernacles). The whole aura of the preparations for the next holiday seemed to begin at the conclusion of the previous one, giving every holiday an ongoing importance and anticipation.

Getting dressed up and going to the synagogue with my parents and brother Tibi was a cherished occasion. As we walked up the road, uncles and cousins joined us. The synagogue was about one kilometer away, situated across the street from the old Brandstein house in the *Dorf* section of town. The whole experience was an absolute delight. I loved the smell of burned candles and the mahogany pews. The prayers were according to the Eastern European Hasidic custom (*Nusah Sfarad*) instead of the Ashkenazi order of prayers (as practiced by the majority of Jews in the United States), but not the *Sfaradi* custom of the eastern Jews.

As we returned home from the synagogue following the evening prayers, I was aware of a certain special, positively charged atmosphere. Everyone was dressed in his or her best. The sky seemed to me like a canopy of stars over our heads and the moon appeared within reach. Our entire extended family and friends were together as we left the synagogue and walked down the main road. Since we lived the furthest from the synagogue, we exchanged Sabbath or holiday greetings with everyone as they turned off the road toward their homes.

On *Rosh Hashanah* (Jewish New Year) and *Yom Kippur* (Day of Atonement) our dark, perhaps somewhat dingy, synagogue was transformed with the solemnity of these holidays that was the highlight of the year. It was an unbelievable sight to witness everyone in white *kittels* (long cotton robes) and prayer shawls. It seemed to me that my paternal grandpa and Papa looked angelic. During these holidays I could feel the presence of our Maker. The holiday atmosphere, the setting of the table with burning holiday candles and the dinners contributed to the aura that turned the holidays into holy days. On these occasions, the synagogue candles in front of the ark were made of beeswax. The flickering of the flames and the aroma of the burning beeswax remain in my mind and nostrils. It was an awe-inspiring experience.

For the Sabbath evening prayers we went next door to the Hasidic *Rebbe* Leifer's *shtiebel*. He was the grandson of the mystical miracle-working Grand *Rebbe* Mordechai Leifer of Nadvorna. He concluded the Friday night service with a unique tune that was preserved from his grandfather. The tune and refrain of "*Shabbis Shulam / Shabbis Mevorach*" (Peaceful Sabbath / Blessed Sabbath) went on among the congregants until the *Rebbe* stopped singing. It happily echoes in my mind to this day. We had a close relationship with the Leifers. The fence between our houses had a few planks removed so that they could come and draw water from our well because it was deeper and colder than theirs. The rabbi's youngest son, Yisroel Chaim, and my brother, Tibi, were close friends.

Since Grandpa Bruckstein, as well as the whole Bruckstein family, went to a different synagogue in the opposite direction from ours, I do not have recollections of their services. They frequented the newer Handal Synagogue, which was situated in the *Handal* section of town, near the bridge over the Talabor River.

Growing up in Buština, nearly everyone I knew or played with was a cousin. My universe consisted of my parents and my brother Tibi, who were the "sun and the moon" to me. The other "heavenly bodies" were my grandparents, aunts and uncles, while my numerous cousins were my stars in heaven. In addition to my grandparents' siblings and their families, I recall a number of other prominent families. They were the Wolf, Schreter and Hillman families who were partners in the water-powered flour mill and oil press. The Kraus family was in the lumber business where my father had his start as a young man. The Schwartz family was in the wholesale general merchandise business. The Simsovic family dabbled in lumber, while the Feigs had a small interest in my maternal grandfather's businesses. The Hillman family was in the alcohol and vinegar business as well as partners in the mill.

Among my fascinations, and there seemed to be many, was Grandfather Bruckstein's general store. It was situated near the top of Railroad Street, within sight of the *Central* crossroads. The store was somewhat recessed, allowing customers to park their horse-drawn wagons near the large cobblestone front. While the store did not refuse the retail trade, it was primarily a wholesale operation. It was the major supplier of general merchandise to the stores of the surrounding towns and regions, handling a broad spectrum of goods including flour, sugar, vinegar, wire, nails and more. It was in competition with the Schwartz store in town. The commerce in Buština was big enough and strong enough to draw a very wide clientele. I used the store as my private stash. All I had to do was show up and someone would shove some goodies into my hand. I loved filberts (a type of hazelnut) and never neglected to secure a fistful of them. I believe the word was out from my mother that everyone should do their best to try to fatten me up. I built a personal relationship with all the employees in the store and I profited from this often.

Board games were popular and everyone learned to play chess. We kids emulated the adults, challenging each other for a game. The ability to play a decent game of chess was a cherished achievement. That was until my cousin Mendi Schreter, an only child who was showered with everything, trumped us with his recently acquired prized possession: a board game called Monopoly (based on the streets of Budapest instead of the original, which is based on Atlantic City in New Jersey). With his new game, Mendi became "king of the hill." We all kowtowed to him and did his bidding just for the opportunity to play.

However, Mendi's "reign" soon came to an end when Doctor Jung, a famous ear, nose and throat specialist from Sighet, recommended to my parents that I have my tonsils removed. I was terrified and did not want to go. My mother ultimately bribed me with the promise of any present of my choice. Of course, I selected Monopoly! However, when my mother later learned that my cousins, Ervin and Vicki, and I were now being mean to Mendi (we didn't need him anymore), she quickly put an end to it. My mother would not tolerate that kind of behavior and made sure we were kind and inclusive.

ELEMENTARY SCHOOL

The first three years of my elementary education, while the Carpathians were still part of the Czechoslovak Republic, is a period that I look back on with a smile. It was sheer pleasure to spend the better part of the day with friends and in the care of wonderful, caring and dedicated teachers. We learned many songs and many interesting things and the preparations and rehearsals for the annual school play were a delightful interlude from the regular school programs.

Every school day culminated in the delight of being greeted by Mother who would hug me tight to her bosom and smother me with the warmest wonderful kisses one can possibly imagine. After a *nosh* (snack) of some freshly baked goods (if it was a Thursday), a hot cocoa or some other delight, Mother enthroned me in her favorite place for me, the foyer right off the kitchen, where she could keep an eye on me and be available for my frequent need of help while doing my homework. When and if the homework passed and met her critical approval, including the handwriting, it was then playtime. I would accompany Ilona on her chores feeding our cow and chickens, or wander off to examine a flower, or just look up at the sky and find some interesting cloud patterns. I found that if I looked at the clouds long and hard enough, I could find a recognizable image.

Papa's arrival home signaled that it was suppertime, and the day would end with a warm bath that provided many opportunities to be close to Mother and be on the receiving end of her wonderful hugs and kisses. The day would be capped off by saying my prayers and Mama's warm, secure tuck into bed. I shared the room with my brother. He had the privilege of staying up a little longer than I, so that by the time he went to bed, I would be sleeping the sleep of the innocent. So ended a typical, perfect day.

Every afternoon after school, including Sundays, I went to *cheder*. It was a one-room school. Like many other community endeavors, our greater family members were the major contributors who financed at least half of its costs. Nevertheless, the school was threadbare, with an income barely meeting its minimum financial needs. A rabbi from the nearby town of Bedevlya was the teacher; he supplemented his income by giving afternoon and evening classes in our school as well as private tutoring for *Bar Mitzvah* preparation. The *cheder* class consisted mostly of my cousins and friends, along with some other boys from the town whom I didn't know.

There was an incident, which took place one winter day, that I particularly remember. It was a Thursday, the day all Hebrew schoolchildren dreaded, because it was on Thursdays that we had the *farheren* (oral test) on the week's material. We had to repeat what we had learned, in all its intricacies, with some passages by heart. This particular Thursday I was less than marginally prepared and I decided that *cheder* had to be avoided. However, the problem was how? Not knowing my lessons or just playing hooky would not meet with approval at home and might have some unpredictable consequences. So, what to do?

I reminded myself of a recently overheard conversation between my brother and his friends describing how easily one could disturb the classroom in the wintertime. At the time I overheard the conversation, I made careful note of it for possible later use. "If the need arises," I had murmured to myself. "Well, if not now, then when?" I reasoned. "It is the winter and the need is certainly here!" I decided that then was the time to put this newly acquired knowledge into action.

At home, before my departure for school, I took a matchbox and filled it with a combination of paprika and pepper. Upon my arrival at *cheder*, I furtively threw my concoction into the little wood-burning stove that the rabbi personally attended and which barely managed to keep the frost off the windows of the room. As the mixture began to burn, it gave off a dense, choking smoke that burned the eyes and throats of the students and the rabbi alike, making it impossible for the class to continue. In the midst of much coughing and gagging, the class was dismissed. While clearing his throat and washing his eyes with snow, the rabbi, his face red with anger and quoting appropriate passages from the Bible to reinforce his words, insisted that the culprit come forward. When his request did not meet with success, he started right there and then an immediate investigation to discover the perpetrator. His investigation bordered on an inquisition. Since I judged his efforts to be totally fruitless, I felt safe enough and left school, although I had no idea where I would go. I was afraid to go home earlier than the usual dismissal time as that would have started a sequence of intense questioning by my mother first and then by my father, a "double whammy" that would have put the rabbi's inquisition to shame. Covering up my perpetration of this "dastardly deed," in the words of the rabbi, I obviously drew a fine moral line to fit the occasion. It was one thing to lie to the rabbi and another thing to lie to my parents. Therefore, I decided that instead of going home and facing the music that would inevitably force me to lie, I would go home at the regular time and avoid the whole inevitable episode. Hence, I stopped off at the blacksmith (where else?), and spent the remaining hours watching him shoe horses and make wheel rims and barrel rings.

It was finally time to go home. As I got within sight of my house, I noticed that the *rebbe* from my *cheder* was just leaving. I caught a glimpse of him as he was coming out through our gate. This was not a very good sign on any day, but considering what had happened in school that afternoon, it did not bode well. I continued home with my heart in my throat. I suspected oncoming doom as I furtively entered the house; I could hear my heart pounding as I ever so softly greeted my parents.

"Andi, I want to talk to you," my papa said in an authoritative voice much like a command. Surprisingly, somehow his voice calmed me down as I thought, "Here it comes; soon it will be over."

I braced myself for the coming questions, but much to my relief, Mother said to Father, "Not now Mordche, let him eat first." Mother would never allow anything to interfere with the slim possibility of my eating dinner.

We were seated at the dinner table in our usual seats. Father sat at the head of the table, Mother sat opposite him, Tibi to my father's right and I to his left. At the end of dinner, my father asked me: "Andi, did anything unusual happen in school today?"

"No," I answered. Thereupon, Father stretched out his left hand and slapped me across my face, causing me to nearly fall backwards.

Papa asked again, "Did anything unusual happen in school today?"

"No," I said once again. Papa, who had seldom, if ever, hit me became livid with anger; I had committed the unthinkable and lied to him! What's more, I lied to him twice!! Papa knocked me and my chair over with another slap.

At this point, I somehow got the idea that he knew about the unusual thing that had happened in school that day, and that the *rebbe*'s inquisition must have yielded my name. Once again, I was told to sit at the table. As I was doing so, I began to cry hysterically. Mother picked me up and smothered me by taking me to her bosom and saved me from any further interrogation. This episode was all the more memorable because Father was a loving, gentle man who usually left the disciplining of the children to Mother. His children's gross misbehavior, freshness or lying would bring shame to the family, which he would not tolerate.

Notwithstanding this particular incident, these were happy days, as childhood days are bound to be. The world's leaders, meanwhile, were jockeying for their prospective positions on the chessboard of the world, especially of Europe. They were brewing the prerequisites for the catastrophe that would soon engulf humanity, but not necessarily themselves or their immediate families, into an unmentionable inferno. We, the innocent, were to be the victims who would pay the price for their ambition, unabated pride and sheer stupidity.

PART II

END OF CHILDHOOD

THE HUNGARIAN OCCUPATION

lthough I had heard adults around me talking about antisemitism, I had no idea what it really meant and it certainly did not affect me. I had neither knowledge nor understanding of the aims of the evil conspirators who were soon to bring the world the greatest disaster ever perpetrated by man upon mankind.

Konrad Ernst Eduard Henlein, a former gymnastics teacher who echoed German Chancellor Hitler's demands and did his bidding concerning Czechoslovakia, founded the German Sudeten Party with the aim of allowing Germany to occupy the Sudeten section of Czechoslovakia. The dominance in the 1930s of Henlein's Sudetenland political party contributed to the Munich Agreement on September 30, 1938, which was due in part to his influence on the British delegate Lord Runciman during the latter's visit to Czechoslovakia. On September 29-30, 1938, the Munich Conference was attended by England, France, Germany and Italy. Notably, the Czechs, whose very existence was at stake, were not invited. The conference resulted in the infamous Munich Pact.

The German partial occupation of Czechoslovakia in 1938, and all of Czechoslovakia in March 1939, came about as a result of a decision made at the Munich Conference. Prime Minister of Great Britain, Neville

Chamberlain, and Prime Minister Eduard Daladier of France acquiesced to the dismemberment of Czechoslovakia, thereby legitimizing Hitler's claim to the northern part of Czechoslovakia, which the Germans called the southern part of Germany, "Sudetenland." Hitler based his claim on the so-called "plebiscite" that was conducted with predictable results. It was a well-doctored sham by Germany's surrogates in the Sudetenland, given that only the ethnic German inhabitants were allowed to vote; it obviously resulted in the inhabitants' preference to be a part of Germany. The German occupation of the Sudetenland and, from March 1939, Czechoslovakia (Reichsprotektorat Böhmen und Mähren), brought an avalanche of claims against Czech homes, businesses and properties by the ethnic German population in the Sudetenland, resulting in many confiscations of property and the deportations of their rightful owners. Since Hitler threatened war if Germany's claim was not resolved in its favor, the western nations chose appeasement of Hitler, and Chamberlain declared he had achieved "peace in our time."

On March 15, 1939, Hungary's claim to the Carpathian section of Czechoslovakia was honored by Hitler and Mussolini, and thus our hometown of Buština became occupied by Hungary. This action resulted in the finality of the dismemberment of Czechoslovakia. Hitler's action, with the agreement of the Allied Powers, ended the existence of our Czech, Western-style democratic republic with its parliamentary form of government. Within a year of the Munich Pact, as a direct result of Hitler's belief that the leaders of the West were weak degenerates who would not fight for their freedom or their countries, Germany and her Axis allies invaded Poland, starting World War II.

It was arranged that there would be a hiatus of ten to fourteen days between the retreating Czech Army and the occupying Hungarian Army, so that the armies would not clash. A demagogue by the name of Voloshin was forcefully advocating an independent Ukraine in the territory of Carpathia, instead of the forthcoming Hungarian occupation. This new entity was to be called Ruthenia. To this end, he aligned himself with a native Nazi warlord by the name of Sich, who had organized his followers into a quasi-army called Sich's Guards, or Sichaki by the Czechs. The organization was under the direct control of the Germans and was a copy of the Hungarian Nyilas (Arrow Cross), a subversive Nazi organization closely following the doctrines and actions of the German Nazi storm troopers or Brown

Shirts. During the power vacuum of the hiatus, Sich promptly pronounced the region as independent Ukraine and declared all previous laws null and void. Following his lead, many priests of the region, who were supporters and advocates of Sich, proclaimed the State of Independent Ukraine in their churches.

Informed of the suspension of all Czech laws and having been bombarded with antisemitic rhetoric, the indigenous population took advantage of the situation and exercised their hitherto suppressed antisemitic inclinations and lawless greed, resulting in complete anarchy and pandemonium. The indigent youth, with Sich Guards in their leadership, went on a rampage. Robbery, rape, chaos and mayhem were the norm. Fearing for our lives, we spent most of the days and nights in our cellar, behind heavy doors. Our maid, Ilona, was our connection to the outside world, from which we could hear the youths rampaging and firing guns. News of break-ins and robberies unsettled us and rattled our nerves. I was eight years old.

As the Czech Army was withdrawing from our town, they were bottlenecked at the bridge crossing the Talabor River. The Sichaks were sniping at them from the nearby Handal Synagogue and managed to shoot and kill a Czech soldier. The Czechs fired a few rounds of artillery at the synagogue, damaging it. A Czech officer sought out Grandfather Bruckstein, since he was the de facto head of the Jewish community. The officer informed him that they were going to neutralize the area so that the Czech Army could cross the bridge, which was totally exposed to sniper fire. They intended to do this by shooting cannons and mortars at our side of the town in order to clear the swath of land that included our houses. He wanted to eliminate the "cover" for the Sichaks, and ordered my grandfather to clear out his people from the designated area within two hours.

Grandfather ran across the street to get Father, and had the officer repeat his statement. After much explanation and pleading to rescind their decision to reduce part of our town to rubble — mainly Jewish property — the parties struck a compromise. My father would become a go-between and act as the emissary to the local clergy. So it happened that my father called upon the clergy of our town, together with the Czech officer, and explained the situation. It was decided that a peaceful demonstration for an independent Ukraine, a parade, would take place on the main street leading to the bridge, shielding the retreating Czech Army, enabling them to cross in peace. While the demonstration never took place, the threat to demolish part, and if need be, the whole town, was proclaimed throughout the town.

The proclamation was made in the usual way: Our town crier stood in various strategic places in town and drummed loudly until a crowd had gathered. He then ceremoniously read the proclamation followed by a drum roll, proceeded to his next position and repeated the whole act. He fascinated many of the town's children, including me, who typically followed him on his appointed rounds as if he were the Pied Piper. Although the town was ultimately spared, the synagogue was nearly totally destroyed. In 1940, the year following its destruction, it was rebuilt to a point of minimum usefulness but was never restored completely, and certainly not to its previous grandeur. Due to the behavior of the Sichaks, by the time the Hungarian Army entered the area, they were perceived as liberators. Everyone, including our parents and grandparents who remembered the Austro-Hungarian Empire, welcomed them as liberators.

It happened one early afternoon while my mother was bathing me in a washtub. A commotion of great excitement broke out outside. People were running on the road and shouting that the Hungarians had arrived. Papa and Tibi ran out to the street to join the excitement, while Mother ran to the window to see this momentous occasion. In her excitement, she left me standing naked, wet and soapy. I finally ran to her and was jumping up and down, screaming and begging to see what was going on. Mother lifted me up to the window, without bothering to rinse and dry me off, in order not to miss any of the spectacle. Just then, the "liberating" Hungarian Army passed our house. It was a sight to behold. In the lead was a general on horseback, decked out in his parade uniform, wearing boots with spurs. A red, white and green sash was strung across his chest that was bedecked with medals. He had a saber suspended from his belt and a horsewhip in his left hand. His beautiful, white steed was walking somewhat sideways, parade style. Officers of a lower rank followed the general, and, in turn, the cavalry. The parade continued with an array of horse-drawn artillery, field guns and ammunition wagons and, eventually, by the Hungarian foot soldiers with their equipment.

The Hungarian Army made a very quick end to the rampaging Sichaks. As the Hungarians were advancing, they hung captured Sichaks on telephone poles along the road. This was instant Hungarian justice that immediately ended the rebellion and restored order by asserting their brutal military authority. The bulk of the Sichak guards escaped across the Carpathian Mountains into Ukraine, where they joined the Ukrainian Nazi Bender Group, which was of its own ilk, and whose members, in turn, joined the German Army and were subsequently at the forefront of many of the atrocities committed against the Jews.

All the townsfolk, including my parents and grandparents, greeted the Hungarians dressed in their finery and displayed red, white and green bunting, the colors of the Hungarian flag. They stood in the street waving flags to welcome the "liberators," believing that these Hungarians were the disciples of the benevolent monarch Franz Joseph whom they warmly remembered. We children were told that the Hungarians were our friends and that it was all right to run around and mingle with the soldiers and play with them. We were to accept them as liberators and behave normally in their presence without fear, as if they were the Czechs. Our parents' opinion of the "liberators" was soon to change abruptly.

The Hungarians did not waste much time revealing their true character. I was witness to the army's punishment of "*kikotes*," whereby they would hang a disobedient soldier from a pole by his wrists that were tied behind his back. In order to prolong the agony, every time the unfortunate victim lost consciousness, he would be revived with buckets of water thrown in his face. I also remember an incident that took place while I was standing with my father in front of our house. A highly decorated lieutenant general in full uniform arrived on horseback, and an orderly ran up to hold his horse's bridle. The soldier was either not holding the horse properly or perhaps a button was not closed on his tunic, but whatever small infraction he committed, suddenly, the officer kicked the orderly in the face. The soldier was badly wounded; nevertheless, he stood at attention while the officer proceeded to horsewhip him. I'll always remember how Father turned to me and warned me to stay away from them, "Andi, these are not Franz Joseph's Hungarians, these are Hungarian barbarians." When I told my mother what I had witnessed, she told me that I should avoid them just like I would a dangerous animal. This was not the last act of brutality I would see committed by the Hungarians.

EARLY ANTISEMITISM

With the occupying Hungarian Army came the Hungarian teachers whose only qualification was that they were the officers' girlfriends. My mother called them "camp followers" (but I didn't understand what that meant). In order to get on the government's payroll they became the new teachers in our schools. The Hungarians had a slogan that "if it's Hungarian bread you eat, then it's the Hungarian language you speak!" Our classes were now all taught in Hungarian.

During the first few days, my teacher, who was the girlfriend of the highest-ranking officer and was staying in my maternal grandfather's house, lectured us about the history and the greatness of Hungary, the Hungarian Army and especially the greatness of its officers. I somehow provoked this teacher by telling one of my fellow students that I knew they were barbarians and that I was at home there, whereas they were the strangers. The teacher came over to me, and while calling me a "shitty Jew," hit me on the head with a ruler and then ordered me to hold up my fingers to be hit. This was a common school punishment in Hungary, called *kőrőmos* (fingernailing). I refused to obey her and started to cry. She hit me on the head once more, and again called me a "filthy, shitty Jew." I quickly gathered up my belongings and ran out of the class with a chorus of snickers ringing in my ears. I ran home sobbing and told my mother what had happened. Without delay, Mother took me by my hand, we went back to the school, and entered the classroom for a confrontation.

"Did you hit my child?" Mother demanded.

As the teacher went into a tirade against Jews, Mother slapped her across the face. The teacher made some noise about the general, threatening that we would hear from him. This ended that particular incident. Within days, the teacher was transferred to another school and nothing more came of it. At that point and time, being too early in the occupation, the authorities took into consideration what kind of family was involved; however, only one year later, the same action would have had dire, life-threatening consequences.

For me, school was a snap. I spoke Hungarian while most others did not. Mother always kept me a few steps ahead of the curriculum by preparing me for the class. The antisemitic teachers would make me stand up, and while pointing at me, admonish the class saying, "Look at the Jew! How come he knows? Shame on you!" At other times, when nobody knew the answer to a given question and I had my hand up, the teacher would say, "All right, Jew, what is the answer?" I somehow never caught on that it would be better to lie low and keep my hand down and my mouth shut to avoid the teacher's retort. My classmates, including my "friends," began to resent me for causing them embarrassment.

Things changed quickly. I was accustomed to being the center or at least the major player in all the school games, but now the Hungarian "colonizer" urchins played a new game, called "Get the Jew." Their feelings at school were reinforced at home, as antisemitism became blatant. In school, it was pointed out that the Jew always finished his assignment first; the Jew always handed in his neat homework on time (my mother would sit with me until it was completed to her satisfaction); and the Jew always had the poems memorized. (Actually, my mother would learn each poem first, and as she was doing her needlework, she would have me repeat it over and over, putting it to a tune and singing it to me. Seldom did I go to bed without knowing it by heart, and then in the morning she went over it with me again.) At school, it wasn't Andi who knew the poem; rather, it was the Jew who knew the poem. Many students could not speak Hungarian, but they knew the Hungarian term "Zsido" (Jew).

I did not understand the term "antisemitism" or that such behavior had a name. I just thought that this is what these hooligans were like and that they just disliked me. I did not think much of them, either; I thought that they were dumb and rough. I did not understand the distinction between my dislikes and their hatred. Mother told me to stay away from them, especially from the "occupiers," and told me not to join in their soccer games. What bothered and grieved me most was the behavior of my former non-Jewish friends. I could not understand why they gravitated to the side of my tormentors, especially when the chips were down. When things got rough for me, I took solace in the fact that soon I would be home, where everything was always all right. Such behavior by teachers and students was unheard of prior to the Hungarian occupation. As a child, I had never experienced antisemitism from any adult in authority. Once in a while, a kid would yell out an antisemitic slur such as, "Christ killer," or "Jew, go to Palestine!" But if their parents heard of their offspring's epithets, the kid would be abruptly silenced, for most likely their livelihood depended on the very same Jew.

Sundays were different: We were admonished by Mother not to pass by or go near a church. On Sundays, as the parishioners came out of church all fired up by the priest about the "Jewish Christ killers," it was unpleasant if not outright dangerous to be within sight. Nobody would come right up to me and call me any derogatory name, but whatever these children did or said was hammered into them by the priests and, to some extent, by what they heard from their parents at home, many of whom could neither read nor write. Illiteracy in our region among the indigenous people, including the priests, was notoriously common.

I do recall one incident that occurred when I was snow sledding far behind the large home of my Brandstein grandparents. There was a terrific hill where lots of kids would gather to sled down for fun. On this occasion, as I reached the bottom of the hill, some local non-Jewish bullies flipped me over and tried to steal my sled. However, Tibi showed up out of nowhere and managed to grab the sled back. He then scared off the bullies by spinning around, swinging the sled and daring them to fight him. Tibi was like a superhero!

In 1940, at the age of nine and a half, I experienced one of the most memorable and painful personal episodes in my young life. It was the passing of my beloved Grandma Ruchele, my mother's mother. Grandma Ruchele was my "second mother," protector and best friend. I loved her with all my heart and soul. I could not come to terms with her loss; I mourned her then, and still do. Grandma Ruchele meant to me everything that is beautiful and nice. I cannot believe that anyone else ever had a grandma like my Grandma Ruchele. Not until I lost my saintly mother and, many years later, my dear father, have I had such a feeling of loss as that of Grandma Ruchele.

In 1941, the Hungarians declared the entire Carpathian region a military zone. They hastily began to reinforce the mountain passes as a barrier to the advancing Russian Army. Enormous amounts of armaments, mostly field guns, cannons and more war materials, were being trucked eastward through Buština, heading to the mountains.

During the following several months, we were awakened nightly by the rumble of heavy trucks that shook the foundations of our house as they passed by, just a few yards from our windows. Many times, the convoys of armaments lasted most of the night. My brother Tibi and I found this exciting and it was a hot topic of conversation among our cousins and friends. We were somewhat disadvantaged, however, relative to others, because Mother usually prevented us from climbing onto the windowsill for a better look. Instead, she instructed us to keep the house in total darkness at night so as not to bring our home and ourselves to the attention of the passing barbarians.

Having been exposed to the "reinforcement" scenario and having had the opportunity to see what seemed to me the mighty Hungarian Army, some of whom were camped across the street from my home in Grandpa Bruckstein's cane sheds, and seeing the comings and goings from Grandpa Bruckstein's house where a wing with three bedrooms was commandeered and occupied by the top Hungarian military officers of whom I was in awe, I could not understand why the adults, including my father, made statements such as, "The Russians will go through them like a hot knife through butter." Unfortunately, we did not get the chance to see this, since the Russians did not attack the Hungarians in the Carpathian Mountains until after we had been deported. When they finally attacked, the Russians did go through the Hungarians exactly as he had predicted.

As the reinforcement of the Russian front approached its final stages, and the activity of transporting war materials began to ebb, the Hungarian military authorities proceeded to their next agenda, namely, the "Hungarianization" of the territory. This was carried out by bringing in indigent criminal elements, the unemployed and, in many cases, criminals from the jails. These "colonizers," whom everyone referred to as "the scum of the Hungarian Motherland," occupied our homes and businesses and soon became our cruel bosses. This "scum" was fiercely antisemitic and introduced persecution on a new grand scale. Their antisemitism was mostly for economic reasons. Every Jewish business was forced to have at least one "true Hungarian partner," as the military authorities referred to them, and they were given Jewish housing, farms, land and business establishments that were confiscated under any trumped-up baseless charges they could think of. Accordingly, they had a vested economic interest in antisemitism, a bonanza that they fervently honed and practiced with clever innovations and inventiveness; simply put, our losses were their gains. They taught their newest vicious, outrageous and ferocious lies about Jews to their urchins who then spread them in school and made our lives intolerable. This colonization heralded the beginning of the official systematic persecution of the Jews.[1] The colonizers were insatiable in their economic and monetary demands on Jews. Every day brought new demands and threats of bodily harm if their extortions were not met. The power of the colonizers' intimidation was the stated or implied threat of going to the authorities with the most outrageous and ridiculous fabricated lies to present their claims. They were encouraged by the knowledge that the Hungarian military authorities, whose lackeys they were, would always, without fail, take their word against that of any Jew for any claim they could dream up, and that Jewish defense against their claims, even if supported by ironclad, undeniable proof, was never adequate. They knew as well as we did that when dealing with the fiercely antisemitic Hungarian antisemitic authorities, a Jew was always wrong just because he was a Jew.

I began to associate the word antisemitism, which I heard everywhere around me, with the baseless hatred and the terrible curses hurled at me and my Jewish friends in school by the urchins of the colonizers and with increasing frequency by the native Ruthenian children who emulated them. Their curses and epithets, as well as being spat at, kept reverberating in my mind long after school and inflicted my soul and disrupted my equilibrium. I began to understand the meaning of antisemitism and its intention. I began to understand and feel the pain of the antisemitic acts that everyone was talking about, acts that were perpetrated on us every day. My parents were unable to quell the fear in me, especially since it was the dominant topic of everyone's conversation. There was just no way a child could be shielded from it. I often inquired of my parents and grandparents whether we would be harmed; their reassurances to the contrary did not do much to quell my fears.

---

1   The first anti-Jewish law, promulgated on May 29, 1938, restricted to 20 percent the number of Jews in commercial enterprises, in the press and among physicians, engineers and lawyers. The second law (May 5, 1939), defined Jews racially: People with two, three or four Jewish-born grandparents. Their employment was forbidden in many areas: government, media, medicine, law and more. The number of Jews that private companies could employ was restricted. Most also lost their right to vote. The third anti-Jewish law, which was passed on August 8, 1941, changed the definition of "Jew" according to the Nuremberg racial laws. The law prohibited intermarriage, as well as sexual relations between Christians and Jews.

Bruckstein family reunion on the occasion of Miriam Bruckstein's
(Andrew's great aunt) return visit to Buština from the US, 1925.

Front row of adults (left to right): Rachel (Andrew's grandmother, holding Sophie),
Yisroel Natan (Andrew's grandfather), Sirka (Andrew's great-grandmother),
Moshe (Andrew's great-grandfather), Miriam (Moshe's daughter) and Joseph Bruchenstein
(Miriam's husband).

Back row (fourth from right): Matilda (Andrew's mother), Vali and Gizi
(Matilda's twin sisters); (fourth from left): Fanny (Matilda's sister).

Yisroel Natan
and Rachel Bruckstein
(Andrew's maternal
grandparents),
Buština.

Rachel Bruckstein (Andrew's maternal grandmother) before her wedding.

Eliezer and Amalia Brandstein (Andrew's paternal grandparents), Buština.

Matilda and Ernest Brandstein (Andrew's parents).

DIE TRAUUNG UNSERER KINDER

MATILDE UND ERNST

WIRD AM 4. JÄNNER 1927. 4 UHR NACHMITTAGS IN SEVLJUS
STATTFINDEN, ZU DER WIR SIE SAMMT W. FAMILIE
HÖFL. EINLADEN.

BUŠTINA IM MON. JÄNNER 1927.

ISRAEL BRUCKSTEIN & FRAU.
LAZAR BRANDSTEIN & FRAU.

ABENDMAHL UM 6 UHR.

TELEGRAMMADRESSE: BRUCKSTEIN, HOTEL EUROPA SEVLJUS.

The wedding invitation of Matilda and Ernest, January 1927.

Left to right: Tibor, Matilda, Ernest and Andrew Brandstein (Burian).

Andrew (left) and Tibor, prewar.

Tibor (left, 9 years old) and Andrew (7 years old), 1938.

Matilda Brandstein with Tibor (left) and Andrew.

Matilda (Bruckstein) Brandstein.

Children going to *cheder* with local rabbi.

Front to back: Herzi [_], Vicki Brandstein, Ervin Brandstein, Mendi Shechter, Gyuszi Woolf, Oti Brandstein, [_] Schwartz, Pali Karausz, Tibor Brandstein.

Matilda Brandstein (center, back) with three of her sisters: Gizi (left), Vali (right), Fanny (front), 1925.

Left to right: Cousins Vicki, Ervin and Oti Brandstein in the backyard
of the Brandstein grandparents' home, 1940.

Brandstein and Bruckstein cousins and friends (Ervin Brandstein on shoulders, Manci Brandstein lying far left, Sophie Brandstein lying in front) on the Talibor riverbank, 1942.

Joseph (Joszi) Bruckstein,
Budapest, 1942.

Sophie (Zofka)
Bruckstein, 1943.

The ramp in Birkenau. Hungarian Jews being subjected to the selection process,
May 1944, Yad Vashem Photo Archives.

Andrew's registration card for Mauthausen concentration camp,
stating that he entered Auschwitz on June 3, 1944 and was transferred
to Mauthausen on January 30, 1945.

The entrance to Mauthausen, Yad Vashem Photo Archives.

Prisoners carry large stones up the "stairs of death" of the Mauthausen quarry. Courtesy of Archiv der KZ-Gedenkstaette Mauthausen, USHMM.

Tibor, 1945.   Andrew, 1945.

Andrew in Liberec
with a non-Jewish friend,
c. 1945.

Andrew's repatriation papers to Czechoslovakia,
August 31, 1945.

THE FIRST DEPORTATION

S oon, the next phase of the Hungarian tyranny was unleashed: All Jews were ordered to register, regardless of age, and state whether they were Hungarian citizens by virtue of residence in the Austro-Hungarian Empire prior to 1918. The registration was to be completed within a period of three months beginning in April 1941. Failure to do so would have dire consequences, the least of which was deportation along with the Jews who were unable to prove that they were Hungarian citizens. Furthermore, all able-bodied Jewish males from eighteen to fifty years old were ordered to report to the military authorities. Once there, they were interrogated about their skills, if any, and many of them were selected for forced labor camps. Those selected were, at first, trucked daily to work sites in the mountains where they installed telephone poles for military communication. Later, they were taken away to work camps on the Ukrainian side of the Carpathian Mountains. There, the work camp was nothing but a concentration camp.[2]

Mother's older brother, Geza, was living in Antwerp, working for the Czechoslovakian consulate, when the war broke out. He married Paulina Brodt and, as a wedding gift, they received a Packard car. When the borders were closed, they decided to get to Tangier by driving across France and Spain and then try to make their way to England. To reach and pass through the French/Belgian border, Geza donned a Czech Army uniform with stripes, put a Czechoslovakian flag on his car and passed himself off as an embassy attaché. They had a chauffeur. So, while Paula sat inside the car, Geza stood on the outboard of the Packard while the Belgian and French police and border patrols ushered them through. In this way, Geza got them out of France, across Spain and into Tangier, Morocco. From there, they made their way to Oran in Algeria, from where they could fly to London. In 1942, they finally obtained their visas for England. Having spent all their money during the long trip and their stay in Tangier, Geza rejoined the Czech Army while Paula assisted in

---

2   In March 1939, a law was passed in Hungary requiring the draft of Jews aged twenty to forty-eight into labor service units. After the German invasion of the Soviet Union in June 1941, the service began to grow. By 1942, 100,000 men had served or were serving in these units. More than 40,000 Jews died there. For further information see http://www.yadvashem.org/yv/en/education/newsletter/31/conscripted_slaves.asp (accessed, March 17, 2016).

a hospital and sold her knitting works. They had their first child, Edward, in England. After the war, they went back to Belgium where they had their second child, Robert.

Mother's younger brother, Uncle Joseph, happened to be on business in Budapest at the time of the edict. Upon his return home, he was selected for forced labor and eventually wound up in a penal labor camp in Ukraine near the city of Kiev. Some inmates of various work camps escaped and returned home, where news of their experiences spread. A fellow inmate of Uncle Joseph, who managed to escape and return home, gave us a vivid description of my uncle's catastrophic fate. Due to the deplorable conditions in the camp, the scourge of typhus broke out among the workers. The Germans isolated the inflicted in a designated bunk, supposedly designated as a sick bay, where Uncle Joseph volunteered as an orderly to take care of the sick. A few days later, as the Germans were sure that all the afflicted were so segregated, they set fire to the bunk and burned it down with everyone in it. This is how the Germans dealt with the outbreak and this is how our dear, darling Uncle Joseph was murdered.

The information from the slave labor returnees was the main topic of conversation. While it was just a trickle of information on the situation of the slave laborers and deportees, it nevertheless initiated intensive discussions between my father, grandfather and uncles as to its meaning. To where would all this lead; and what and when should we do anything about it? Father reported the horrific firsthand report by one returnee from the East, who described killings in the woods. The witness had escaped because the Germans had left him for dead. German soldiers and Ukrainians in German uniforms were killing the Jews, some of whom were marched off into the woods and never heard of again. Grandpa realized it was murder, not just robbery. The entire community was in a panic. This information from the slave labor escapees turned out to be just a very tiny part of the atrocities that were actually being perpetrated on the deportees by the Germans and their eager co-conspirators, the fiercely antisemitic Ukrainians. Yet, it was but an overture of things yet to come. Just a few months later, the Hungarians began summoning those Jews who either admitted to or were suspected of not having official Hungarian citizenship.

Giselle Goldberger ("Gizi," who survived the war and became my stepmother after the war) and her entire family — her father, stepmother, sister and younger brother — were deported from the town of Mukačevo (Munkács). Her older brother, Geza, happened to be in Budapest, where he managed to escape arrest. After their arrest, together with other Jews, they were trucked over the Carpathian Mountains to the Ukraine and deposited in the woods in the German-occupied zone. I remember Gizi later telling us of their ordeal: "We were just dumped across the border and abandoned to the mercy of the local Ukrainians who proceeded, at first, to rob us of our belongings and later perpetrated mayhem, untold hardships, rape and unspeakable horrors on us. Some local youth gangs acted as 'bounty hunters,' seeking Jews whom they then turned over to German military personnel. Jews who found themselves under German control were among the victims of infamous, bestial atrocities. Jews who managed to reach cities in Ukraine were rounded up by the Germans and transported to concentration camps. Those few of us who managed to survive did so by bartering for our lives or by our sheer tenacity and fantastic ingenuity and, undoubtedly, with help from our Creator."

Antisemitism in Hungary was well established and the fascist Arrow Cross guards were running rampant, especially in the capital city of Budapest. Escalating atrocities against Jews was tolerated, if not encouraged, by the authorities. The Hungarians deported Jews in 1941 from the Carpathian regions with the excuse that the deportees lacked Hungarian citizenship, a criterion applied only to the Jews. Nevertheless, Horthy Miklós, the Hungarian regent, steadfastly refused Hitler's demands until March 19, 1944. When the Germans occupied Hungary and ordered the arrest and segregation of all Jews in ghettos, the Hungarian authorities complied, much too willingly. By then, the systematic deportations of Jews in 1941 served them well. I give the Hungarians no credit for their "benevolence" in delaying the mass deportations. To put my feelings in perspective, I note that it was the Hungarians who took me out of my home, it was the Hungarians who deported me to the ghetto, and it was the Hungarians who loaded me into a cattle car and, while sealed, turned me over to the Germans, knowing that it was for the purpose of extermination.[3]

---

3   The author refers here to the Hungarian cooperation with the Germans, their part in anti-Jewish acts and their cooperation and role in sending Jews to ghettos and transfer camps in Hungary. One must also remember that the Germans were the main force in carrying out the Final Solution of the Jewish Question in general, and concerning the Hungarian Jews in particular.

TIBI'S BAR MITZVAH

Meanwhile, autumn 1941 was a momentous time in my nearly eleven-year-old life. For months now, I had been witnessing numerous *Bar Mitzvah* celebrations for Cousin Oti and many of my brother's friends, but now, in October, my brother Tibi was about to become *Bar Mitzvah*, the coming of age as a Jewish man. It is very difficult to describe the pride and escalating excitement I felt as the big day approached. For months, with the help of our Hebrew school *rebbe*, Tibi had been preparing for his reading of that week's *Torah* portion as well as the *Haftarah*, the portion from the Prophets read in synagogue every Sabbath. What's more, he was preparing a *Pshetl* (a scholarly discourse of a passage from the Scripture) to deliver on the day of his *Bar Mitzvah*. Reciting the portions is considered a difficult achievement, worthy of a smart, mature and studious young man; reciting them nearly flawlessly is rewarded with high praise and brings honor to the boy's parents, grandparents and siblings.

The Friday night Sabbath dinner on the eve of the *Bar Mitzvah* included the entire extended family, with our grandparents, aunts and uncles all dressed in their finest outfits. Mother went all out and set the dinner table, which was extended to its maximum, with her finest Rosenthal porcelain dishes, silverware and crystal. The light of the burning Sabbath candles reflected off the happy and proud faces of all the participants. Our beautiful mother, perhaps more than most, had the God-given gift of setting the mood with her graceful beauty, style and manners. That night, she was particularly delightful to behold. Tibi, the guest of honor, sitting in his usual seat on Papa's right, looked angelic as accolades from the family cascaded on him as if he stood under a waterfall. I swelled with pride and made mental notes of everything that was happening.

The occasion and the dinner marking it were the most festive and meaningful in my young life. Tibi had always been, and remained all his life, my guardian angel, to whom I looked up as he looked over me. While I was a young, relatively weak and sheltered child, Tibi was a big, strong and resourceful boy who was Papa and Mama's right hand in coping. He was unflappable, even under the most intolerable situations. In addition to being Father's indispensable partner in helping our immediate and extended family, he never shirked from helping all within his reach. I always felt safe just knowing that he was my brother. Our family's closeness and love for each other were legendary, and it established a lifelong unbreakable bond between us. Those who knew us will attest that we were bound with an everlasting brotherly love for each other, a love and respect that grew stronger and more meaningful with each passing day. It is my greatest wish that our children should be as close to each other as we were.

The following day, the Sabbath, Tibi was placed, once again, at center stage. As was expected, he performed flawlessly and deservedly received congratulations from the entire congregation, family and friends. The Sabbath celebratory meal took place at our maternal grandfather's house. Tables were set the length of the veranda, which spanned the entire width of the house and could accommodate all the invited guests. Adhering to proper custom, Rabbi Leifer, the Buština *rebbe*, was first to speak. He expounded on the spiritual meaning and responsibilities of a boy reaching the age of thirteen and concluded that he was fully confident that our Yitzchak Itzik (Tibi's Hebrew name) would be a fine example. Grandpa expressed his appreciation for the pleasure, the *naches* (joyful satisfaction) with which his grandson provided him, and that he was looking forward, please God, to be awarded with additional *naches* from all his grandchildren. The long festive lunch, which had been prepared by all the Bruckstein women, was highlighted when Tibi stood up, bravely looked at the assembled and learned audience — particularly at Grandpa who was *kvelling* (swelling) with pride — and recited the *Pshetl*, which defined his coming of age. Everyone was astounded by the maturity and ease with which Tibi met the challenge. He established himself as a mature person who was sure to fulfill the family's hopes and great expectations.

Tibi's *Bar Mitzvah* heightened my anxiety at the thought of my own *Bar Mitzvah*. Although Tibi "raised the bar" of achievement, I hoped and resolved that my *Bar Mitzvah* two years hence would be no less lavish and that the standard of my performance would be no lower than what my dear brother had established. Not that I ever hoped to surpass or even equal my brother's accomplishments, but I hoped that when my day came, with God's help, I would do my very best. I knew that when the time came, Mama would see to it that I was well prepared and that I, too, would receive my share of accolades. However, our situation as Jews was rapidly deteriorating, and while my *Bar*

Mitzvah two years later was the greatest thing to happen in my young life, it had to be measured by the currency of the time.

TÉGLÁS

The situation for the Jews in the Carpathian region was becoming more and more precarious. It became ever clearer that even the citizenship of those Jews who had been citizens of the Austro-Hungarian Empire was being questioned. My parents had automatically become Czech citizens when Czechoslovakia was created in 1918. Nevertheless, the Hungarians were playing with the idea of not recognizing the Jews' previous citizenship. This denial would only affect the Jews of the region since they were the ones the Hungarians sought to deport. Certainly, those with a lesser claim or lacking Hungarian citizenship were in dire danger of deportation.

Grandfather Bruckstein's father, Great-Grandfather Moshe, was born in Poland. He did not feel that his family's citizenship was secure enough and sought to strengthen their claim to it by acquiring a "clean" and uncontestable de facto citizenship. For that purpose, he asked Father to go to Budapest to see what he could do concerning the matter. My father, regardless of the dire consequences that his action might have elicited, managed to contact a person in authority in the Hungarian government from whom he "acquired" Hungarian citizenship that was "clean and authentic" for all of the Brucksteins at a cost of 5,000 Hungarian pengő plus a fifty-liter barrel of wine. The sum was a king's ransom, a fortune of money; a bookkeeper's monthly salary at that time was less than 200 pengő, while the average monthly salary of an unskilled laborer was twenty pengő. Grandfather was elated with the result of the trip; he felt that Father had saved their lives. Papa, on the other hand, although he thought that our citizenship was authentic, assessed the prevailing situation in Buština. He decided that it would be prudent for our family, including Grandpa and my aunts as well as his mother, Grandma Amalia Brandstein, to leave temporarily, until, in his words, "the dangerous situation clarifies itself or blows over."

In the early spring of 1942, my parents decided to take up temporary residence with my Aunt Emmus, the widow of my father's eldest brother, Jeno. Aunt Emmus lived in Hungary proper with her three daughters, Lilly,

Vera and Cuna, in a small town named Téglás. One could not find a town more Hungarian than Téglás. It is adjacent to the main railroad tracks near the city of Debrecen and ideally located for our purpose of "getting out of the hellfire," as Papa put it. Aunt Emmus reported that, so far, the authorities had not harassed her family nor anyone else she knew. Being sufficiently secluded, Téglás was certainly off the beaten path of the Jew hunters and out of the way of the antisemitic authorities. Papa judged it to be a safe choice since it was not in a war zone. Since her husband's passing, Aunt Emmus had operated their lumberyard alone and, therefore, welcomed my father's expert help.

My parents and grandparents devised complex plans for leaving. The idea was to avoid any noticeable action on their part, lest they come to the attention of the gendarmes or the military authorities. The only preparations to leave of which I was aware took on the air of a conspiracy with military logistics. The *kinderlach* (children) were not told anything about leaving. There was no mention of Aunt Emmus or of our cousins Lilly, Vera or Cuna, and the name "Téglás" was certainly not uttered. However, there was a supercharged atmosphere that prevailed in the house with hectic comings and goings, and Mother was especially busy and preoccupied with packing. While the scope of the packing operation was noticeably unusual, it did not seem to arouse my concern, since Papa often traveled on business and perhaps, I thought, he was going away for longer than usual. Nevertheless, I became upset when my parents stopped talking when I entered the room, which led me to wonder what I may have done wrong. I was told that all was well. Still, there was a certain unfamiliar tension that I was unable to readily identify or to ascertain its cause. There was no mention of leaving among my cousins, whom I also suspect had no knowledge of anything that was going on.

The preparations in my grandparents' homes were certainly no less hectic. They had also determined to leave temporarily. Grandpa Bruckstein decided to take his daughters living in Buština to his married daughter Valerie Wieder (Aunt Vali) in Budapest and the logistics of Grandfather's move was no small task, considering that his family consisted of three unmarried daughters. The girls, Aunts Edith, Judith and Sophie, all had considerable wardrobes that they were unwilling to leave behind. Grandmother Amalia Brandstein had been a widow since 1937 and she left Buština to stay with her daughter, Aunt Helen, who lived in Mad, Hungary. Aunt Helen was the mother of my cousin Laci who was later with me briefly in Birkenau. My parents did not leave Buština until they had overseen and aided the rest of the family's departures. We were the last to leave and were most dangerously exposed to discovery and possible treachery by the authorities. Papa disguised our luggage by packing it in wooden crates and managed to ship it from our lumberyard by rail freight. I was still unaware that anything particular was happening even on the day that we unceremoniously made our way to the railroad station, each one indirectly, and left.

Our strategy was worthy of a military plan. Since Téglás was to the west of Buština, Papa went to the town of Técső to the east and boarded a train going west. Mother and I went to the railroad station in Buština and boarded the same train that Papa was on. My brother Tibi went to Visk, the next town to the east and boarded the same train. This way we avoided the spectacle of all of us going together to the Buština station. Such an action would have unavoidably raised the suspicion of us running away, an action that would have certainly had dire, if not fatal, consequences.

As far as we children were concerned, life in Téglás was fun. Having our cousins to play with and a familiar lumberyard to play in was wonderful. The setting of the town, which was flat like a prairie with no mountains or hills in sight, was a novelty to us, since we were used to the Carpathian Mountains scenery. However, the hot and dry temperature in Téglás was not to our liking and we did miss the cool breezes and cool nights of Buština.

Cousin Lilly was already grown up and, therefore, I found very little in common with her. Vera, who was closer to Tibi's age, and Cuna, who was approximately my age, were our playmates. Mondays, Wednesdays and Fridays were special days that we looked forward to with great excitement. It was on those days that the high-speed Árpád Nyilas train (named after a highly esteemed Hungarian hero) rushed by just a few yards from the house on its way to Budapest. On those special days, we would rush through our lunch and stand in an advantageous spot where we could see the tracks for a few kilometers each way. At exactly one o'clock in the afternoon, we could hear the ever-increasing sound of the oncoming train. Our hearts pumped with excitement in proportion with the nearing of the train. Then, the blunt-nosed phenomenon with the ever-increasing crescendo of the rushing wheels on the steel rails and the train, which a moment before was just a speck on the horizon emanating a muted, rapidly increasing sound, now sounded a frightful blast of warning as it neared the ramps of the Téglás crossroad. Never slowing, the mammoth, bullet shaped, awesome, gigantic "wonder machine" rushed by. As we turned in the direction of the passing train, we were aware that our hearts were pumping wildly and our blood rushed to our heads. It took some time to recover from the unbelievable excitement.

That summer, with cousin Lilly's encouragement, the Brandstein children, now comprising two families, produced a show and invited the town's children along with their parents. A script was written and rewritten until it met with the "producer's" approval, lengthy rehearsals were held, Lilly made fantastic costumes and a carpenter made the scenery. The show ran for three days and was, by all standards, a huge success. The show was the talk of the town and was the highlight of our Téglás summer of 1942.

As it turned out, the "temporary" stay in Téglás turned into months—six months to be exact — during which time we escaped many roundups in the Carpathian region, with Buština being no exception. At the end of the summer of 1942, Father decided that the situation had calmed down enough for our safe return. The families' extended absence must have been noticed by the local authorities; it must have raised some eyebrows as to where and what we were up to. Nevertheless, I heard of no detectable or visibly overt consequences of our absence. Father seemingly dealt unequivocally with the small consequences, if any, which may have arisen.

HIGH SCHOOL IN TÉCSŐ

S oon after our return from Téglás, I started attending the nearest high school in the town of Técső (formerly Tačovo), seven kilometers east of Buština. Although Tibi went to the gymnasium in the town of Chust, twenty-one kilometers west of Buština, my parents decided in favor of my cousins, who were nearer to my age, and sent me with them to the high school in Técső, rather than with Tibi. My mother judged me as not mature or independent enough to manage in Chust with the bigger boys and did not particularly look forward to me being away from her for an entire week at a time. Frankly, I was happy to go to school with my cousins, Ervin and Vicki, my playmates and best friends. Their father, Adolph Brandstein, was my father's brother. Ervin was just a little older than me and Vicki was about the same age (but his birthday just missed the school cut-off, so his parents had to push him ahead to be in my grade). Their older brother, Oti, was Tibi's age and they were very close.

Técső was within walking distance and on the same highway as Buština; therefore, the shorter distance did not necessitate an overnight stay, as Tibi was forced to do. Tibi took the train to Chust carrying a contraption containing six meals for his week's sustenance. While in school, he stayed in a rented room with Oti. They came home only on weekends and holidays.

In the fall and spring, I often rode the family bicycle to school, if and when it was available to me, otherwise Mother would arrange a carriage or wagon to take me and, usually, some cousins. The Hungarians, as a form of harassment, did not excuse a Jewish child who was absent from school on the Sabbath (Saturday), and enforced Saturday attendance to a point that they made it almost impossible to graduate without attending all classes. Luckily, Grandma Ruchele's brother, Great-Uncle Eber Goldberger, lived in Técső, within walking distance of my school. So, Mother arranged for me to stay with him on the weekends. On Sabbath mornings, I first recited the morning prayer and then walked to school where I managed not to desecrate the Sabbath by writing or doing any other forbidden work. After school, I returned to the Goldbergers for the Sabbath meal.

Uncle Eber was a God-fearing Hasidic Jew who conducted himself in an admirable, impressive and pious fashion. He was a tall man who commanded and demanded respect by his presence alone. His impeccable Hasidic garb and his white, well-kept beard made him a striking figure. He also had a beautiful countenance and a deep baritone voice. Uncle Eber had an air of pride, yet the Goldbergers were paragons of modesty. Trying to emulate the table manners of the Goldberger children who were older than me, I learned to speak when spoken to and to use polite formal language when addressing my uncle or aunt. I had experienced a Hasidic lifestyle on a more modest scale at my Bruckstein grandparents' home, but without the formality to which I was now introduced. My home and upbringing were pretty strict and I was certainly taught to mind my manners, but it was nothing like what I experienced in the Goldberger house, which had a certain atmosphere of, "Don't you dare! It's the Sabbath!" Since I was there only on Friday nights, when I slept overnight and joined them the next day for the Sabbath meal, I was only familiar with this particular part of the week, preceding and during the Sabbath, with its own particular atmosphere. The formality at the Sabbath table in the candlelit dining room and the candles' reflections on the book-lined mahogany shelves intimidated me. As a twelve-year-old, I had an uncomfortable, yet admiring feeling toward the Goldbergers. While I did not refuse to be there, and in many ways was drawn to their lifestyle and respected it, I would not have liked to have it in my home.

In our living room we had a glass-fronted curio cabinet where Mother displayed her cherished objects, such as her many beautiful silver pieces, Bavarian crystal, Meissen and Dresden porcelain figurines and other various *objets d'art*. Among the most admired of them was a masterfully hand-carved chain attached to an intricate globe with a ball inside it. The entire object was made from one piece of mahogany wood. It was truly a superb and much-admired work of art and a testimonial to the artist's patience. This treasure was one of my mother's prized possessions; it was made by Uncle Eber who had given it to my mother as a token of his admiration for her.

In Uncle Eber's house, there was an entire bookcase with glass doors filled with his art. On the Sabbath after lunch, I spent a lot of time standing in front of the bookcase, admiring the pieces of art from all angles through the reflections in the mirrors that were strategically placed in the cabinet for that very purpose. I remember being in awe of the intricate one-piece birdcages with birds in them. I can still visualize some of the pieces that I most admired. While Uncle Eber repeatedly admonished me not to open the glass doors and certainly not to touch anything inside, he enjoyed my appreciation of them. I questioned him about the technique, wondering how he made things inside each other when there seemed there was not enough room to put one's hand inside the object. I still remember his answer, "With a lot of patience and love."

One Friday afternoon, Uncle Eber took up the subject of his hobby with me, and expounded on the pleasure of creating beauty with one's own hands. I was then privileged to gain entry to his *sanctum sanctorum*, the little den where he had his hobby desk. I was elated when he unrolled a neatly rolled cloth pouch containing his tiny, very delicate carving tools, some of which were no larger than and indistinguishable from a needle. The tools were designed to reach every conceivable angle and were neatly arranged according to their edges and purpose.

Uncle Eber showed me some of his works in progress and demonstrated the use of some of his tools. Upon noticing my interest and admiration, Uncle Eber asked me to work a piece of wood. He must have been impressed with what he saw because he proceeded to encourage and shower me with compliments for my ability to handle the tools and the respect I had for them. He then suggested that I take up the hobby. I was elated by his compliments and excited by the prospect and the possibility of creating beautiful objects such as these.

If the weather on the Sabbath was beautiful, as it often was, I walked the seven kilometers from Técső to home; otherwise, I would stay at the Goldbergers until the following day, for it was too dangerous to walk home after sunset, especially for a Jew. On my arrival home the following Sunday, I excitedly told Mother about all that had happened and how, in addition to respecting him, I now loved and admired Uncle Eber. I spent the better part of an hour inspecting Mother's chain and globe and making vivid mental notes of the tools that Uncle Eber had probably used in creating its intricate pattern. I must have bored Mother with my now "expert" explanations as to how Uncle Eber managed to make it. Alas, due to my fast unraveling childhood bliss, I never had the chance to pursue this beautiful hobby.

Whether by bicycle, carriage or on foot, the trip to and from school was a memorable event. It was exhilarating to be on the road with the sky providing a blissful canopy and being surrounded by ever-evolving natural scenery. I was seldom, if ever, alone on the road; there was always at least one cousin or friend to be with. We greeted the farmers and laborers along the way, and much to their amusement, we chased each other while playing catch. As part of the game we played, we sometimes ended up walking or running ten kilometers instead of seven by running in all directions, including backwards rather than forwards, trying to avoid being caught and becoming "it." Sometimes we sang military marching songs and marched to them in military style. Other than on the Sabbath, we indulged in the variety of seasonal fruits. We ate apples off the fruit trees, sunflower seeds right out of the sunflowers and picked berries from the bushes at the side of the road. We admired the progress of the growth of the corn and potato fields and identified the various plantings as we went along. Cousin Ervin always bested us with his agricultural knowledge. It seemed to us that he knew everything there was to know about domestic animals, fowl, produce and agriculture. He demonstrated how to tell if a chicken was with an egg. It was a method I do not wish to describe.

As the year 1942 progressed, events that we described as "incidents" increased. During our blissful walks, we began to encounter, slowly at first and then noticeably increasing, incidents of antisemitism. We were berated by passersby, especially by the Hungarian "transplants"[4] and their urchins, who were later joined by the native Ruthenian youths who rapidly learned from them. The beautiful, seemingly peaceful cornfields would harbor a stone thrower and sometimes a menacing bunch of thugs who were lying in wait. They would materialize seemingly out of nowhere and rob us. By the autumn, after incidents of bodily harm, it became outright dangerous for us to be on the road all together and, therefore, we were forced to forgo the privilege of the open road. Our parents were forced to make other, safer arrangements to transport us to school, namely, by hiring a trusted adult with a horse and wagon.

In the winter, we went by sleigh. The carter started out at Grandpa Brandstein's compound where he picked up my three cousins — Aliza, Ervin and Vicki. Aliza was a daughter of my Uncle Izidor. Although there were only three passengers, by the time they reached my house, the sleigh already seemed full with children sprawled out at every angle. It always took some maneuvering and coercing on the part of my mother to make room for me. A horse, which was no prime candidate to win a prize for being an outstanding example of its species, pulled the sleigh. The winter weather in our part of the Carpathian Mountains was bitterly cold, so much so that one did not dare touch a metallic object exposed to the weather lest his hand freeze to the object, which was painful to unstick. A coarse, layered, homespun blanket covered the horse while at rest, for it was in dire danger of freezing to death. Later, as the horse warmed up and steam rose from its body, layers of the blanket were peeled back, only to be reapplied as soon as we arrived at our destination. Small brass bells, which rang with every step the horse took, decorated the harness. The bottom of the wagon was bedded with sheepskins. Additional sheepskins, with their suffocating odor, covered us, the passengers. The way home was somewhat better due to the

---

4   Hungarians brought to areas that were annexed to Hungary during the war years.

fact that we were tired and therefore less frisky and the weather was usually much milder.

The memory of those winter rides lingers on till this day. One can very well imagine what was going on under the sheepskins with four cousins consisting of one girl and three boys. Four cousins of course, have eight feet attached to eight legs and therein was the problem. I must say that Cousin Aliza, who was the eldest among us, was the chief instigator of whatever horseplay was going on. Somehow, she never had ample room for her feet. Some of us claimed that that would be true even if she were alone in the sleigh. When setting out in the darkness of winter, Ervin and I pointed out to each other the intricacies of the kaleidoscope effect of the overture to the oncoming sunrise. We delighted in the colors of the sky evolving from indigo to red and then with orange and blue streaks that illuminated the scarce clouds and then to a brilliant sunrise. Every sunrise provided us with a magnificent thrill, as the sun rose and seemed to linger on the road right in front of us, giving us the illusion that it was very near and that we would soon drive right into it.

It was with great promise and expectations that I started my first year of high school, the beginning of which lived up to and, in many measures, surpassed my expectations. As the term progressed, the teachers began to address my fellow Jewish students and me as "Jew." Yesterday's "Hey, Andi!" became "Hey, Jew!" However, was I too naïve to notice, or did I choose to ignore the little innuendos of antisemitism among my schoolmates as well? The insinuations seemed to be clearly understood by my cousins, who pointed them out to me, but did not ring an alarm bell for me. Perhaps I had lived too much of a sheltered life, or maybe I just wished away all of the insults and threats and made believe they did not exist.

Reality soon set in when one day at recess, as I happened to be standing in the schoolyard at a construction site in front of a barrow of wet cement, a fellow student and a known bully, a Hungarian "transplant," forcibly and intentionally bumped into me so that I fell over his fellow conspirator. Following their prearranged plan, his friend had furtively snuck behind me and assumed a crouching position for the desired effect, namely, propelling me into the wet cement. Their plan succeeded famously as I fell into the cement and nearly drowned. The offenders, as well as many other students, including some of whom I considered to be my friends, doubled up with laughter. My predicament, that is, "the Jew's" predicament, amused them. I was rescued by some of the Gypsy construction workers who extended a broomstick to me and pulled me out. While I was crying uncontrollably, they stripped me naked and dowsed me and my clothes with buckets of water, managing to wash off the wet cement to a manageable extent. This episode devastated my confidence and shamed me; it hurt me physically as well as mentally. After that incident, Mother had a difficult time convincing me to return to school and when I did, they, the know-nothings, continually taunted me. It was a punishing experience without recourse on my part.

The absence of retribution by any of the teachers or the administration for this behavior encouraged more daring and overt tormenting of the Jewish students. By the time 1942 ended, antisemitism had achieved an officially approved status. As the Hungarian "transplants" were bad in all school subjects and the Ruthenians had trouble mastering the Hungarian language, which was entirely foreign to them, it was we, the Jews, who excelled in our studies. The frustrated teachers, who could not get a suitable answer to their questions on any subject, constantly taunted the laggards with the now-familiar retort, "You should be ashamed. I'll bet that the Jew will know it and you do not," which the teacher spat, whereupon he commanded me, "Get up, Jew, and give us the answer." When I gave the right answer to the question that Mama had rehearsed with me the night before, the teacher's admonishments to the students, comparing them to the Jewish students, only served to infuriate them more. They gave vent to their frustrations by intensifying their actions of their antisemitic fervor.

THE WIEDERS AND THE BBC

As the calendar turned to the year 1943, there was no indication and no hope that things would soon get better. Businesses were being confiscated, including ours, and given to our "partners," the "transplanted colonizers." The Hungarian antisemitic national press was evermore vindictive and overtly inflammatory. The Jews…the Jews… always the Jews; they were responsible for every misfortune, fire and disease in Hungary. Every calamity from military reversals to the onslaught of influenza was blamed on the Jews. If there was a kidnapping, someone burgled and stole, or someone committed murder, extortion or rape, it was immediately "solved"! The morning papers carried the identity of the culprit, and, of course, it was a Jewish conspiracy! It was the same conspiracy that set *all* the fires, poisoned the wells and killed little blond Christian girls for their blood for Passover. Headlines called for "cleansing" the "mother country" of all the Jews.

Typical news broadcasts were along the following lines: "The brave, heroic, vastly outnumbered Hungarian Army acting for the betterment of world order has attacked, defeated and massacred the cowardly Russian hordes near the putrid Ukrainian city of Kiev, only to be pushed back at a great loss by the actions of the cursed devilish Jewish conspirators and the Russian puppets under their control. We shall long remember those perfidious Jews that caused the massacre of our heroes and shed their blood. We stand resolved to destroy the Jews first and then go on to destroy the exposed and unprotected Slavic slobs who threaten our women and children and conspire with the Jews for our very existence. We shall rejoice in our victory only when we rid ourselves of the Jewish plots and interferences." I remember asking my father, "Tell me, Papa, do we, the Jews do all this? If so, shouldn't we do more of the same?" I was proud to be a Jew since, from all accounts, it seemed that we were winning the war single-handedly.

My mother's twin sisters, Valerie (Vali) and Giselle (Gizi), and their families lived in Budapest. In those days, it was the custom for people from the cities to stay in the country during the summer to escape the stiflingly warm weather. For this purpose, Buština, with its crisp fresh air, crystal clear water and temperate summer climate, was ideal. The convenience of having a three-week summer vacation and visiting Grandma and Grandpa and the Buština uncles, aunts and cousins was an opportunity not to be missed. By 1943, Giselle was divorced and seldom came to visit the family, but Valerie, with her husband, David Wieder, and their two daughters, Kitty and Erika, were regular summer visitors. Uncle David owned the "Bobby" razor blade factories whose products were sold in competition with the imported and expensive Gillette product. In addition to the "Bobby" blades that were sold all over Europe and beyond, Uncle David was involved in other endeavors, such as real estate and fabric manufacturing.

I loved the Wieders. Uncle David and Aunt Vali were special people. They were always beautifully dressed and coifed in the latest styles that we soon became acquainted with through the fashion magazines they brought with them. At the first encounter with Uncle David, as I greeted him, he would press into my hand a gift of a silver pengő. The Buština children were not accustomed to having money since there was hardly anything to buy except ice cream or dragées, the sugar-coated nuts I loved. I needed Mother's permission to buy either treat and, if granted, she would give me the few pennies for the purchase. Now I was the owner of a whole silver pengő! This was a fortune for me that I would save together with the previous year's pengő gift. Wow! I had two pengős and my *Bar Mitzvah* was not until the following December. Who knew what I would get then! We were well-to-do, but not with liquid assets. I don't think I ever saw anything larger than a fifty-pengő note in my father's hand.

The summer of 1943 was no exception. The "city-slicker" Wieder family came for their yearly pilgrimage, descending on us with their dozen suitcases, some of which contained gifts for Aunt Vali's sisters, their spouses and kids. Seven-year-old Erika, the younger of the two girls, who was closest to my age, hung out with my friends and me. We were amused by her comments about the country; how she would love it "if only it was not so full of dirt and things would not crawl, fly, creep, bark and howl; if just everything would be paved." She would complain, "Oh, no! Look at the puddles and all that mud! Why doesn't Grandpa do something about it? In Budapest the rain disappears and there is no mud, isn't that better?"

One fine late afternoon, Erika joined the boys for some horseplay in the field among the fruit trees. Anticipating her reaction, I threw an insect into Erika's long hair. Her reaction did not disappoint us. Her shrieks and flailing of her hands were a delight that could sustain us throughout the following harsh winter. We did it again the following week, even though her mother, Aunt Vali, made us swear not to torment Erika again. With every good intention, who could resist such a delight? The second time, the incident was not without repercussion. Aunt Vali complained to my mother, who assured her that Andi could not have been totally responsible for this dastardly act, and that boys will be boys. Nevertheless, Mother proceeded to admonish us and demand that we not do it again. We promised, but silently added to ourselves, "This year, but wait till *next* year." Unfortunately, the opportunity the following year never came.

When at home, we children were deliriously happy, for we did not comprehend the ominous clouds that were gathering momentum towards our demise. We were unable to weigh the consequences of the oncoming developments that were soon to engulf us and bring upon us the world's greatest disaster perpetrated by man. When we returned from Téglás, we were confronted and became acquainted with new laws imposing progressively worse restrictions on the Jewish population. I remember meetings of the Jewish community being held in Grandpa Bruckstein's home and Father telling me how Grandfather opened the meeting with, "*Wus titmen, kinderlach?*" (What should we do, children?) It was a question that brought on such diverse opinions that the meeting derailed into nonproductive arguments. Realizing the dire situation they were in, each person not only contributed his opinion, but also shared with the others the latest news and/ or rumors.

At subsequent meetings, some, including Father, advised everyone to run and hide, but one uncle called it ridiculous. He explained his position, stating "the Germans would not kill us, maybe the Ukrainians would, for those peasants would do anything; but Germans? After all, they are intelligent people, university people, people from Berlin, Nuremberg, Munich and Cologne; these people will do no such thing! How can these stories be true?" Unfortunately, many of those present agreed with him, and the meeting ended without a consensus. Any decision on what should be done, if anything, was postponed to await further developments.

A radio was a precious commodity, but for Jews, it was life-threatening to own one. I noticed that after we came back from Téglás, Papa would listen to our radio in the cellar with the volume turned down so low that he literally had his ear touching its speaker. It seemed strange to me that Mother acted as a lookout; she would always lean out the window facing the front of the house whenever Papa went down to the cellar to listen to it. Ilona, our maid, was kept totally ignorant of the radio's location or even of its very existence. Discovery of the radio by the Hungarian authorities, God forbid, its very existence and clandestine use, would be considered a subversive act that would result in certain arrest and charges that could culminate in incarceration or deportation.

From listening to the radio, I knew the name Churchill. I heard Hitler in his harangues sneer with venom, deriding him as he mentioned his name, which he would pronounce as "Herrrrrr Churrrrrrchill," with a guttural, mocking voice. According to the German broadcasts, Churchill, the Prime

Minister of Great Britain, was the puppet agent of the Jews and they alone, of course, were singularly responsible for the unspeakable horrors of the war. I saw Hitler in a newsreel; he reminded me of our rooster as it strutted around our backyard. He did everything that the rooster did except crow, which, come to think of it, for all intents and purposes, he did.

Papa never missed the BBC, which was broadcasting its news programs in all languages for the benefit of those in Nazi-occupied territories. On one occasion, I overheard a broadcast where Hitler was pontificating on his favorite subject *"Ich werde die Juden ausradieren!"* (I will erase the Jews!) I did not comprehend the meaning of it; why would anybody erase the Jews? You erase what you write; how do you erase people? From my parents' attitudes I gathered that it was bad. Father was an expert in handling the radio as it had to be fiddled with and positioned in just the right way. Then, and only when it was positioned just right, was the sound of the BBC signature tune heard, followed in Hungarian by, "This is the BBC, the British Broadcasting Corporation from London." We put our lives on the line to keep ourselves informed about the true state of the war.

Father and Mother had clandestine discussions, which I overheard. I remember that Father wanted us to hide in the woods among the Romani loggers, or to try to get to Fiume in Italy where his good friend and customer would help us. He pleaded with my mother to agree to go into the forest for a few months, where his laborers would hide the four of us. He explained that he had already made the arrangements and wanted to sneak away, but Mother would not hear of it. "What, and leave my father behind? Never!" was my mother's response. He begged Mother to leave, and although he said it would be impossible to hide more than four people, he promised he would make arrangements for the others and send for them later, but Mother was adamant. I'll never forget hearing her respond, "I am not hiding and will not have our children hide in forests like animals, nor am I leaving my father." That was it. We remained.

Some people did run and hide and survived, while others were found out. There were instances where some were turned over to the Hungarians or Germans, depending under whose jurisdiction they were, by the very people who accepted a king's ransom to hide them. Some of these reports got back to us; hence, many who otherwise would have made arrangements to leave and be hidden, became scared and discouraged from doing so.

After the war, we heard that the famous Dr. Jung, who had removed my tonsils, had had prior knowledge of his imminent arrest and deportation. It was said that the soldiers found the doctor, his wife and children sitting at their dining room table dressed in their best outfits. Dr. Jung had a syringe in his hand and they were all dead. He had obviously injected them all and then himself in order to deprive the Nazis of their pleasure.

THE YELLOW STAR, CURFEWS AND RESTRICTIONS

The law enacted in 1944, ordering all Jews to wear a yellow star with the marking "*Jude*" (Jew) alarmed, humiliated and ridiculed us. We were now visually marked out as targets.[5] We were spat upon and insulted by some folks, including townspeople who were still dependent on our family for their livelihood. Some sheepishly spat on the floor or in our direction as we passed by. They were constantly harangued and reminded by the authorities and their clergy that everything that was bad and wrong, including the weather and certainly the war, their unemployment, hunger and nonexistent healthcare, was the fault of the "evil, perfidious Jews," who were now marked and deserved their ridicule.

I felt ashamed to be wearing the yellow star, which covered almost my entire chest. I complained about it and cried to Mother, who reassured me by pointing out her own yellow star, and telling me it was not so bad, as she caressed my tearful face. "But Mama, the children are spitting and calling me terrible names, sometimes they throw things at me, they even hurt me sometimes," I retorted in a whiny voice as I paused in my sobs. Mama's assurances had a temporary effect that held only until the next spit, insult or threat. I just could not understand why this was happening, or why neither Mama nor Papa was able to explain it. Do we Jews really do all the bad things

5   Nazi Germany exercised its influence and authority in the satellite countries and dependencies in order that "their" Jews would be "marked," too. In December 1942, Hungary refused to impose the yellow star obligation on the Hungarian Jews. However, after the German Army took over Hungary in March 1944, the first decision concerning Jewish affairs by the new government, led by Döme Sztójay, from March 31, required the wearing of the yellow star.

that the Nazis say we do? Do we really deserve this? And if Jews do, I know that I have certainly not done anything to anybody. So, why me?

Discriminatory laws against the Jews were increased another notch when the Hungarian authorities instituted a 10 p.m. curfew for all Jews. Later, the curfew was set at 9 p.m. and then changed once again to the earlier time of 8 p.m. Realizing that crimes such as robbery, pillage and looting perpetrated against the Jews and their property were seldom, if at all, punished, the indigent townspeople soon learned what the Hungarian "transplants" knew all along, namely that it was all right to rob a Jew. This realization brought about brazen attacks bordering on pogroms against all that was still Jewish property.

A law restricting any Jew from owning his own business without a Hungarian partner soon followed. A native Carpathian was not good enough for partnership. The partner had to be one of the colonizers, a pure-blooded Hungarian appointee who became a so-called partner in the business without any compensation to the owner. My father's appointed "partner" was one of the town's most vehement antisemites, who clamored for and received the position. However, he grossly overestimated its monetary rewards, for by then the business hardly made any profit. On his very first day, the "partner" walked in and demanded money. No amount was enough for him; whatever he was given he would take and then threaten bodily harm and a report of various imaginary wrongdoings to the authorities if not given more. Soon, within weeks, the "partner" took away the whole business, which he proceeded to liquidate, while pocketing all the proceeds.

Every month, and sometimes every week, tighter restrictions were announced: Jews could not purchase property, new levies were enacted against existing properties, and eventually came the laws of confiscation of all Jewish property. Grandfather had a very successful wholesale general supply business in partnership with two of his brothers, in addition to his own businesses in cane products and in medicinal herbs. They were forced to take on a "partner," and just as had happened to my father, the new "partner" soon kicked them out of their own business. As 1944 approached, a Jew could no longer attend school, so Tibi and I stayed at home where Mother continued our secular education. I may add that I learned more in the few months that Mama was my official teacher than during an entire year of formal instruction. Our Hebrew school was disbanded, since it became too dangerous to keep it open.

My parents continued our Jewish education by having the rabbi of the school come to our home or one of my cousin's houses to tutor us.

By this time, my whole disposition had changed; I was no longer the "happiest child in the world," but had become gloomy and cranky. My aunts said that I looked as if I carried the whole world on my shoulders. To the best of my knowledge, everyone I encountered looked no better than I did. Everyone had the look of the condemned. Insecurity, moroseness and despair were the rule of the day. I no longer thought that the world was a wondrous place created for my enjoyment. I learned to hate and despise our tormentors, but disagreed with those who said that some people were like animals. I loved animals and understood that they were driven by their innate instincts and one always knew what to expect from them. Some men, I came to believe, were worse than animals; they were creatures who devised instruments of war and torture, and, what's more, they devoured their own species. As a child, I concluded that this world would be infinitely more wonderful if there were no human beings in it at all. I was in a quandary to accept what I was taught — that our God created the world and everything in it for the benefit of man. If so, I thought, humankind had certainly botched things up and deserved to be banished from it.

It was under these conditions that we celebrated my much-awaited *Bar Mitzvah* in December 1943. It was to be a day of bliss and so it was. However, one could not help but realize that it was a very thin sliver of joy among the daily calamities. Ever since I could remember, I had been orienting myself toward the big day of my *Bar Mitzvah*. It was the day that I was to pass from childhood to manhood. Being the youngest in our family, together with my cousin Vicki, the youngest among all the cousins, I'd had ample opportunity to experience many *Bar Mitzvah* celebrations. Above all, that of my brother, Tibi, twenty-six months previously, had made a lasting impression on me. It had invigorated my enthusiasm and raised my expectations. I could hardly wait for the big day to arrive. I conjured up in my imagination every possible scenario, each one surpassing the other in my anticipation of the pleasures and joys I would experience on that day.

The times notwithstanding, it was still singularly the greatest day in my young life. Mama and Papa did everything, within the constraints of our situation, to make it a momentous day for me. Brother Tibi was as proud as a peacock, being my older brother and adviser (and remained so his whole life). Grandfather Bruckstein, together with all my many aunts, uncles and cousins, showered me with their love, their warmest congratulations and many presents. In addition to my receiving *tefillin* (phylacteries), three presents in particular stood out for me. The first was a pair of long pants. Children wore knickers, but now I was a man! The second was a fountain pen. And the third, the most special, was a Tissot watch — the same brand as my mother's watch. How proud I was of those presents. Looking back, the adults who all participated, branded with the yellow Jewish star on their clothes and under great personal stress, did a great job of making me feel special. My *Bar Mitzvah* day was a ray of sunshine in a very ominously overcast world.

JULIANA'S RESCUE AND THE ROUNDUP

Sometime in March 1944, the wife of the Hungarian chief of police, a close and genuine friend of my mother's, who worked as the teletype operator at the police station right next to us, ran over to our house one evening with a telegraph in her hand. The telegraph was an order to round up all the Jews early in the morning, confiscate all our property and take us to the railroad station where we would be taken by train to work camps for the duration of the war. The order went out to all police stations in the region. Mother's friend advised us to hide whatever possible that night.

Panic-filled, unmitigated terror engulfed our closely knit circle. Messengers were sent out to warn other families. The shocking news generated another round of discussion, from which I remember hearing the arguments. Some of the Buština Jews were essentially saying, "How bad can it be? We already heard on the radio that the Nazis are being pushed out of Russia. They are being killed left and right. How long can they go on taking these enormous casualties? The Russians are on the other side of the mountains and the Americans are in the war; how long will it be until the Germans capitulate and everything will be all right and the war will be over? So, they will take us to a work camp, so we will work, how bad can that be?" I feel that this was an expression of the typical "pogrom mentality" prevalent in countries where Jews were second-class citizens, always thinking that everything that happens is all for the good. I felt that they were essentially saying, "Let's cut our losses, for it's not so bad. So there is a war, so we will lose some, but with the help of the Almighty, this too will be over and we will prevail."

Father and Tibi went down to the cellar with shovels and hid our jewelry under the floor of the potato bin. Some more "treasures" were hidden in the chicken coops and the barn. We had no aluminum foil or plastic wraps. Some photographs were wrapped in tablecloths or butcher's paper. Valuables were put in jars or other receptacles. When Father and Tibi finished with our belongings, they proceeded across the street to help Grandpa do the same.

True to the warning, the Hungarian gendarmes, the "*tollasok*" (feathered ones), in their very impressive uniforms and hats with rooster feathers, which gave them their nickname, burst into our house at 5.30 in the morning. They already displayed their animal mentality by using the butt of a gun to burst through the front door instead of simply using the door handle. They posted themselves at all the room entrances and ordered us to move to the middle of the house, to the living/dining area. One of the gendarmes spread a tablecloth on the floor and ordered us to put all our valuables in it. It was instantly clear to us that they were preparing to rob us. They knew where we were ultimately going, so they figured they should have "first dibs."

The gendarmes made Father empty his pockets and made Mother remove her pearls and rings. I did not think that I had anything to throw in, but then one of the gendarmes whom I knew well and regarded as a friend, as he used to allow me to play with his rifle and police paraphernalia, grabbed my arm, ripped my watch off my wrist and grabbed the fountain pen from my pocket. He threw them both to the tablecloth on the floor. I was in total shock at how they dared to do this to us. After all, they were our next-door neighbors. I cried out to them to leave us alone, but it was to no avail, as I was held by my wrist and told to shut up, or else. The watch was the Tissot that had been presented to me only three months previously at my *Bar Mitzvah*. It was my prized possession, my treasure and I wore it on my wrist as a badge of honor. My watch was the insignia of my manhood. Now the Hungarians were violating my very being, my soul; they stripped and robbed me of my newly acquired dignity and personal identity. I was in a continued state of bewilderment from that violation; the injustice perpetrated on me, on our family and on the Jewish people as a whole. This shock was, of course, soon to be exceeded by subsequent actions against us, and then surpassed upon our arrival in the ghetto. But these devastations in my young life were my passage from the cocoon in which I lived into the reality of the world of 1944.

The gendarmes marched us out of our house as if we were common criminals. They took us to the Handal Synagogue near the Talabor River, the synagogue attended by Grandfather Bruckstein. We were gathered there along with some of our uncles and aunts and their families, as well as other prominent families of the town. I clung to my parents and brother, for they were my safety net. New arrivals were brought in every few minutes, but Grandpa and his family were not brought to the synagogue until six o'clock in the evening. The gendarmes had gone for the "big fish," rounding up the ten wealthiest families, hoping to get enough loot to satisfy their larcenous greed. Expecting to find Grandfather's "fortune," they had targeted him and had interrogated him in his home from 5.30 in the morning and continued throughout the day.

The gendarmes threatened to burn down the synagogue with all of us in it, unless we came forward and revealed to them where our "wealth" was hidden. They constantly interrogated us, including the children. Certain men were singled out and taken outside to the back of the synagogue. Once these men were removed, the gendarmes informed the men's wives that unless they told them the whereabouts of the "hoard" of jewels and money their husbands had stashed, their men would be shot. As soon as one wife said that she knew of no horde of jewels or money, shots rang out outside, often followed by the wife fainting. What followed was pandemonium. The people were in total panic and terrified. (The man, as we found out later, was not shot. The gendarme would not shoot the goose that might lay the golden egg. The man was not returned to the synagogue, however, in order to keep up the perpetual terror and maintain the gendarme's believability.)

When Father and Grandfather were marched out at bayonet point, Mother became hysterical. She attacked the gendarme with her fists, while screaming and kicking. When threatened with a bayonet, Mother grabbed the bayonet with her bare hands, pushed the rifle aside, and kicked and slapped the gendarme. She kept on screaming, "How dare you do this to us, you filthy pig!" and, "Watch your mouth, you uncouth louse!" and, "I demand that you release my father and my husband and let us go home." While at it, she informed the gendarme of his lineage and had some choice words concerning his mother. She kept on demanding to be released at once and be restored to her home. Either Mother did not realize how the world had changed, or, if she did, she refused to accept it. The Hungarian gendarmes in their blind lust for money did not understand that there were no "hordes of jewels and money" other than sentimental personal jewelry. They did not understand that we were a community that had lived in one valley for nearly 300 years. Unlike city people, our wealth consisted of land and standing timber. Money was kept in the banks to finance business transactions, and we had pledged accounts receivable against loans. The gendarmes believed their own antisemitic stereotyping that all Jews had vaults of jewels and cash.

We were held captive for three days, at the end of which they announced that they had received orders to cancel the deportation roundup due to a lack of trains for transport. It appears they had jumped the gun with the deportation arrest. We were, therefore, released and allowed to return to our ransacked homes where the walls had been smashed, floorboards ripped out and cellars dug up. The frenzied vultures had done a thorough job, although, luckily, they had not searched under our potato bin. We had reason to believe that the actual order canceling the deportation came on the day following our arrest. However, they kept us captive until they had finished the search to satisfy their blind lust to devour their prey. What was supposed to be a deportation arrest, turned into a pre-deportation robbery.

Once we were home, Mother began her preparations for Passover. According to Papa, our troubles were over, and the Russian Army would break through the Carpathian Mountains within two weeks. Everyone laughed at my father for his opinion, and thought that he was either underestimating the Russians or overestimating the Hungarians. Everyone but Father thought that the Russians would be held back for perhaps two days at most, as the Hungarian Army was "like a flock of birds on a telephone wire — you shoot one bird and the rest fly away." Father expected that a Russian officer, entering town as part of a liberating army, would join us for the Passover spring celebration.

All the adults, while looking at maps, followed the radio reports of conquests of the nearby Russian Army with great interest. They "conducted the war" by arguing among themselves as to what would be the Russian Army's next move. Most Jews in Buština felt that since we had not been deported and were now back in our own homes, even though they had been ransacked, we were safe. After all, the Nazis were retreating, so the local Jews thought that the Germans were too busy to bother with their obsession of killing Jews. The feeling was that we would be able to sit out the remaining few weeks of the war in our homes and await the liberating Russian Army. If the war took a little longer, then perhaps, in the worst-case scenario, the Nazis would take us to the mountains to work. After all, they needed laborers, they needed us then.

The BBC broadcasts fueled our false delusions. Most of the Hungarian Army and its officers were hurriedly sent to the front, and an air of upcoming doom and panic prevailed among the ranks. We even heard some soldiers saying that they were being sent to the mountains to be slaughtered. The Allied advances delighted us. Losses sustained by the Axis Armies was the topic of joyful conversations and rumors. The Americans were advancing on all fronts, and the Russians were teaching the Nazis a lesson that they would never forget. All this certainly fueled and reinforced our false illusions of safety. Our gloom was interrupted by a slight sliver of sunshine through the delight of the outcome of an episode worthy of a whodunit.

My Aunt Fanny, one of my mother's younger sisters, married to Uncle Zoltan (Zoli) Simsovic lived in Buština and had an adorable blond, blue-eyed one-year-old daughter named Juliana. Aunt Fanny and Uncle Zoli happened to be in Budapest during the time of our aborted deportation arrest and the child had been left in the care of Aunt Judith (Juci) in Buština. While in Budapest, they became alarmed over the arrest and near deportation and undertook a very risky, intricate scheme to rescue their baby daughter from Buština, a scenario worthy of a spy thriller. Aunt Judith, who, with her blue eyes and blond hair, did not look Jewish, was asked to purchase a peasant outfit for the child and gave the peasant-clad baby to our authentic peasant maid, Ilona, who had been with us since she was a child and was completely trusted.

Ilona took the baby by way of the fields to the house of Dr. Davidovic, who was a friend as well as the only doctor in town and was the Simsovics' neighbor. Once there, Dr. Davidovic's peasant maid took the child, wrapped in a peasant shawl, as peasants were accustomed to do, to the railroad station, where they embarked on a train to Budapest. Once on the train, Dr. Davidovic's maid followed the explicit instructions she had been given. After the first stop, she proceeded with the baby to the first-class car that was at the front of the train. There, she identified her contact and sat down next to her. After making eye contact with each other, the contact called the child by her name, effectively giving the password. Realizing that this person was the prearranged designated courier, the maid got off the train alone at the very next stop, leaving baby Juliana in the courier's care. The courier proceeded to take the child to Budapest and turned her over to her mother, Fanny. Juliana and her parents survived the entire war in Budapest, and she now lives in Israel with her family.

DEPORTATION

Our actual deportation, this time without the benefit of any warning whatsoever, took place in the spring, thirty days after Passover, on May 16, 1944.[6] The bubble of our latest illusionary euphoria burst. The Hungarian gendarmes burst into our house with bayonet-fastened rifles at the ready and with a rough and determined attitude they pushed and shoved us, while shouting crisp orders designed to intimidate us. Papa believed that this action would be nothing but a second round of robbery, a continuation of the first raid. The yields of that first raid must have whetted their appetite and now, when they thought that we least expected it, they were there for more. However, it soon became clear that this time their action was not just a raid to rob us of our personal possessions. Our parents shuddered as if thunder

---

6   The extermination phase in Hungary began after the German invasion of Hungary in March 1944. Until then, Horthy refused to succumb to Hitler's pressure to hand over the Jews. At this time, there were more than 800,000 Jews living in Hungary, as a result of annexations of regions from Slovakia, Romania and Yugoslavia. In May 1944, the deportations to Auschwitz began. In just eight weeks, some 424,000 Jews were deported to Auschwitz-Birkenau. After October 1944, when the Arrow Cross party came to power, thousands of Jews from Budapest were murdered on the banks of the Danube and tens of thousands were marched hundreds of miles towards the Austrian border. In all, some 565,000 Hungarian Jews were murdered. For further information see http://www.yadvashem.org/yv/en/education/newsletter/31/jews_hungary.asp (accessed, March 17, 2016).

had struck and they turned chalk-white in fright as they heard the sergeant announce his orders to take us straight to the railroad station where a train was waiting to deport us.

Mother was clutching at her heart and nearly fainted while I clung to her, screaming "Mama!" I was extremely frightened and began to cry. I sensed the terrible calamity that was gathering momentum and enveloping us. From the look on my parents' frightened faces, I sensed the dire consequences heralded by these agents of the devil. After the announcement, the sergeant in charge of this detail displayed his discomfort with his official duties by constantly squaring his jaw and squirming his neck, as if his collar were too tight. I became captivated by the sequence of his squirm and the movement of his ample Adam's apple as he swallowed. Then, in quick sequence, this was followed with an exaggerated squaring of his shoulders and a jerky fidgeting with his rifle that he grasped in his left hand and then quickly grabbed again with his weather-beaten right hand. He then clicked his heels while he snapped at attention and drew his weapon close to himself. He repeated this entire cycle every time he uttered an order. His uneasiness was not caused by his compassion towards us, but rather, by his inflated ego and concern to "do it right," since our town of Buština did not afford him many opportunities to be in charge of orders of this magnitude. He revealed his lack of compassion by his rough behavior as he ordered us to pack some personal belongings into two bags that were to be taken with us. He followed my mother, to whom I was clinging as if for dear life, as she attempted to gather all the available suitcases. He quickly informed us that only two pieces of luggage per family, rather than for each person, would be permitted. Needless to say, after packing the bare necessities for the two children, there was little room left for our parents' belongings. Mother's plea to be allowed a third bag brought her to tears that caused me to cry once again and gave me the impetus to flail my fists at the gendarme while shouting at him, but caused no dent in his demeanor.

His nearness afflicted me with a combination of his body odor, foul garlicky breath and gun oil. The whiff caused me to gag and throw up, which, with my hysterical crying, made quite a mess that was just another thing that Mother had to contend with. Mother's plea for an extra bag was rebuffed rather gruffly, upon which she, having run out of patience, gave the sergeant a long, piercing look that was not lost on him. Defensively, the sergeant, as he went through his routine of fidgeting, refused her, citing explicit orders from headquarters, without any personal discretion in the matter. He looked ahead toward no one in particular as he clicked his heels, putting a definitive period on the end of his disavowal.

Mother hurriedly dressed us in suits of homespun Romanian wool. The knickers and woolen socks were well suited for the coming "journey," as were the belted jacket and warm sweater that defied the weather. At the other end of the house, Papa also had his hands full. All of the gendarmes — other than the sentries who were posted at the exit — seemed to be preoccupied with their interrogation and forceful requests to disclose the location of our supposed treasures. Their grilling was well laced with threats of bodily harm and much worse. The search of our house that was conducted by the most seasoned members of the group yielded some portable items and gadgets that were of no great value; nevertheless, they appropriated them for the "state," i.e., their own pocket, thereby depriving the pleasure of the town scavengers to get their thieving hands on it. The gendarme's meager take prompted their ultimate threat to take the house apart brick by brick, and if they found anything, we would be summarily shot. We were then ordered, or rather pushed, out of the house. We left with the threat ringing in our ears. Mama and Papa spared themselves the agony of looking back.

The exit from our house led to our backyard. We then turned right toward the gate that led to our bridge-like overpass that spanned the relatively deep trench, which served as a run-off ditch down both sides of the road. Crossing the fifteen-foot bridge, we joined other fellow Jews, people who lived further east from us, who were also being marched under guard from their homes, including the *Benesco* section of our town. They were carrying or dragging the allotted two pieces of luggage of various sizes. There were some large families with little children, including the fruit-peddler widow, Shaina Rivka, with her whole brood of little ones hanging on to every possible space on her elaborate ragged skirt. Somehow, she managed to balance her obese body, the width of which seemed to me greater than her height, on her two grotesquely swollen feet and still half carry, half drag her two pieces of luggage. Infants were carried by various, sometimes ingenious, means including wooden dough-kneading bowls. There was Blinde Mima, with a makeshift pack on her back and a cane in her hand, being led by a young girl. There was Ruven Chaim, the proverbial poor man, with his wife and children being deported for the second time (previously in 1941), walking with the same dough-kneading tub under his arm containing his ninth child. As we were ordered to join the sad spectacle of marchers, we noticed Grandfather Yisroel Bruckstein with his unmarried daughters, Aunts Edith, Judith and Sophie, being forcefully evicted from their home across the street. We lingered just long enough so that we would be together in this horrible procession.

Word spread rapidly that the Jews were being deported and the indigenous population, mostly from the *Dorf* section of town, soon lined up at the *Central* to watch as we were being shamefully driven out. A few of them yelled something derogatory at us, but most were dumbfounded and just stood there watching silently. I did not understand then, but can well appreciate today, the embarrassment that our parents and grandparents felt being paraded through the streets with our prominently displayed yellow stars on our chests and under armed guard, as if we were common criminals. However, I did have the sensation that a calamity greater than the loss of my dear Grandma Ruchele was unfolding. Then again, my mind played a placating role, thinking to myself, "How bad can it be? Here is Papa, Mama, Tibi and my grandparents. All my cousins are with us; the entire family is together! That's good, no?" Obviously, I did not understand fully what was happening, but I was very aware of the pain and panic that my parents and everyone around me were conveying and I was swept up by it. From their conversations, I was able to gather a glimmer of the catastrophe that was being played out and I began to catch on. I was growing up fast. My mind began to prepare and train me for what was to come.

Our destination was the railroad station one and a quarter kilometers from our house. Other Jewish families joined our sorrowful column as we passed their homes, including our relatives and friends. We saw the Schwartzes, the Wolfs and the Hillmans emerging from their homes. At the *Central*, the main crossroads, long columns of deportees merged with us as we turned right into Railroad Street. At this time, it became clear to us that the entire Jewish population of our town, not just a selected few, were being deported. On Railroad Street, we were joined by my papa's brothers, Uncles Izidor, Adolph and Joseph, and their families. Like tributary rivers joining the main stream, columns of Jews coming from *Handal* and a larger column from *Dorf* joined us, among whom were my Bruckstein Great Uncles Lippa (Leopold) and Zindu (Alexander) with their families.

These were the conditions under which all Jews, including us, the Brandstein and Bruckstein families, were forcefully removed from their homes in our town of Buština in the Carpathian valley. Our family had lived there continuously ever since the middle of the seventeenth century, for approximately 300 years.

At the railroad station we were herded towards a waiting freight train with closed cattle cars, to be transported to an unknown destination. It is not difficult to imagine the tumult that ensued at our small railroad station by the arrival of nearly 4,000 terrified men, women and children under military guard and in a state of panic. We were pushed and prodded into the cattle cars at bayonet point by the Hungarian gendarmes with the aid of a large contingent of Hungarian soldiers who were assembled at the station for this purpose. The "loading" seemed to have a particular urgency, as if to meet a schedule, and its progress was enunciated by the metal-on-metal clanging of the fully loaded cattle cars as the doors were shut.

It is not easy to climb into a high cattle car without the benefit of a platform. Family and friends were helping those who could not make it. People who were separated from their loved ones were screaming, while children were being exchanged between cars. A child separated from his family by either being left out of the car or being pushed into a different car was a frequent occurrence. Communication by a parent shouting over the general hysterical tumult and the concerns of others would sometimes successfully locate the lost family member, but by no means always. Gendarmes and soldiers were eager to help the girls and young women into the cars with their hands lingering under their skirts and on their chests. Somehow, it always took twice as long to "load" a girl or young woman into the cattle car than a male. From the soldiers' smiling faces and sly remarks, the kicking and screaming of the girls prolonged their duration in a compromising position and contributed to the enjoyment of the lecherous perpetrators. The elderly and the children had to be either helped by a lending hand or endure the additional disgrace and physical harm of being literally thrown into the cars by the soldiers.

Our family, under Mother's watchful eye, managed to get into the same cattle car along with her entire extended family — her father and all of his brothers and their families. Father's family — my uncles, aunts and cousins — managed to be together in an adjacent car. Finally, our car was fully loaded and the soldiers shut its heavy door. A solid thud at the end of a rolling clang announced that the door had met its sill, and a lesser click at the end of another clang confirmed us that the door bolt had securely shut us in. Grandfather audibly said that the lid of our coffin had been sealed. Papa and Tibi quickly arranged the extended family's luggage to serve as benches for the elderly, the sick, women, children and the infirm. Grandpa and Mother sat and the children sat on their laps. There was much hysterical crying and praying. There was neither water, nor toilet facilities. It was almost midday and nearly two hours after our being loaded into the cattle cars that the train, perhaps mercifully, began to move. The car was yanked and bounced back and forth between the adjacent bumpers as the freight train began to make its way.

The cattle car had a window approximately one foot square with iron bars and laced with barbed wire. As our car passed the cemetery, Papa and Grandpa paused their speculative conversation about our possible destination. The most eminent person buried there is the much revered miracle-working Grand Rabbi Mordechai Leifer of Nadvorna, may his soul rest in peace.[7] I remember standing next to my grandfather by the window, curious to see out, and he was looking out towards the cemetery where his wife, his dear Ruchele, was buried. As he sighted the cemetery from the freight car, Grandpa cried, tears running down his cheeks, wetting his vest and shirt. He looked out the window and said in Yiddish, "*Ruchele, ich kim shoin, es vet nisht lang doiren.*" (Ruchele, dear, I am coming, it will not take long.) I did not realize it then, but later it became obvious that my grandfather not only suspected the catastrophe that was being played out, he somehow knew the fate that was awaiting us. Yes, he knew. This incident left such a lasting impression on my young soul that I can still see and hear the particulars whenever I recall them, which I sometimes do involuntarily.

The love that Grandpa Yisroel Bruckstein and Grandma Ruchele Malka had for each other was legendary in the community and much admired. Grandpa constantly demonstrated his love for his Ruchele by showering her with gifts that he bought on his frequent business trips all over Europe. People used to say that they were like *toibelech* (doves). My father, who

---

7   *Rebbe* Mordchele Leifer is buried in a private mausoleum in the Buština cemetery. The author's great-grandparents, Moshe and Sirka Bruckstein, grandmother, Rachel Bru.cksten, and grandfather, Eliezer Brandstein, are all buried in honored positions alongside the wall of the mausoleum.

was present when Grandma Ruchele passed away, witnessed the ultimate devotion they had for each other. Papa described the moment of Grandma's death in the arms of her beloved Yisroel. As Grandfather was hugging his dear Ruchele and as her sweet unblemished soul left her body, passing to her rewards in Heaven, Grandpa screamed out her name and Ruchele turned her head, one more time, towards my anguished grandfather, who was crying uncontrollably.

As the train moved on, the adults took turns keeping watch through the limited view from the cattle car window that afforded them an opportunity to see signs in Hungarian. The fact that we were in Hungary gave us some degree of hope, since we were seemingly not headed to the dreaded killing fields of the Ukraine or Poland that we had heard about. However, this train ride was the most torturous experience that we had endured so far, for we were not yet seasoned to the hardships, which, at best, were to be our daily fate. Just six hours of hell, six hours that seemed an eternity; six hours that were filled alternatively with rapt prayer, crying, fainting, loose bowels and hysterical howling that drowned out the hysterics of the children. Mercifully, perhaps, we arrived at our destination, the ghetto in the town of Mátészalka in Hungary.

MÁTÉSZALKA GHETTO[8]

The cattle cars were opened with much clanging, revealing our wretched conditions, which were in contrast to the beautiful spring day. The sun provided a ghoulish disparity to our condition, both physical and mental, as we were half-dead due to the lack of air and wet from perspiration and fear. Hungarian soldiers ordered us to get off the train with our possessions. Many, especially the elderly, were hurt as they fell disembarking the high cattle cars. As soon as the guards were able to

---

8   The last national census conducted in Hungary prior to the German occupation, taken in January 1941, recorded 1,555 Jewish inhabitants in Mátészalka, accounting for roughly 15 percent of the total population. Most were merchants and artisans and a number were clerks. The town had an Orthodox Jewish community that comprised a Hasidic community with a separate prayer house. Educational institutions included a Jewish elementary school, a Talmud Torah and a *yeshiva*.

achieve some semblance of order, they herded us into a compound that was surrounded by barbed wire and guarded by sentries. Once inside, we were ordered to assemble, and then the Hungarian commandant of the ghetto addressed us. "You are in the Mátészalka Ghetto under the command of the Hungarian Army and under martial law," he barked at us. "Anyone who attempts to escape will be shot," he continued. "Every infraction will be dealt with brutal force if not by execution," he conveyed to us as a matter-of-fact and with an obvious smirk. And lastly, motioning in the general direction of the front gate where we had entered the compound, "You are to remain assembled and wait for your turn to be registered, which will take place inside the brick building behind me." "The registration," we were told, "will be accomplished with two families at a time and with your entire

The German Army occupied Hungary on March 19, 1944. A census conducted in the second week of April 1944 showed that 1,625 Jews belonged to the Orthodox Jewish community of Mátészalka. The Hungarian administration remained intact and in force after the occupation. Dr. Gyorgy Fogarassy, the Hungarian chief administrative officer of the Mátészalka District, ordered the establishment of the ghetto in Mátészalka. Ghettoization began on May 9, 1944. The ghetto was established in the center of the town beside the Szalkai factory and the Schreiber lumberyard, both of which were connected to the railway system by tracks. In addition to local Jews, other Jews from various localities in the vicinity, some 16,300 people, lived in the Mátészalka Ghetto. A Jewish Council headed by Rabbi Frigyes Gruenbaum operated in the ghetto. Several Jewish physicians set up a sick bay in a Jewish house outside the compound with the help of a gentile physician neighbor. The Jewish elementary school building was transformed into a hospital, prompting the municipal authorities to cast out the Jewish patients from the town hospital.

The Mátészalka Ghetto was severely overcrowded, and the majority of the inhabitants lived without shelter. A soup kitchen provided food, which, however, was insufficient. The town authorities allocated 200 grams of bread daily per person. The Mátészalka Ghetto was guarded by Hungarian gendarmes, while internal order was maintained by the Jewish Order Service under the command of Nathan Spitzer. The name of the ghetto's Hungarian commander was Kulifay, infamous for his cruelty. The gendarmes tortured the inhabitants of the ghetto into revealing the whereabouts of their hidden valuables. Several Jews died during and as a consequence of the torture. The gendarmes also raped young Jewish women in their headquarters.

The inhabitants of the ghetto were deported to Auschwitz in five transports between May 19 and June 5, 1944. The SS officer *Hauptsturmfuehrer* Ernst Gierzick supervised the entrainment process.

See Guy Miron and Shlomit Shulhani, eds., *The Yad Vashem Encyclopedia of the Ghettos during the Holocaust* (Jerusalem: Yad Vashem Publications, 2009).

belongings." It was at this "reception" where I got the third shock of my young, by now, turbulent life.

A couple of hours passed until our turn finally came to be "received," and — Papa and Mama, Tibi and I — were paired up with Mr. and Mrs. Elefant, two of the most virtuous and prominent elderly citizens of our town. Mr. Elefant was a known and widely respected sage and Talmudic scholar. Mrs. Elefant was highly respected and widely known and admired as a woman of valor and a pillar of piety. Two guards escorted the six of us into the designated red brick building. We were led into a room that was bare of furnishings, except for a light bulb shaded by a simple reflector that hung in the middle of the room, a low cabinet that served as a receptacle for garbage and two tables that were placed end to end to form one long table behind which stood an officer and two guards. Slivers of sunshine peeked into the room through the two windows, illuminating the dust in the room, which rose from the bare wooden floor and swirled wildly in direct concert with our movements.

The officer behind the tables ordered us to place our luggage on the table. As we did so, the two guards unceremoniously pounced on it like vultures and proceeded to help themselves indiscriminately to anything that their thieving hearts desired, while we helplessly stood by. After a short wait, which was spent watching our last possessions being robbed, we were escorted to an inner office that contained only the same hanging light in the center of the room under which a chisel-faced Hungarian Army officer, framed by two guards standing on each side of him, was seated on a low chair. All three of them had walking canes in their right hands. The guards' left hands rested on the exposed butts of their side arms that were holstered and attached to their belts. A strap across their chests and over their uniforms supported these belts. Curiously, the seated officer held his cane by its end with its crook extended as he ordered Mrs. Elefant to step forward to be searched. Given that there were no female personnel to conduct the search, Mrs. Elefant hesitated and showed her reluctance to obey the order. One of the guards standing behind the seated officer stepped forward and hooked the crook of his walking cane around Mrs. Elefant's neck and forcefully pulled her forward. The officer then ordered her to crouch. While she was still reluctant, the two guards forced Mrs. Elefant's knees apart with the crooks of their canes and held her so, while the seated officer violated her dignity by lifting her skirt and roughly probing her with the crook of his walking cane. He proceeded to exercise his expertise by pushing and twisting the cane as he searched her for hidden treasures. Her elderly husband shouted at them to stop. As he approached the officer with his arms outstretched, intending, if need be, to physically stop him, the two guards beat him mercilessly with their walking canes; they beat him into a bloody pulp, nearly killing him. The episode did not deter the officer from continuing the search.

My mother was next. Mama was searched while Mr. Elefant was on the floor bleeding from his head and Mrs. Elefant was screaming hysterically. The Hungarian officer menacingly lifted his cane over Mama's head and yelled at her to crouch, whereupon he proceeded to violate her. As it was well demonstrated, if Mama disobeyed or anyone protested, the cane would come down on our mama's head. Papa and my brother were stunned, while I screamed, "Mama!" The search continued unabated while Mr. Elefant was being removed from the room and Mrs. Elefant, crying hysterically, was pushed out the back door.

When this macabre episode was thankfully over, we were led out, with our now-diminished luggage, through the rear door where a waiting sentry marched us toward a line of sheds. I could not come to terms with what I witnessed. Such brutality! I could not imagine that anyone could do such a thing. My mind was racing with the thoughts of, "How can this be? How can anybody do this to any woman, particularly to a saintly woman like Mrs. Elefant, and nearly killing dear Mr. Elefant? How dare they touch our dear mother! How could my father just stand there while these hooligans insulted us? Why did we let them get away with this crime? How dare they!" As a child, I thought that Papa was omnipotent; after all, he was Father! Is there anything that he could not do? Why was my papa standing there helpless? This was the first time I experienced adults as helpless, especially adults of my family. This realization shocked me out of my innocence. My nonchalant attitude of thinking that nothing bad can happen as long as I am with my parents changed to one of apprehension and fear.

Later in the day, I asked my father the very same questions, wondering how it was possible to have let anybody do this to Mama. My father's answer was simply, "Son, these are terrible times." I said to him, "I understand that there are terrible times, but, what does it mean these are terrible times? How can times be terrible?" Papa looked at me while his hands were caressing my face and said, "You will understand, my sweet child, you will understand." Soon enough I came to understand and, like many, assigned the brutality around me to the times that were terrible. However, I was wrong in thinking that I understood, for today, I still do not understand how people suffer from "the times that are terrible." People make the times terrible. We lived in times when the people were terrible.

The antisemitism, deportation from my home and then entering Ghetto Mátészalka were my introduction to the "terrible times" that were to escalate exponentially with every passing day. At home, during the so-called "prior-to-deportation roundup," the Hungarian gendarmes robbed us. Then, during the actual deportation, the gendarmes told us to take with us a limited amount of our personal possessions and stole the rest. Now, in Ghetto Mátészalka, the Hungarian Army guards robbed us once again. They removed everything of real or perceived value from our meager possessions, including, sometimes, the valise itself. The clothing on our backs did not escape their gluttonous appetite if it caught their fancy. They robbed our combs out of our pockets or from the children's hair, leaving us with less than the bare necessities. Their actions emanated from their lust to "rob the dead," for they knew where we were destined to go and they wanted to get their murderous hands on whatever they could before the Germans got to us. Throughout our stay in the ghetto, the Hungarians conducted selective searches for contraband goods; they repeatedly searched women as well as men and children. The officers of the guards were relentless in their fiendish pursuit; every possible body crevice was thoroughly searched.

Ghetto Mátészalka was a fenced-in, abandoned or commandeered brick factory with wooden cooling and storage sheds. The sheds ran the entire length of the property that was adjacent to the railroad tracks near the railroad station of the town. In addition to the brick kilns and storage sheds, there was a sizable closed-off section where the sheds served as equipment storage facilities. The brick building near the main entrance where we were "welcomed" had served as the offices of the establishment. In addition to the working part of the property, the fence extended and encompassed undeveloped adjacent fields. The location was well chosen for the intended purpose of being a transient ghetto. The fact that the whole complex was abutting the railroad tracks provided the tyrants an efficiency of transport that could otherwise not have been easily attained. The disembarkation of an arriving transport or the embarkation of a departing one was within a mere block of the ghetto so the pitiful victims did not have to be marched or trucked through the town.

There were no bunks in the sheds; this was not accommodation for human beings. The spring weather was still chilly, especially at night. It was absolutely forbidden, under penalty of death, to destroy any ghetto property, and they especially prohibited burning wood from the shed. Nevertheless, some people literally took the risk of facing death when they ripped up some of the floorboards or pieces from the rafters for firewood to keep a little bit warm and perhaps cook something edible if and when anything edible was available.

Due to overcrowding, our family was assigned one of the ten feet by ten feet makeshift upper parts of a two-story shed. These spaces were created with boards being placed between the rafters and were accessible only with the aid of rickety ladders that were difficult to scale, but they had the advantage of giving somewhat better protection against the rain and cold by the overhang of the roof. Papa and Tibi placed our belongings in an advantageous way to create a semblance of a human habitat. We were so crowded that it was impossible to reach our spot without stepping on someone else's belongings. I, as a child, had no trouble sleeping, but my parents found it almost impossible to sleep at night, being kept awake by children bawling and people lamenting their situation. Their sleep deprivation contributed appreciably to their despair that became more pronounced as the days went by.

I found a couple of broken bricks and with them I made a fireplace. I was, and still am, very good at adapting to a given situation and, therefore, was put in charge of making a little fire to roast a root or a potato on a stick in the hot coals. Money was either not available or had no value. Bartering was the only form of exchange. The guards robbed much of the food that was allocated to us; they ate as much as they could, bartered some and sold the rest in town. The puny rations that were distributed to the four of us were hardly enough to feed Tibi and me, so our parents were literally starving. Later, Papa told me that, even in the concentration camps, he was never as hungry as he was in Ghetto Mátészalka.

To understand the starvation that our parents experienced, one must weigh their uncharacteristic actions considering food. Outside the non-electrified barbed wire that surrounded the ghetto were private potato, radish and cabbage fields. When we arrived we were warned against making any attempt to escape, or going outside the wire fence as we would be summarily shot. There were warning posters displayed on the fence at various intervals stating this and the guards unceremoniously executed anyone caught outside the fence. Despite these warnings of dire consequences, Father would act as a lookout and permit and actually encourage me, my mother's "frog," her skinny boy, to slide under the wire, get into the fields and dig up some potatoes or roots. If I were caught, I would have been shot, just like others were, but it was simply a matter of survival.

The Hungarian goons, the so-called guards, organized a semi-official brigade of selected young men from the ghetto to help in the policing of the camp's daily routine. Tibi, who was fifteen years old but could and did pass for two or even three years older, had a minor role in the brigade that afforded him the opportunity to supplement our meager rations, thwarting our starvation. Besides the hunger, we had to contend with the guards constantly threatening our lives and demanding our money and valuables. Robbery was the theme of every moment of our stay.

The days were spent looking for or talking about food, discussing our situation, listening to rumors and avoiding the guards. There was a rumor that a certain army camp needed workers. People had illusions that we were waiting for railroad cars to be taken to work camps and the sooner the better, we assumed, because when we got to the work camps they would presumably have to feed us. Thus, we were anxiously waiting for the opportunity to leave. Labor-related rumors that were officially fostered upon us by our tormentors, once again worked their magic. Our self-illusion kept us hopeful and hope made an unbearable ordeal marginally, but nevertheless, bearable. Nobody thought that we were destined to be fodder for extermination camp crematoria.

Ghetto Mátészalka was a misnomer; it was not a ghetto in any sense of the word, rather a holding pen for those in transit. The authorities never intended to keep people there for any extended period and certainly the place had no provisions or facilities for mass housing and feeding beyond a few days. It was a cramped, cold and awful place. We were incarcerated in Ghetto Mátészalka for nineteen long terrible days, hellish days of starvation, worry and despair that once again seemed an eternity, without any provision for bathing or any other health-related activities. We thought things could not get any worse; after all, these nineteen days stretched human endurance to the limit. No human being could withstand more of it and certainly not anything worse. Or could they?

On a late Sunday evening on the nineteenth day of our incarceration, we heard rumors that our departure for a work camp was imminent. We believed the news to be good. We felt as if we were being liberated. That sleepless night was filled with speculation as to where we might be going. After all, the prevailing opinion was that wherever we were being taken would be better. People reinforced this opinion with the hope that in a work camp they would have to feed us. After all, weak or dead men can't work. However, things did not turn out that way. Illusions and self-hypnotic hopes are just that. In comparison, Ghetto Mátészalka would soon seem like heaven on earth. How much can a human being endure? We would soon find out.

CATTLE CARS

The next day was a beautiful sunny Monday, one of those days that I used to associate with a good omen. The sky was blue, with a few fluffy clouds floating in the distance. The temperature was warm with a gentle breeze providing a breath of fresh air in the sheds. It was a day that someone may describe as a "glad-to-be-alive day" and none would dispute it. None of us, however, would have described it that way. It was just another day that would surely be filled with misery and hunger. It did, so we believed, bring us closer to the end of the war and liberation that we not only hoped for, but believed with all our hearts and souls was imminent. The belief in our real or imaginary liberation from the inferno somehow sustained us throughout our incarceration.

The stupor of that current daydream was suddenly shattered as a convoy of army trucks rumbled through the gate of the ghetto and disgorged an army group made up of perhaps a hundred Hungarian soldiers with their guns and bayonets at the ready and brandishing clubs. They began to drive us towards the gate and then we were ordered to get ready for transport. Despite the rumor of our imminent departure, we had no real prior notice of our actual transport; therefore, we were not even able to take all of our meager belongings. The rush tactic was a final and clever way of getting us to leave behind whatever we might have hidden as well as our meager possessions. Hence, we were driven en masse, like cattle, the entire short distance to the rail tracks.

The embarkation should have been an omen of things to come. The train did not pull up to the station; therefore, besides the difficulty of embarking into a cattle car that was very high, we had to surmount the additional height of an embankment to reach the tracks. We were literally tossed into the cars without any regard for keeping family members together. The freight cattle cars were filled to the utmost limits. The unprecedented brutality of the Hungarian soldiers was terrifying. Their action burst many of our preconceived notions as to our destination. They literally squeezed us into the cars as they wielded their clubs to force us in and then shut the doors and locked them. The screaming in the closed car was deafening, with the children's as well as the adults' hysteria on an exceptional scale. People were throwing up, others could not control their bowels, while many fainted from despair and fear, mostly of the unknown. With the separation of many families, a new draconian, horrifying dimension was added to the scene. The separated families were inconsolable, beside themselves with terror.

If the six-hour ride from Buština to Ghetto Mátészalka was a nightmarish ride to purgatory, then the next forty-eight hours were a ride to hell, a calamity of biblical proportion. The trip was inhumane beyond comprehension and therefore beyond description. We had neither water nor sanitation. We were not provided with the minimum of human needs. The cattle car had the standard one-foot by eight-inch window at each end that had metal bars and barbed wire and supplied the minimum air to thwart suffocation, but barely enough for survival.

When man is stressed to a point where his mind perceives this to be the limit, he cannot imagine worse conditions. We believed that we had reached the ultimate, the pinnacle of hell on earth. None would dispute that the transport from Ghetto Mátészalka qualified as that outer limit. Nevertheless, later, I experienced even more horrifying conditions, which the mind cannot grasp, and which dwarfed any previous experience. The worst part in this case was the hysteria enveloping me. Some shouted that we were all going to die, while others countered with admonishments to hush and not scare the children. Intensely aggravated by the suffocating conditions, the hysteria seemed to break out in waves; it ebbed for a while only to rise to ever-greater heights.

The pain of seeing Mother's cheeks wet from her gushing tears, and seeing Grandfather's chest heaving and his beard, shirt and vest also wet from tears, was an experience that became embedded in my conscience. I was numb and bewildered. I sought the safety of Mother's lap and her reassuring touch. Seeing my parents, aunts and uncles crying reminded me of the immediate aftermath of Grandma Ruchele's passing, and in my mind, I evaluated the current situation on the same scale. I was terribly upset. I had experienced Grandma's funeral and the crying of adults. That had seemed to me like a calamity. I wondered where we were going that could be so bad. I still hoped that being together with my entire family meant that things could not be so terrible.

The temperature in the car was like an oven; the heat was beyond human tolerance. Many children became feverish. I remember feeling Mother's hand on my forehead and hearing her announce to Father, "The child is hot," and she proceeded to lick my face in order to wet it, then fan me with her kerchief, thereby succeeding in reducing my temperature. The conditions, exacerbated by the lack of food and water or sanitary provisions of any kind were unbearable. The pungent odor of vomit, diarrhea and perspiration was suffocating in the still air of the cattle car. Quite a few people died. I remember one person dying and another person just folded him over to sit on top of the dead man. It was insufferable.

People wondered out loud how anyone would survive, and how much a human being could endure. Everyone was trying to figure out where we were going and what would become of us, and most pressing was the question, "Why?" No one could have even attempted to venture an answer. No conceivable, bizarrely outrageous scenario could have formulated the outcome. Yet, the Devil and his Nazi advocates here on earth were devising means to raise the ante of inconceivable ruthlessness. The bar was being raised exponentially to new heights that defy human comprehension.

We were delayed at the rail hub of the Czech city of Košice, now occupied by Hungary and called Kassa (the Germans called it Kaschau). There, as those who had the advantageous lookout positions at the window of our railcar told us, our guards, the Hungarian soldiers in their brownish-khaki uniforms, were being replaced by guards in blue-gray uniforms, some with SS insignia, and shouting to each other in German. The lookouts announced, in the tones of a death sentence, that the Hungarians were turning us over to the Germans, which had its predictable effect on us — instant havoc. The realization of what this meant was instantaneous, yet everyone was looking for a line of thought that would give us a sliver of hope, real or imaginary. And so, someone offered the "consolation" of us still being on Czech soil. Although it was occupied by Germany, this was a reasonably sensible and acceptable argument, if for no other reason than because it was the only consoling line of reasoning that anyone could think of and had some semblance of credence.

The cattle cars of our train of the doomed were never opened; we were just transferred like cargo with a bill of lading. The Hungarians, who were at this point the partners and lackeys of the Nazis, finished their part of this macabre undertaking by turning us over to the much more experienced "professionals," the angels of death, their German bosses. The train was heading northwest and the boxcar resonated with the rhythmic sound of the wheels on the steel rails in a somnolent beat that sometimes, in its monotonous fashion, had an intoxicating effect that numbed our minds. But mostly, the rhythmic sound had the effect of a blacksmith's hammer striking the anvil as it painfully ticked off the seconds, minutes and hours left to the condemned.

As the train droned on, it passed some of the world's most fertile fields that bless the Slovakian section of Czechoslovakia. On the way, our train of sorrow and grief stopped to wait for the track to clear of oncoming traffic, or for the locomotive to take on water. Along the way, the train backed up and switched tracks many times as additional cars full of additional victims were hitched to it, or as it was being maneuvered onto tracks leading northwest from Košice, towards the slaughterhouses that were its destination. Every back-and-forth reversal jarred us out of our stupor. It woke the children and induced them to wail for hours. Under armed German guards, who were aided by German Shepherd dogs, the train continued to roll on through the Carpathian Mountain passes that led to a valley of lush green fields and orchards.

The following day, there was a deadly despair in our cattle car as the lookouts reported that the stations that we were passing had Polish signs. The meaning of the possible consequences of being in Poland, the sorrowful land that was being soaked with Jewish blood, created an appalling situation of despair. The previous consolation of being on Czech soil disappeared like a dream. The sounds of prayer, wailing, lamenting and cries to the effect of "We will be butchered," were now prevalent.

All previous attempts on the part of the adults to stifle the expression of their anguish and heartache, for the sake of the children, were involuntarily abandoned. The children, taking their lead from their parents, rose their wailing to a new crescendo. I clung tightly to my mother as she held me in her tight embrace, and wet her neck and shoulder with my tears as I joined the chorus of hysterical children. I wondered to myself, "My mommy is crying. What did she do to anybody to make her cry? What is happening to us? Where and what is this monster Poland and why is everybody so afraid of it? Why is it bad to be there? What is it going to do to us? Nobody is lost; we are all here together, so why is everybody crying worse than when somebody died? Look, *Zeidy* (Grandpa) looks funny, his cherubic face looks ashen and his eyes are like glass, it is scary. He does not blink but his lips are moving. Is he sick, God forbid? Maybe he is praying. Why is Tibi talking to Papa so quietly? What is the secret? I am old enough to know, since I have had my *Bar Mitzvah*, I am a man now. So, why doesn't anybody tell me what is going on?" All of these questions ran through my mind, but I could not ask them out loud, because as soon as I began a question, Mama said, "Hush, my sweet child. With the Almighty's help, everything will be all right." Then, someone came up with a typical self-delusionary statement claiming that being in Poland may not necessarily mean that it's as bad as everyone imagines it to be. However, the situation soon reverted to the previous, by now normal, frantic panic.

Hunger was the underlying foundation of the inhuman conditions that prevailed in the freight car. No food or water was given to us prior to our transport's embarkation, nor did anybody have any food reserves to fall back on, since everyone had been starving in the ghetto to begin with. Anything that was chewable was given to the smallest children. It was under these conditions that we had to endure the psychological torment, other than during the illusionary moments of fantasy, the slow realization that we were being hurled towards our slaughter.

It had been forty-eight hours since we left the ghetto at Mátészalka in Hungary; forty-eight hours that comprised an eternity in hell, when we finally arrived at our destination: the infamous Birkenau extermination and concentration camp (also known as Auschwitz II) on Friday, June 2, 1944. The camp was located a few kilometers outside the city of Oświęcim, Poland.

PART III

LIFE OR DEATH?

AUSCHWITZ-BIRKENAU[1]

O ur arrival on June 2, 1944, at the notorious Auschwitz-Birkenau Concentration Camp, also known as Auschwitz II, a *Vernichtungslager* (extermination camp), can never be adequately described. Words cannot express the tumult, the constant screams of children and their mothers who were separated from each other at embarkation and were now frantically searching for each other, mostly unsuccessfully.

---

1   Auschwitz-Birkenau was the largest Nazi extermination and concentration camp, located near the Polish town of Oświęcim, thirty-seven miles west of Kraków, which was established under order of SS chief Heinrich Himmler in April 1940. One-sixth of all Jews murdered by the Nazis were gassed at Auschwitz. Auschwitz-Birkenau was a complex of camps including Auschwitz I, Birkenau (Auschwitz II), Buna-Monowitz (Auschwitz III) and more than 40 forced labor sub-camps. Approximately 1.3 million people were murdered in the camp: 1.1 million Jews, 70,000-80,000 Poles, more than 20,000 Sinti and Roma, 15,000 Soviet POWs and about 15,000 Jehovah's Witnesses, homosexuals, Ukrainians and more. Auschwitz was first run by Camp Commandant Rudolf Höss, and was guarded by the cruel regiment *SS-Totenkopfverbände* (Death's Head Units).

No adjective in any language can adequately describe that experience. The constant German shouts of "*Los! Los!*" (Let's go! Let's go!), and the commands coming through the loudspeakers and by the guards with rifle butts, bayonets and dogs, created an extraordinary panic, a catastrophe of biblical proportions, a commotion that boggles the human mind to comprehend. A surreal feeling of doomsday blanketed our pale, stunned faces.

Arrival at our final destination was announced by our train grinding to a halt and hearing the frighteningly loud clunking noises of the heavy doors of the freight cars being rolled open. The clunking began at the front of the train and came closer and closer to our car that was in the middle of the train. The sound was much like approaching rolling thunder. As it got nearer, the clunking was mingled with the noise and screams of people disembarking onto the concrete platform below and the constant yelling of the guards, "*Los! Los! Raus! Raus!*" (Let's go! Let's go! Out! Out!) While we were still shut in our tomb that was our freight car, our fears escalated to the point of irrationality. When our door was finally opened, it was dusk.

Until early 1942, the Nazis deported to Auschwitz only a relatively small number of Jews. In March 1942, trains carrying Jews began to arrive daily. By July 4, 1942, regular selection was introduced for the Jews arriving on RSHA (Reichssicherheitshauptamt — State Security Headquarters) transports. Throughout 1942, transports arrived from Poland, Slovakia, the Netherlands, Yugoslavia and Theresienstadt. By the second half of 1942, the prisoner population comprised mostly Jews. The majority of them died either while they were in Auschwitz or after transfer to other camps. Jews, mainly from Poland, Greece and the Protectorate of Bohemia and Moravia, Germany, Belgium and Italy, as well as Sinti and Roma, continued to arrive and to be murdered throughout 1943. Between May and June 1944, about 430,000 Hungarian Jews were brought to Auschwitz, alongside Jews from the remaining Polish ghettos yet to be liquidated. The majority of them were murdered. By August 1944, there were still more than 130,000 prisoners in Auschwitz camps, the majority of them Jews.

In the second half of 1944 and the first two weeks of January 1945, about 65,000 prisoners, including almost all the Poles, Russians and Czechs remaining in the camp, were evacuated to various industrial plants in the depths of the Reich. Between January 17 and 21, 1945, the Nazis performed the final evacuation of the camp, sending most of the 58,000 remaining prisoners, the majority of them Jews, on a death march to Germany, during which about 15,000 were killed or died en route. The Soviet Army liberated Auschwitz on January 27; soldiers found only 7,650 barely living prisoners throughout the entire camp complex. For further information see: http://www.yadvashem.org/yv/en/holocaust/about/05/auschwitz_birkenau.asp (accessed, March 17, 2016).

We were first greeted with a rush of fresh and relatively cool air and then with the commands, *"Raus! Raus!"* being shouted by the guards in a guttural German accent while brandishing their machine guns and bayonet-mounted rifles. Some guards mounted the cars and literally threw the people out onto the platform, much as one would hurl a sack of potatoes. The turmoil and commands were intermingled with the snarling and barking of the dogs. One could clearly hear mothers yelling for their missing children, while children were screaming, "Mamaaa! Papaaa! *Mamiii! Tatiii!"* The elderly, who were mostly under the care of their families or friends if they were nearby, were disoriented and looked helpless and forlorn. As the platform filled with disembarking people, the guards were intensifying their commands to move faster, *"Los, Los! Macht schnell! Heraus mit dem verfluchten jüdischen Dreck!"* (Let's go! Let's go! Make it fast! Out with this cursed Jewish filth!) All the while, additional doors were clanking open with the sounds of a receding thunder.

Every command from the moment of arrival was *"Los, Los!"* or *"Mach schnell!"* (Hurry up!), followed by a threatening gesture, which was much too often followed through. We were never asked to walk; we were forced to run, and then to run faster. No speed was ever fast enough and no order was ever conveyed in a civil manner; everything was yelled or rather barked at us with implicit threats of physical harm to life or limb. From now on, *"Schweinehunde, verfluchte Juden"* (swine, cursed Jews) or just plain *"Scheissdreck"* (filthy shit) were among the most often hurled epithets.

We were ordered to leave all our possessions behind. Nevertheless, mothers, especially mothers of infants, grabbed some clothing for their children and clutched it to their bosom, hiding it from the guards' view. As we disembarked, we became acutely aware of the barking, crazed, German Shepherd dogs straining at their leashes, held by helmeted guards with their automatic pistols at the ready. The Birkenau arrival platforms were inside the camp. There were at least five tracks separated by four platforms. Our train backed into the camp through the arch of the camp gate. Once the locomotive was disconnected and had left, the gates of hell closed upon us.

Looking back toward the rear of our long train, we saw a brick building with an arched gate that straddled a single track entering the camp. Once the arch was passed, a complex of tracks and switches, much like at a train station, embraced the platforms. Our view to the right was obstructed by our freight arch was passed, a complex of tracks and switches, much like at a train station, embraced the platforms. Our view to the right was obstructed by our freight train. To our left were two more tracks separated by another platform. Behind the last track and running the entire length of the camp, as far as the eye could see, was a barbed-wire fence fastened to concrete poles with ceramic insulators supporting the barbed wire. Every other concrete pole had a low, downward-facing electrical fixture that illuminated the fence. The fact that the light fixtures derived their power from the barbed wires that were connected to the poles by the insulators, divulged the fact that the fence was electrified. Behind the fence were rows of barracks. Since the guards strictly enforced a curfew that was imposed on all inmates within sight of an arriving transport, the barracks were shut tight, seemingly empty. There were intermittent guard towers with guards manning spotlights and machine guns. Other than one particular section with cypress trees, which was not totally visible, the whole scene was bereft of any trees or vegetation.

The platform was soon packed to capacity with a multitude of sweating and swirling people in various stages of despair. Everyone seemed to be in motion, attempting to keep his or her family together, while trying to stay within sight of the cars containing their meager belongings. Just as one might have thought that the platform could not possibly have room for one more person, a phalanx of guards forcefully cleared the way for a detail of ghouls, skeleton-like emaciated inmates with a cart in tow. They were under heavy guard and clad in striped prisoner uniforms. The macabre detail mounted the cars and with their broomstick-like legs, twig-like arms and fleshless fingers began to unload, or rather throw out, the possessions from the cars into their carts that were equipped with straps to be pulled by other prisoners who were standing by wearing a harness, much like emaciated beasts of burden.

"What is this terrible vile smell and why are ashes falling from the sky?" I could hear people inquiring of one of the beasts of burden, who was within earshot. The man, or rather the skull on stilts, turned, showing his grotesque teeth with some skin pulled tight over them where lips should have been. "They are burning gassed people," the skull furtively answered matter-of-factly, but to no one in particular. "Tonight they will be burning you," it added as it went into a coughing spasm or perhaps a laughing spasm that heaved his shoulders wildly and culminated in a large spit of a globule of blood. Recovering from the coughing fit, he continued, "You are all dead," adding emphasis with his bony hand for good measure. The remarks were dismissed as the words of an insane person.

Although a self-appointed *maven* (expert) berated the "ghoul" with a barrage of epithets, and waved his hands to emphasize their irrelevancy, others took note. Like the spreading concentric rings created by a stone dropped in a calm lake, the "message" was carried to an ever-greater audience. Soon the entire platform was gripped with a new type of fear and in a cold sweat and despair that one could smell as well as feel. One could see the bulging eyes of those who had reached their limit and were displaying the breakdown of their endurance. All the while, the guards intensified their brutal shouts and insults and made good on their threats by using the butts of their rifles while herding us forward in the direction of the head of the column, towards the cypress trees.

My thoughts were in a turmoil. "What did I hear? What was that poor sick man saying? Did he say that they would be burning us? Who burns people? He was obviously wrong when he said that we are all dead. Look, nobody is dead! We are all alive! The other man is certainly right; the poor man is a *meshuganer* (crazy). Besides, what am I worried about? Papa, Mama, Tibi and Grandpa are here, so everything is all right. But I am awfully tired, hungry and thirsty and badly need a bathroom."

The loading of the luggage onto the carts proved to be a monumental task. The walking skeletons could not possibly keep up with the sheer volume of the luggage and certainly not in the time that they were allotted. The guards, who must have had their orders to clear the cars forthwith, ordered the detail of ghosts designated as beasts of burden to join the others in throwing everything indiscriminately onto the platform to be carted away later. In any case, the train was not to be delayed in leaving for another macabre trip to feed the Nazi killing factories.

Soon, the loudspeakers began to roar their commands, and the guards with their dogs enforced them. Every command was preceded by "*Achtung, Achtung*" (Attention, Attention). We were ordered to keep a steady motion forward. As all commands, it was followed by the warning that anyone disobeying a command would be shot. Moments later, the loudspeakers commanded over the din of the multitude, "The old, young, sick and pregnant women or women with young children and those who wish to take care of the old, the sick and the children, are to take the right fork in the road at the end of the platform as we approach the gates." As we were being driven towards the gates, the command was repeated every few minutes, intermingled with additional orders and threats. Disobedience, regardless of how trivial, whether suspected, unintentional or unavoidable, carried the penalty of death.

The constant shouts of *Los! Los!*, being driven forward by the guards who hit and prodded us with their rifle butts and their bayonets, while the dogs barked and growled menacingly and sometimes actually bit us, were fueling our hysteria. People who were being driven from the rear were pushing and climbing over the people in front in order to escape the rampaging dogs. The Germans maintained this constant panic on purpose, and it served their macabre goals well. They maintained a constant rush so that we would not have a chance to think of anything other than the moment at hand. They made the survival of the moment our uppermost concern. We were prodded and driven like cattle to a slaughterhouse holding pen. If someone deliberately disobeyed the guards' command, he was clubbed to the ground and then the dogs would get to him. The guards formed a solid wall along both sides of the platform. With guards and dogs driving us forward, there was no choice but to obey. Twins or triplets, as well as their mothers, were ordered to identify themselves as they reached the front, to receive "special treatment." They were grouped separately from the rest of us. All of us, together as a family, were heeding the command of the loudspeakers and were inching forward toward the front. It was the later part of the afternoon by the time we reached the vicinity of the front of the platform.

My grandfather was dressed in his customary black suit and wore a black hat, the proper attire for a distinguished gentleman of his status. My Great-Uncle Leopold Bruckstein was my grandfather's younger brother and a carbon copy of Grandfather, in looks as well as in his attire. He was his partner and best friend. Until then, we had all managed to stand together. However, as per the instructions given over the loudspeakers, the two elderly brothers were to separate from us. They were to keep to the right, while we, the "fit," were to keep to the left. At first, in order to be together, our entire family planned to go to the right, thinking that this action would take advantage of the better treatment that the elderly, the children and the sick were surely going to receive. After all, Papa reasoned, they will be better taken care of and, as an additional benefit, this action would even save us from slave labor.

Our delusion was so complete that while we were standing there in Birkenau, inside the most notorious and efficient killing factory ever devised by man, we were thinking of "working the angles" of possible advantages. We still held on to our self-hypnotic, self-serving illusions.

As night slowly crept on, mercury vapor floodlights, which gave off an eerie atmosphere, illuminated the train platform. The lights on our left, all along the electrified barbed-wire fence, shone dimly. The setting sun illuminated the clouds in the western sky and above us some stars became visible. The twinkling stars seemed to mock us. The moon was so bright that it seemed near and within reach. This canopy, an otherwise serene scene, was intermingled with the terrible smell, smoke and a fine gray ash that emanated from the chimneys that were in the compound in front of us, beyond the cypress trees.

As we walked forward, we had ample opportunity to look for any sign of life all along the other side of the electrified barbed wire that was to our right. Other than the work detail of emaciated "ghouls" who were unloading our belongings and carting them away, there were no other inmates in sight. It was by the Nazis' design that we were shielded, albeit, sometimes unsuccessfully, as I described above, from any negative confrontation with our fate.

A few hours passed, with no food or drink. Our hunger was excruciating. The absence of any possibility to relieve oneself created an inevitable major problem that brought on beatings and derision from the guards. As we got relatively close to the head of the column but had not yet reached the front, SS men standing in the middle of the oncoming crowd were forcefully separating the elderly, the sick, the very young and their mothers who had not heeded the orders over the loudspeakers or had not yet kept to the right. The separated people were literally torn from the embraces of their loved ones and handed over to the jurisdiction of the other guards who, with prodding rifle butts and bayonets, forced them toward the right fork in the road to join the hundreds upon hundreds who were slowly making their way, as commanded. The scene of the separations undoubtedly ranks among the most bestial, painful and sorrowful episodes that I have ever experienced.

We were now very near the front, near enough to see the fork in the road and the commotion associated with the separation of families, sometimes by force. Realizing that this is how far we could go together as an extended family, Grandfather turned to Uncle Leopold and said to him in Yiddish, "*Kim*

Lippa, lomir shoin gain." (Come, Leopold, let us go.) When Mother saw her father leaving, she held on to Grandpa's sleeve and said, "No, *Tateh* [Father], wait, I am going with you." She turned to Papa and said, "Mordche, you take the boys and I'll go with Grandpa to take care of him."

"Matu, you can't go, they won't let you," Papa retorted.

"I am going to report sick, they want the sick to go with the elderly, and so I will go with him."

"Mama! Mama! I want to go with you, Mama! Let Tibi go with Papa and I will go with you. Please, Mama, let me go with you." I was tugging on Mama's hand.

"No, my child, I am going to take care of Grandpa, and you go with Papa and Tibi."

"I want to go with you, Mama! Please, Mama, why can't I go? Please take me with you; I'll be a good boy! I can help you take care of Grandpa, please, Mama!"

"So be a good boy and do what I say, stay with Papa and Tibi and help take care of each other." I continued with my attempt to go with my mother, crying and whining, but to no avail. Mother hugged and kissed me; she held and caressed my face with both hands (one on each cheek), as she whispered in my ear, "Please, Andika, do what Mama says. Be a good boy and remember that you are now a big boy and take care of Papa and Tibi."

"Mama, I want to go with you, don't leave me," I kept repeating as I tasted my mother's warm tears that were mingling with my own torrent of tears.

There was not much time left before we were to be separated; all of us kissed and hugged each other as we said our tearful "temporary" goodbyes. Mama held my head tightly to her hip while she hugged and kissed Papa and Tibi. We parted, reassuring each other that we would see each other soon, after all, the war could not last much longer and we would see each other after liberation, and perhaps as soon as in a few days, or a few weeks at the most.

The scene of our parting is forever etched in my memory and embedded in my mind. The picture of these three saintly people is permanently engraved in my mind's eye. I can clearly recall Grandfather arm-in-arm with his brother Leopold, and my mother arm-in-arm with her father, my grandfather, walking away to our right. Unbeknownst to us then, they walked straight to the gas chamber. I did not know it then, and find it impossible to believe it now, that I was never again to feel Mother's warm embrace, feel her warm hand stroking me, or hear her soothing voice. I would never again see her beautiful face or smell her sweetness. Her heavenly embrace would never again lock me in. That was the last time I ever saw Mama, Grandpa or Uncle Leopold. The day we entered Auschwitz-Birkenau, June 2, is the date I keep for my mother's *yahrzeit* (the anniversary of the day of death).

Within minutes, Papa, Tibi and I approached the front, the head of the column at the end of the platform and we had no idea what to expect. There stood an SS man who, I believe, was the infamous Dr. Josef Mengele.[2] He was decked out in a sharp, beautiful black uniform. He stood with his feet apart, wearing brilliantly polished boots. His right hand was tucked in his jacket, Napoleon style. He had the medical insignia of the coiled snake on his sleeve and the lightning SS insignia on his collar. He wore a snappy black SS hat with the eagle symbol on top and a rim, which shielded the stern eyes of this executioner. He had a Luger on his belt and a riding whip in his gloved left hand with its strap around his wrist. There were two battle-ready SS men on each side of him, with canes in their hands, and a company of armed guards behind him. As his victims approached, Mengele would rock up and down on the balls of his feet and point with his thumb to his left or to his right, determining the fate of his victim. With a motion to his left he condemned the person standing in front of him to their immediate death; while a motion to his right gave the person a reprieve, the lesser of the two evils, allowing entry into the camp, where likely death would just take more time. If one did not notice the motion or meaning of the thumb signal and therefore did not instantly obey and move towards the indicated direction, Mengele's whip struck the right side of the face and ear, rupturing the skin and causing blood to spurt. His SS guard companions, brandishing their machine guns, would then clearly indicate the direction the unfortunate was to take.

A tortured life, perhaps for a while, or immediate death was determined by the motion of Mengele's thumb. The group that was allowed to enter the camp and thereby be reprieved from immediate death amounted to less than

2   Mengele was not the only doctor to perform the selections. Several doctors also performed the same role as Mengele, who arrived at Auschwitz in May 1943.

one-third of the arrivals. As our turn came to stand before Mengele, Father, who was then forty-four years old, was first in line; he was sent to the left, into the camp. I was next. I was a little "shrimp," my mother's little "frog," a very skinny fellow. Mengele flipped his thumb to his left, my right. Tibi, aged fifteen and a half, but who easily passed for a much older youth, was next. Seeing that we were being separated, he spoke up, and said to Mengele, "Why? He is already thirteen, he is strong and he can work." Tibi promptly received a hard blow of a cane to his head, while Mengele simultaneously ordered him to keep his mouth shut, and motioned him into the camp. Tibi's skull was cracked and he suffered headaches from this event for the rest of his life.

Suddenly, I was left alone and was crying while running to my right, looking for my mother and Grandfather in order to catch up to and join them. I ran back and forth and side to side, yelling "Mama! Mama!" If I had seen her, I would have gone with her, but my voice was just a whisper among the screams of other children. Mama and Grandpa were nowhere to be seen, for the throng of people that were going that way swallowed them up. Nor could I see anyone else I knew, or anyone even familiar to me among the hundreds of people who were within my sight. Fearing total abandonment, I ran to the edge of the throng and strained to look in the direction of my father and brother. Fortuitously, I caught a glimpse of them. They were walking slowly and looking over their shoulders towards me, trying to see whether I had caught up with Mama and was safe. I was positive that Papa and Tibi did not actually see me for they were dodging people who were coming up from behind them, despite making a great effort to locate me. It was useless to yell for I could not possibly be heard over the din of the multitude.

From the very second that I located Papa and Tibi, I did not let them out of my sight. The fear of being left alone and neither quite comprehending nor caring about the consequences of disregarding Mengele's orders made me defy fate, although not consciously, and I headed towards them. Without any consideration of the SS guards, I kept Father in sight and just simply walked towards him and Tibi. I furtively, perhaps nonchalantly, passed right behind the backs of Mengele and the SS guards without being stopped. I was maybe twenty or thirty yards behind them and as soon as I felt that I was in the clear, I began running and shouting, "Papa! Tibi!" Moments later, exhausted and breathless, I caught up to them. The first question my father asked me was whether Mama had let me go. I responded that I had not seen Mama and had not caught up with her, explaining that I had been unable to find anybody I knew. I assured him that I had made a good effort to find Mama. After lingering as long as we could trying to see what became of Mama, the three of us together walked with the crowd to where the "new arrivals" were supposed to go. I was in the middle, with Papa's and Tibi's arms over my shoulders.

This life-saving occurrence was the first of many outright miracles that happened to me in quick succession. I have often wondered if someone was holding my hand, perhaps Mother. I knew she would if she could! Could she? Did she? Was it happenstance? I say "happenstance" because I have difficulty claiming Divine intervention, for I do not have the audacity to feel worthy of it. Besides, that claim would necessarily beg the question of why me. I am not suggesting anything supernatural and only recount what happened; however, I am convinced that, notwithstanding human beings' free will, everything happens by the will of our Creator.

I made it among the living and thereby became one of the youngest inmates in the camp.[3] Later on, at the first *Appel* (roll call), I had the opportunity to observe my fellow inmates standing in row upon row in front of their barrack without seeing anyone even close to my age. Later, another child named Michael Ruvel arrived in my barrack and we became very good friends.

We were herded into a complex of barracks that was set aside for new arrivals; some of the barracks were joined together by short passageways. As we were rushed through one of the large barracks, which was more like an airplane hangar type of building, containing mounds of articles of clothing, we were ordered to strip and to throw each article of clothing onto designated piles that contained similar articles. By the time we undressed, the piles of shoes, pants, jackets, shirts and underwear that were already there were approximately fifteen feet high and some piles that contained larger articles of clothing were at least twenty-five feet high and nearly as wide. Anyone who

---

3   For more information on children and adolescents in Auschwitz, see Helena Kubica, "Children and Adolescents in Auschwitz," in Wacław Długoborski and Franciszek Piper, eds., *Auschwitz 1940-1945: Central Issues in the History of the Camp*, vol. II (Oświęcim: Auschwitz-Birkenau State Museum, 2000), pp. 201-291.

wore glasses had to throw them on a separate pile, creating a three-foot-high stack. There was a mountain of shoes and a foot-high pile of false teeth. We had no time to contemplate the meaning of these piles of articles. All we did was strip, throw our clothing on the pile and run to avoid being beaten, all the while being yelled at and cursed. The German SS guards referred to us as "*Schweinehunde*" (swine) as we ran past them.

Once naked, the guards herded us into the next room, known as the "Sauna," where some inmates in striped uniforms hurriedly cut our hair with hand cutters without any regard for the pain they inflicted by ripping out partially cut hair that was held between the dull cutters. As we progressed to the rear of the barrack, other inmates manned containers that looked like fire extinguishers with hoses attached to them. As we ran past this gauntlet, they sprayed our entire bodies, including our heads, with stinging and stinking chemicals. The chemical, which the inmates referred to as a disinfectant, covered us from head to toe. The spray burned our eyes; it ran into our ears and all the crevices and wounds of our bodies. I was beside myself with pain and fear. The first onslaught of the chemical blinded me and as I was screaming from the intolerable stinging pain, the chemical entered my nostrils and mouth and caused me to cough and throw up. Someone kicked me and then, perhaps mercifully, someone else caught me by my arm and flung me away from the spray. There was no way to wash away the stinging chemical from my eyes and mouth. While everyone was screaming in pain and most of us were blinded and wandering around in circles with one hand on our eyes and the other hand extended in wild gesticulation, we were beaten, cursed and driven to move on to an adjacent room. Father managed to calm me down to some extent by wiping away as much of the chemical as he could with his hand and forearm, only to be reintroduced by my hand wiping the oozing disinfectant from my ears, which also ran down my cheeks. My arm felt as if it were broken. For weeks following, any attempt to make any use of my arm resulted in unbearable, agonizing pain.

While being rushed through the adjacent room, we were issued with the Birkenau striped uniform and wooden shoes, all of which were thrown at us, irrespective of size or fit. It did not matter to them whether one received two left or right shoes or two different sizes, for that matter. I was issued a pair of pants and jacket at least three times my size. We were expected to get dressed while being chased out into an adjacent courtyard. My attempt to dress myself proved fruitless, regardless of the rifle butts and bayonets that were threatening us in conjunction with shouts of the dire consequences procrastination would bring about. My entire body could have fit in just one pants leg alone. There was no way I could manage to put one leg in my huge pants while hopping on the other leg and, at the same time, avoid the rifle butts and the prodding bayonets while maintaining the rush towards the outside. I remained naked, carrying the clothing.

Once outside in the paved yard surrounded by a high concrete wall, the night air felt cold to my naked, stinging body. Within moments, I was shaking uncontrollably. My eyes were still burning so that I could hardly see and I felt as if they were dissolving and running out of their sockets. I was clinging to my father and crying hysterically, while everybody was exchanging uniforms. Tibi, being older and stronger and not being a whiner, endured his pain silently. Father managed to "organize" a uniform for me by exchanging my pants with someone for a pair that was only twice my size. Keeping any personal articles was absolutely forbidden under penalty of death (death being the only penalty in the vocabulary of the SS). Nevertheless, due to sheer necessity and ignorance, I had managed to keep my suspenders; otherwise I would have needed both hands to keep my pants from falling down. I did not really fully understand the potential consequences of my doing so, and obviously, neither did Papa, since it was an act that could have resulted in my being shot immediately on the spot.

As we were standing in despair on the cement floor of the courtyard, weak from hunger and shivering from fear and the cold air, and preoccupied with our stinging bodies and our clothing, we were acutely aware of an atmosphere of doom surrounding us. The smell and taste of the air as well as the light provided an atmosphere of Dante's Inferno. It was a feeling of an oncoming, imminent catastrophe. The courtyard was surrounded by high cement walls on top of which were low-wattage lights and barbed electrified wires. The sky itself was ominously and totally dark, spotted with a few stars that were still mocking us by every means other than sound. The moon must have been obstructed, for it was not within sight. Everyone was screaming, crying, praying, shivering or hugging each other.

In contrast to the darkness, there was an ominous, flickering light that licked eerily at the sky and provided a supernatural illumination. The light emanating from nearby chimneys was reminiscent of a gigantic bonfire. Even in normal, happy times, bonfires create a certain unsettling "pagan" atmosphere with a mood-changing effect. The horrific flames, thick with hot ashes, were in contrast to the dark sky and created a "doomsday" atmosphere. The ashes were covering us with a gray dust, as if spewed out from an erupting volcano. And there was a horrible smell of burning flesh. Remembering what the "crazies" at our arrival told us, some men yelled, "We will be killed and burned." Others screamed, "Shut up or they will." While others prayed, "God, sweet God," or "*Shema Yisroel*" (Hear, O Israel). I held onto my father while I was hugged tightly by my brother and I screamed, "Mama!! Mamaaaa!!!"

One of the kapos (overseers), a Polish Jewish inmate worker, charged with expediting our progress and obviously crazed by working in this section and by what he was being forced to do, forcefully grabbed me by the chin. He twisted and turned my head so that I lifted my gaze towards the chimneys and their flames shooting twenty to thirty feet into the air, spewing out gray ash that fell on us and on the floor of the yard. While holding my head up with one hand, he pointed at the flaming chimney with his other hand, and yelled in my ear, "There! Your mama, there, there is Mama!" He pointed at the huge chimneys of the crematoria and the flames that were so intense that the lightning rods on the chimneys melted and formed into grotesque shapes. This was my welcome to Birkenau Concentration Camp.[4]

My mind was numb. As a sheltered child of thirteen years old, I had no concept of the meaning of all this. It must be said that people who were older than me couldn't understand it either. No one could. Everything was happening so fast that I could not grasp, nor could I possibly understand, that

---

4   The process of selection and murder was carefully planned and organized. When a train stopped at the platform, veteran prisoners received the victims and gathered their belongings in several barracks in an area known as "Kanada." The arrivals were lined up in two columns — men and boys in one, women and girls in the other — and SS physicians performed a selection. The criterion was the appearance of the prisoners, whose fate, for labor or for death, was determined at will. Before they entered the chamber, they were told that they were about to be disinfected and were ordered to undress. The doors of the chamber were locked and the gas was introduced. After the victims were murdered, their gold teeth were extracted and women's hair was shorn by the Sonderkommando (see note 10, p. 142). The bodies were hauled to the crematoria furnaces for incineration, the bones were pulverized and the ashes were scattered in the fields.

it was not only actual people, but even people from our transport, who were being burned. I asked my dear papa if what the man had said was true, and he assured me that it was not and that soon it would all be over. He squeezed me tighter and planted a kiss on my forehead.

"Why is the man saying that about Mama?"

"He is a bad man. Stay away from him."

"Papa, where do you think Mama is? Is she all right and safe?"

"Hush, hush, everything will be all right. You will see."

I found consolation in Papa's words. Other than the escalating cruelties during the period before deportation, the ghetto episodes, the rail transports and the disembarkation and separations here in Birkenau, episodes that were certainly not on the scale of this new experience, I was not aware that human beings were capable of perpetrating such cruelty and inflicting such suffering and with such inhumanity on fellow humans. I did not recognize the monstrous bestiality even when I was in its midst. And, still, I thought that since I was with Papa and Tibi, nothing bad could happen to me. After all, they would take care of me.

We were later told, but I don't know if it was true, that the only reason we survived that night is because they couldn't gas and burn us fast enough. The fact that there was an "overload" of victims beyond what they could possibly handle, saved us; otherwise we would all have been gassed and fed to the ovens that same evening. This was our welcome to the most efficient killing factory ever devised by man.

I arrived in Birkenau on June 2, 1944, right in the middle of the killing frenzy. Although Birkenau had the capacity to gas 6,000 persons daily in each of the four gas chambers, a total of 24,000 people per day, during the heyday of arriving transports, such as ours, the killing and burning were backed up for many hours.[5] In addition to the gas chambers and crematoria, the Nazis

5   Shortly after construction had begun at Birkenau, the decision was made to change its designation and turn it into an extermination camp. The first murder experiments with Zyklon B gas were carried out in Block 11 in the main camp on Poles and Soviet POWs early in September 1941. It soon became obvious that using the cellars of Block 11 was inconvenient for several reasons, and this was mainly why the SS set about converting the crematorium mortuary, which was adjacent to the room with the furnaces, into a gas chamber. However, this gas chamber caused several problems and difficulties too, and due to the large numbers of Jews who began to be sent to the camp, at the turn of

used auxiliary gas chambers and pyres to burn the corpses outdoors. The inmate who had grabbed my head and forced me to look at the burning chimneys of the crematoria was correct. There, somewhere in the flames and the smoke that rose toward the sky, were my mama and grandpa. It was their ashes that spewed down on us and covered us in gray dust. Surely, as my mama's tortured pure soul rose to heaven, she looked down on her beloved husband and adored children, consoling herself that at least we were alive, and confident that since we were in Papa's good hands we would be safe. As for her, she would take care of her father. They rest in peace in Heaven, I have no doubt about that, where they enjoy the grace of the Almighty and await the coming of the Messiah when we will once again be together as a family. In the meantime, Mama interceded on our behalf, I believe, and guided our fate towards survival and throughout our lives.

We were marched five abreast out of the crematoria compound, then walked through a corridor approximately twenty feet wide. There was an electrified barbed-wire fence on each side of us, with guard towers strategically spaced all along the way. We walked from the rear of the camp where the gas chambers and crematoria were located, toward the front of the camp near the rail station. We were placed into barracks of the E Camp, known as the *Zigeunerlager* (Gypsy Camp), where thousands of Gypsies and Jews were being held. There were mostly grownups in my barrack but this was the first time for me to meet other children in the camp.

The Gypsy kapos (overseers) who were in charge of a barrack or

1942, Höss started searching for a place where one could kill hundreds of people, keep it secret and, at the same time, solve the problem of the disposal of large numbers of corpses. After Himmler visited Auschwitz on July 17-18, 1942, and in order to "cope" with the large numbers of Jews who were about to be sent to Auschwitz, the SS decided to build four "modern" and permanent installations in Birkenau, which began operating in May 1943. They each included an underground undressing room and gas chamber, and a crematorium for incinerating the bodies of the murdered. These facilities had the potential to kill 6,000 people daily, making the murder of the Jews a far more "efficient" process. The extermination reached its peak in the spring and summer of 1944, with the deportation of some 430,000 Hungarian Jews to the camp, and the subsequent murder of the majority of the deportees. During this period, the pressure on the extermination machinery was so great that the Germans also reactivated the makeshift gas chambers that had been operating in 1942. For further information see: http://www.yadvashem.org/yv/en/exhibitions/auschwitz_architecture/overview.asp (accessed, March 17, 2016).

work detail enjoyed a semi-authoritative position over us Jews, which they exercised with eagerness, vigor and brutality. Since their usefulness as kapos, orderlies, etc. seemingly shielded them from the daily selections, they seemed to us to be the untouchables. Nevertheless, by the middle of 1944, their numbers significantly dwindled.[6] Most of the kapos, especially the non-Jewish German inmates, were murderers, bank robbers, socialists, Communists, homosexuals and pedophiles who had been incarcerated and given kapo authority, or placed in lesser positions of authority. Many were sadists and perverts, ready to do anything in order to keep their position in the camp hierarchy. According to the hierarchy of authority, above the Gypsy kapos were the German kapos, then the German SS guards, the SS officers and the camp commandant. Since the Gypsy kapo was on the lowest rung, he would show off his abilities with a flourish of brutality towards his wards in order to impress his superiors.

Each designated group of misfits had their own identifying insignia on the left breast of their jackets, followed by a serial number. There were those with red triangles, green triangles, pink triangles, etc.[7] Some triangles

6   In 1943 and 1944, thousands of Sinti and Roma were deported to Auschwitz. They lived under horrible conditions. Many died of starvation, from illness or from being used for medical experiments. Others were murdered. In total, about 23,000 Gypsies, primarily from Germany, Austria, the Protectorate of Bavaria and Moravia, and Poland, but also from other countries, were sent to Auschwitz-Birkenau. A group of about 1,700 Polish Sinti and Roma were murdered immediately after arriving at the camp, without being entered in the records. Of the approximately 23,000 Sinti and Roma deported to Auschwitz, some 20,000 were murdered in the gas chambers or died.

7   Red triangles marked political prisoners (*Schutzhäftlinge* — Sch.), in other words, those who were imprisoned on the basis of a "protective custody order" (*Schutzhaftbefehl*). Green triangles marked criminal prisoners (*Berufsverbrecher* — BV), imprisoned as a direct consequence of committing a forbidden act, or, although they had been released from prison, the criminal police regarded the sentence imposed by the court as too lenient. Prisoners in this category were mostly Germans. Black triangles marked asocial prisoners (*Asoziale* — Aso.), imprisoned in theory for vagrancy or prostitution, but in fact for a wide range of other deeds or behaviors loosely and arbitrarily interpreted by the police. The Roma in the Birkenau Gypsy camp were classified as asocial. Purple triangles marked prisoners imprisoned for belonging to the Jehovah's Witnesses (*Internationale Bibelforscher-Vereinigung* — IBV), regarded as enemies of the state because of their pacifistic beliefs. Pink triangles marked homosexual prisoners who were, in practice, exclusively German and imprisoned on the basis of paragraph 175 of the German criminal code.

pointed up and others pointed down. The markings identified different types of criminals, political prisoners, sex offenders and others incarcerated by the Nazi state. A few were marked with a *Fluchtpunkt* — a mark placed just over the triangle on the chest of an inmate who had either attempted to escape or was suspected of plotting to escape. Hatred of Jews, despite providing them with the opportunity of authority, was everyone's common denominator.

In E Camp of the Birkenau *Vernichtungslager* (extermination camp), there were two rows of wooden barracks, which had barn-like doors, one of which was the exact width of the rear of the German military trucks. The floors of the barracks were paved with cement. A wide road separated the two rows of barracks, and between the road and the opposite barrack was an *Appellplatz*, a clearing for the purpose of roll call as well as for access to the barrack. The *Appellplatz* ran the entire length of the camp, so that during roll call, looking left and right and then across the road to the other rows of blocks, each with their own *Appellplatz* in front, one could see the entire population of the camp.

Just inside the barn doors on the side of the barrack was an enclosure that was the private domain of the kapo. Each barrack had a brick oven that began after an approximate clearing of twenty feet from the entrance and ran the entire length of the space. The chimney was at the other end, thus the heat and smoke going through the whole oven had the capacity to keep it entirely warm but never hot. At the end of each barrack was a somewhat closed-off area containing two steel drums for latrine use; an arrangement that many, including myself, never could make use of, for the barrels were difficult to reach and were perpetually full.

The entire camp was enclosed with an electrified barbed-wire fence, with a guard tower at each end. There was a double electrified fence facing the main road that was the entrance to our E Camp. The fences between camps were especially secured. In addition to our electrified fence and the guard towers was a "dog run" approximately four feet wide, and then the electrified fence of the next camp. Since the individual camps were narrow and long and the camps abutted each other on the long side, the space between the electrified fences was wide enough for a guard and his dog to patrol.

The first barrack to which we were assigned was just an empty shell. It had no bunks. We were ordered to lay down head to foot on the cold cement floor, literally like sardines in a can. Once we were packed in as tight as possible, some blankets were haphazardly thrown over us while the Gypsy kapo, clutching a walking cane with the crook of the cane pointing down, walked back and forth along the length of the oven yelling for quiet as he threateningly brandished his cane while looking for and identifying his victims.

The kapo had his unique way of keeping several hundred frightened, hungry and thirsty prisoners quiet. Upon detecting an inevitable sound, he went down on one knee and threw his walking cane in the direction of the noise. The cane made a whipping noise, much like a propeller, as it careened over our heads. It inevitably wounded, if not split, a few heads on the way to its intended destination that he rarely missed. Breaking heads was his favorite pastime. Following this maneuver, he then demanded his cane back. The cane was returned to him by passing it from hand to hand, or else he would jump off the oven and run to retrieve the cane without regard to whom or where he trampled. The kapo had many opportunities to practice his well-honed craft. There was no way for anyone to go to the barrels that served as latrines so we had to relieve ourselves right where we were lying. If one as much as turned or allowed his spot to be taken, he was left exposed to the kapo's virtuoso expertise. I was well insulated and protected by being wedged in between my father and brother who shielded me from the kapo's view.

During the night, if someone detected that the person next to him had died or was about to die or was too weak to resist, he would throw the person out of the spot next to him in order to gain some more space for himself. Whomever the body landed on threw the body once again. This could go on so that some dead people were bouncing like rag dolls from person to person until the Gypsy kapo jumped off the brick oven and, while trampling on people's heads, reached the dead body. The kapo would hook the crook of his cane around the dead person's neck and pull him away to a clearance. He would then order two designated orderlies to drag the body to the latrine. This mode of what was called "sanitation" in the camp was also part of the kapo's "expertise" that he practiced nightly.

I was one of the few people who came into the barrack wearing suspenders, which were spotted by the Gypsy kapo. He grabbed me by my throat and while I struggled, cried and screamed in panic, he forcibly removed them from me. After I freed myself from his grip and lifted my pants which, without my suspenders, fell to the floor, I hit him with my strongest weapon in my arsenal: angry threats to tell my father. I began screaming at him to give me my suspenders back, "or else." Luckily, someone yanked me away from his presence just in time to avoid the cane coming down on my head.

At that point, after all that I had seen, heard and gone through, I was still not aware of the reality of our situation. Holding onto my pants with both hands, I went crying to my father, complaining that the Gypsy had taken my suspenders. I wanted Papa to get my suspenders back for me, and Tibi was eager to be allowed to go and get them. After all, my past experience taught me that all I had to do was ask my father and that would be the end of anything that was wrong. My father would fix everything. But, instead of the answer I expected, Papa said to me, "It's alright, son, we will manage without the suspenders. It is OK, hush, these people are gangsters and we don't want to mess with them." This was another lesson that I learned well and filed it in my mind under the heading, "These are terrible times." I had begun the lesson in Ghetto Mátészalka and now it was continuing here, again. Perhaps this was the time when I became convinced that things that had been true in the past were no longer true. I learned once again that Father was no longer omnipotent, and that nothing mattered. We were in the hands of gangsters, there was no decency or politeness and what's more, there was no justice. There was no right or wrong, only survival. There was only the might of the upper hand and in order to survive one had to endure and bide his time. I was growing up fast!

The next morning, we were driven out of the barrack for roll call. The Germans were killing over 20,000 people daily, but they were obsessed with counting every person. Sometimes the roll calls were used for "selections," usually to feed the gas chambers and sometimes for slave labor.

It was still June 1944, fifteen days after our arrival, when Papa and Tibi were selected. This selection was unlike other selections. So far, the seemingly unending arrival of transports of Hungarian Jews overwhelmed the enormous capacities of the four crematoria. The overabundance of victims had provided a temporary reprieve from the fate eventually awaiting us. However, this time, German civilians came with Polish and Hungarian interpreters with whom they walked up and down the rows of inmates standing at roll call and announced that "anybody who is a tradesman,

knows timber, a carpenter or is a cutter of stone or wood should step out."
Usually, nobody stepped out for anything. My father, who did not yet know
any better, did not know that the Germans often used the ruse of labor and
better treatment to "select for gas chamber fodder, to thin out the ranks."
Hence, Papa stepped out with Tibi. I missed his signal to step out and so
remained standing. The German in civilian clothes asked my father, "What
is your occupation?"

"I am a timber and lumber man," my father answered.

"Who is this?" the SS man asked, his riding whip pointing at my brother.

"He is my son, we work together," my father said.

He looked at my brother, who was a big boy, and let him pass. They
were then both ordered to join the few others selected who were separated
from us by about five feet. Seeing that he and Tibi were selected for work,
my father motioned to me to step out so that perhaps I too would be selected.
I obeyed immediately and stepped out, for which a guard smacked me across
the face and literally kicked me back into the ranks. I was standing there with
tears running down my face while watching Papa motioning to me with his
finger on his lips to be quiet, not to cry out. We stood there for what seemed
to be hours.

When trucks arrived and orders were given to the guards to load the
selected for transportation, it became obvious that we were being separated.
Papa said to me in Yiddish, "*Mein Kind* [my child], I have three things to say
to you, listen well. I don't know what this world will come to, I don't know
where we are going and I don't know what's going to become of us. Keep
yourself clean so you don't get sick; be a *mensch* [a person of integrity] and
don't let them make an animal out of you; and remember, whoever lives
through this inferno, goes home and waits for the others. God willing, we
will all meet at home." With these words, the selected group was marched
off. I watched and my eyes caught the eyes of Papa and Tibi and then they
disappeared into a truck, leaving me behind, dumbfounded and scared.
My blood drained to my feet as I realized that I was left alone in Birkenau
without parents and without a sibling. All I could do was attempt to stifle
my sobs and hold my hand across my mouth as I called for my mama, papa
and Tibi.

ALONE IN BIRKENAU

A few days after Father and Tibi's departure, for what I hoped was forced labor, I was assigned to a "regular" barrack in the same Gypsy camp but with a different Gypsy kapo. Each side of the entire length of the barrack was lined with continuous wooden bunks made of planks, three bunks high. The ten men who were assigned to each bunk could only fit if they turned on their side and slept head to foot. Because I took up very little space, I was a much sought-after commodity as a bunkmate.

On the second day in my new barrack, the new Gypsy kapo treated me to one of the many significant shocks I was to receive in my young life. One of the young fellows who occupied the bunk next to mine, managed to smuggle in a pair of *tefillin* (phylacteries) and a small prayer book. In the morning, he put on his phylacteries and stood in the aisle totally submerged in prayer. A lookout was posted and as soon as the kapo's presence was detected, a prearranged alarm was given, alas too late and to no avail. The Gypsy kapo had noticed the commotion associated with the alert and the fellow jumping into a bunk to hide. Everyone scattered as the kapo ran up to the bunk. The kapo reached into the bunk and grabbed the young man by his feet and pulled him out into the aisle. He then quickly grabbed the leather straps of the phylacteries and wound them around the young man's neck strangling him to death. I will never forget the young man's bulging eyes as he was being choked, or the sounds he made as his life was being extinguished. The kapo removed the phylacteries from the lifeless body and threw them into the latrine barrel. He then picked up the dead body and threw it on top of the oven so that everyone could see it, and declared authoritatively, "Let this be a lesson to you." Yes, a lesson expertly taught and well learned.

The daily ritual of roll calls began with an order for everyone to clear the barrack and line up five abreast out front. It was always five abreast in order to facilitate the counting. Being the youngest and smallest, and therefore the slowest, I was usually among the last to leave the block, which usually resulted in my being on the receiving end of a few kicks and curses. However, I also often observed the guards performing the ritual of bayoneting the piles of blankets, making sure that no one was hiding in them and I made a mental note that in case of a raid, the blankets were not to be used as a hiding place. Sometimes, the guards succeeded either to kill outright or to wound and then kill someone who was hiding. It is hard to imagine what difference it made to the Third Reich if one more or one fewer victim was present at roll call. In the first few weeks, roll call was usually once a day and took a few hours. By the middle of the summer or thereabouts, they were twice a day and later, three times a day was the norm, in order to feed the gas chambers. After a while, we heard the SS refer to the roll calls as *selektionen* (selections).

No effort on our part to clear the block for roll call was ever fast enough. The kapo and his orderlies always drove us with clubs and shouts of insults that went to the core of our very souls. Neither rain nor even a snow blizzard prevented their cruel obsession with this procedure. There we stood for hours in the rain or cold, half naked, hungry and frightened. Inevitably, someone would faint and his fate would be sealed. After we'd been standing for hours, an SS officer, accompanied by several guards, would begin his counting by walking down the length of the assembly, while audibly counting the rows of fives, *"fünf, zehn, fünfzehn"* (five, ten, fifteen), etc. When he reached fifty, the officer yelled out the number and one of the guards recorded it.

Ninety percent of our time was spent standing in rows waiting to be selected. The SS used a variety of methods to accomplish the selections of their victims. Once in a while, they would indiscriminately take the first five, last five or ten or more rows of fives. Other times, the selection was accomplished by choosing individuals from the ranks who were deemed to be the most vulnerable. All it took to be selected was for the SS officer to point at or hit the man with his riding whip or walking cane across his face for the accompanying guards to remove him brutally from the ranks and then the man was, for all practical purposes, dead. After the guards separated the selected victims from the main group, the officer would command them to *Rechts-um* (face right) or *Links-um* (face left). The group would obey the order and march away; otherwise they would be taught fast and furiously what it means to disobey. The selected ones never came back. Obviously, they took up the slack in the gas chamber that day.

The barracks were constantly being replenished with newcomers. New transports were arriving in greater numbers than the Nazis could immediately kill; therefore, the overflow would enter the holding pen that was Birkenau and inevitably some of them would wind up in our camp and barrack. When the arriving transports were below the capacity of the gas chambers and crematoria, furious *selektionen* at roll call took up the slack. Nevertheless, somehow, it did not register in my mind the possibility that the *selektionen* at roll call meant the possibility of my own imminent death. "Those selected must have done something wrong and, after all," I reasoned to myself, "I did not do anything wrong to anyone." It had now been almost two months since my arrival in Birkenau, and I still believed that being innocent would win the day.

We were issued a daily portion of one slice of so-called bread, a portion of which consisted of one-tenth of the one-kilogram loaf. The bread, as little as there was, was mostly sawdust. The loaves were tapered; therefore, the ends were much smaller than the middle slices. Some seasoned and savvy inmates would jockey for a position in the bread line to avoid the end cuts. This behavior often resulted in massive beatings administered by the kapo. I, of course, never got a middle slice; I never had a chance to be in the right place for it. Additionally, on more than one occasion, bread was grabbed out of my hand by other prisoners, or my jaw was forcibly squeezed open to steal the food that was already in my mouth. I couldn't chew and swallow fast enough. That is how hungry and desperate they were. I soon learned that I quickly had to take a bite or two in front of the German guard or kapo who was supervising the handing out of the bread rations. I would then hurriedly, while still standing there, roll the rest of the ration into my oversized shirt and squeeze it close to my body, under my armpit. My method of preserving my ration was many times severely tested, but any attempt to steal it seldom succeeded. They would have to kill me before I would let go. I accomplished the stashing of my ration in the relative safety of standing before the kapo, but I had to work fast and clear out so as not to invite the kapo's cane over my head for delaying the line. After a while, I learned the ropes, became an old-timer, and there was an understanding that this type of theft was only done to newcomers.

I also learned that I was safer by myself. I felt safer when I was insulated from my fellow inmates. For further safety, I hung out at the front of the barrack near the kapo's dwelling where any commotion would come to his attention. In addition, I noted that for greater safety, outside the barrack was preferable to inside in the company of strangers who were my fellow inmates, and I began to spend more and more time outdoors on the side of my barrack where I was shielded from direct view.

In addition to the "luxury" of the bread, we were given soup. The food detail would bring in two garbage cans that contained the so-called soup, which consisted of lukewarm water with potato peels, half-cooked sugar beets and garbage that had sunk to the bottom. Some said that there were rodents in it and many people got diarrhea from it. People perished from diarrhea more often than any other illness. Once again, my position in the line determined whether I got water from the top or some solids from the bottom. So it was, that there was a lot of pushing and fighting for the "right" position, which, once again, resulted in beatings and yelling to keep people in line. If one attempted to sneak in for seconds, the men in line would beat him. The commotion would bring the situation to an early end and the intruder stood a good chance of being clubbed by the kapo. Many times the dispensing of food was halted altogether as punishment.

I learned from the so-called "old-timers," those inmates who had managed to survive a few months, about the meaning of the *selektionen*. When I requested one of them to clarify the meaning, I was informed that "they mean your death." Being forewarned, I began to realize what the disappearance of those who were selected meant. At first, I wasn't alone in being unaware, or perhaps not wanting to be aware, that the people who were selected were not coming back; I certainly had no idea that they may have been killed. It was the buzz, the talk of the inmates concerning the selections, to which my ears were always open. Some people remarked that of all the people who had been taken out over the last few weeks, no one had come back, while others assured their listeners that they must have been taken to a work camp. Reality finally hit us when someone overheard the guards saying that soon we would all be killed off and would go up in smoke.

In the beginning, the old self-delusion of hearing and thinking what we wanted was in place. The confirmation from the guards could not be wished nor dreamed away, and from then on, I lived in constant fear and my heart would race whenever I was within sight of a German guard or kapo, especially at roll call. Being by now a seasoned old-timer, I watched the folks standing at roll call who were within my sight and noticed that the SS conducted the selection methodically. A system was being employed, or perhaps it was just a pattern that they fell into. Often, they would select and march off either the front or the back rows of fives, and seldom the middle unless they noticed a child or an especially emaciated person. I therefore always managed to be in the middle and avoided being seen as a child by standing on my shoes to make myself appear taller, while still managing to make myself visible enough to be counted. A short count resulted in hours of standing and exposing myself to additional danger. No one was dismissed until the count was right. Many times I was selected but managed to slip to the part of the assembly that was dismissed, while the others were marched off.

In the summer of 1944, there were days when the weather under other circumstances would have been described as beautiful and ideal. Nevertheless, regardless of my miserable circumstances, I never failed to notice the beauty of nature and managed to enjoy it and accept it as a gift of God. In the late afternoon of one particularly beautiful day, when the waning sun seemed to be mocking us with its beauty, all the Gypsies, including the kapos from the Jewish barrack, as well as ours, were summoned to roll call. They were ordered to assemble in front of their barracks in the Gypsy section of the camp and following a standard roll call, most of them were ordered to return to their barrack. However, the kapos were not allowed to return to the Jewish barrack where they exercised authority. Rather, they too were ordered into the Gypsy barrack. Later, at dusk, I noticed from my vantage point on the side of our barrack where I was hiding in fear of being trapped, a convoy of canvas-enclosed trucks rumbling into our E Camp. Each truck had a squad of SS guards in it, wearing helmets and equipped with clubs and the dreaded Schmeisser machine guns. I was wondering if we were possibly the victims, since we hadn't been summoned for roll call, and if not, who could possibly be their intended victims. Was this perhaps a new system to trap us in our barrack without a roll call? I began to prepare myself and to think of scenarios for possible action in order to have the slimmest chance of survival. It did not dawn on me, given that E Camp had only Gypsies and Jews, that the Gypsies (rather than the Jews) could possibly be the intended victims.

I watched the trucks backing into the barn door of the Gypsy barrack, just like backing into an open garage. When each truck was in place, the SS proceeded with their patented system of clearing the victims from the barrack. The sound of a whistle blow gave the signal for the squads to jump off the trucks and enter the barrack. With two SS officers guarding the tight spaces between the truck and the doors and another two guarding the rear, the barrack was effectively sealed off. The rest of the squad beat and drove the screaming and bleeding Gypsies onto the trucks. Knowing the barrack, I knew that they had no choice; there was nowhere to run except into the truck. The SS guards raised the back gates and lowered the back canvases of the trucks, after which the convoy drove off. For the next few days, the crematoria chimneys spewed flames and ashes that illuminated the night sky. During the previous week, there had been no new transports arriving to feed the crematoria, so it was simply the Gypsies' turn. Our turn would come; it was just a question of time and availability of the killing machines. If, in one single night, they could clean out all the Gypsies who were our overseers, what were our prospects? We were well aware of our fate. From that point on, German criminals, murderers, gangsters, robbers, Communists, socialists and homosexuals who were in the camp as prisoners became our new kapos, our overseers.

A few days later, or perhaps it was weeks, since I had lost my sense of time, I was taken on a work detail and soon found myself on the same railroad platform where I had first arrived. An arriving transport of Jews was being disembarked and this time we were the "ghosts" who were to unload their meager possessions and clean the cars. We wore our striped uniforms so that we were easily identifiable and we were not allowed to mingle with the arrivals. After the newcomers got off the train, we were to climb in and throw out all their belongings onto the platform and shovel out all the excrement, including dead bodies, onto waiting pushcarts. I looked at the faces of the arriving transport of Jews as if I were looking into a mirror; I saw ourselves — my grandparents, parents, aunts and uncles, cousins, sisters and brothers — but what stood out and haunted me for years were the mothers and the children. They tried to speak to us. "Where are we?" they asked in Polish. Not one of us answered, for it would have meant our death.

"Speak to us! Where are we?" they insisted, this time in Yiddish. Seeing their anxiety and sheer terror, I could not take it any longer, I could not stay silent.

"Auschwitz-Birkenau," I answered in Yiddish as I bent over the cart.

"With God's help it will be good," I continued and disappeared into the freight car.

They were Jews from the Łódź Ghetto in Poland, thousands of them.[8] I expected them to enter the camp, but instead of being told to go left or right, they were marched straight to the right, to their deaths. Once again, the crematoria were spewing flames and ashes for days. The entire camp smelled of death. The ashes were falling on us like in a volcanic eruption. The crematoria could not keep up with the load, so the Nazis were burning people in open pyres on the side and at the back of the crematoria. A few days later, a new Hungarian transport arrived and since the gas chambers were busy with the Łódź Jews, the newcomers were instead packed into E Camp, including my barrack. I looked to see who was being pushed into my bunk, and was dumbfounded to see that it was my cousin Laci, the son of my Aunt Helen, my father's sister. He was a year older than me and had lived in the town of Vajan in Hungary. We hugged and kissed each other. He told me that his family had been arrested and deported to a ghetto and then transported here.

As an "old-timer," I taught him the ropes — what to look out for and how to survive. He was a tall, lanky, sheltered and laid-back fellow who

8   The ghetto in Łódź, Poland's second-largest city and major industrial center, was officially sealed on May 1, 1940. It was the second-largest ghetto in the German-occupied areas and was the most severely insulated from its surroundings and from other ghettos. Some 170,000 Jews were interned there, to whom were added tens of thousands of Jews from the district, other Jews from the Reich, and also Sinti and Roma. The ghetto, although intended to be a temporary transit facility, lasted for more than four years after the interests of local Nazis led to a decision to exploit the Jewish labor force.

The first Jews to be deported from Łódź, in January 1942, were sent to the Chełmno death camp. Deportations continued until September 1942, with more than 70,000 Jews and all the Sinti and Roma being sent to Chełmno, after which deportations were all but halted. For the next two years, the Łódź ghetto residents worked, hungered and mourned.

In February 1944, Himmler decided on a gradual liquidation of the ghetto. To this end, the Chełmno death camp, which had been closed in March 1943, was reopened in June 1944. During the three weeks from June 23 to July 14, 1944, more than 7,000 Jews were murdered there. With the Red Army approaching and Chełmno's limited extermination capacity, in early August, the Germans redirected deportations, sending more than 67,000 Jews to Auschwitz.

See www.yadvashem.org/yv/en/holocaust/about//03/lodz.asp (accessed, March 17, 2016) and Miron and Shulhani, eds., *The Yad Vashem Encyclopedia of the Ghettos*, pp. 410-411.

did not seem to have the aggressive pursuit of survival. He did not seem to comprehend the severity of his situation. He could not fathom that someone would want to kill him. We were together for a while. Then, one day, while standing with him side-by-side at roll call, a German SS officer cut the line between us. Laci, unfortunately, was marched a few steps from me, while I was left standing exposed. I was amazed that, although I had tugged at his sleeve to try to pull him across into my line, away from the group that was selected, he shrugged me off and stayed in his line. "Come here. Come here. Laci, come here. They will kill you," I whispered, and motioned to him to jump into my ranks, alas to no avail. He ignored me and did not even indicate that he had some other plan that he thought would meet with more success. He might have been afraid to leave his row, but he made no effort to find an alternative way to save his life, nor did he even look distressed.

I struggled with an explanation for his lack of action to save his own life. I came to the conclusion that Laci either did not realize what was happening, or did not comprehend what I was telling him about our situation. Perhaps he was simply frozen with fear, although he did not say so or look it. If Laci had tried to come over to my side, he most likely would have succeeded, especially given that he was the last in the group being marched off. The SS officer who "cut" the line had already left and the guards who were on their way to us had not yet reached the last row where Laci was standing. Unfortunately, Laci did not even try. I suppose that he did not have enough experience on his own. He had not had time to observe the process of being selected. Obviously, my explanations of the life and peril in Birkenau overwhelmed him. Personal experience like I had was obviously superior to only learning from others. That was the last time I saw my cousin Laci.

SELECTIONS AND SURVIVAL

I was selected and survived several times. I had many near misses and escapes in Birkenau as well as in other camps. I would like to state for the record that my survival is no virtue of mine, nor was it a brilliant deed on my part; it was not heroic, nor the result of the execution of a well-thought-out plan or even the result of a conscious effort. One might think that a "guiding hand from above," or at least miraculous "coincidences," were the instrument of my survival. I certainly subscribe to that theory, although I fail to see why I was saved or why I would be the recipient of such grace. If one does not wish to pry into that which we do not understand, then the theory of survival instinct, coupled with a strong, non-relenting will to live, with a good dose of luck is a very strong argument.

I learned my lesson from the Gypsy misfortune; therefore, I always hung out up front, close to the main doors of our barrack. I watched out for any unusual activity. This vigilance saved my life. Being out front had additional benefits, such as the chance of being chosen for a work detail that would get me out of E Camp and give me an opportunity to look for my mother. I never came to grips with the possibility that Mother had perished. To this day, I have difficulty accepting that obvious fact. Every time I stood for roll call, I constantly searched through the electrified wires for the possibility of seeing her. I would shout across the fence if I saw a woman, "Do you know Matilda Brandstein from Buština? If you meet anyone from Buština, tell them to tell her that her husband and sons are alive and that Andi is here." I was forever looking for my mother. Once, I spotted and made contact with a female family friend. She had some contact with the kapos who made illicit forays into the women's section. When she heard that I was to be selected, she managed to use her connection with the kapo to have me replaced in the head count.

One day, just after noon, I was in my usual position hanging out in front of the barrack, when a work detail brought in two garbage cans with "food" consisting of the usual fare, namely slop. Normally the kapo of the barrack whose "office" was by the door would order the work detail to start ladling out the soup. Since I understood some German, I overheard the German kapo tell the work detail of prisoners, "Out with this crap, they don't need it anymore," followed by the command, "*Raus! Los! Los!*" (Out! Let's go! Let's go!) That was typically followed by a cane to the head, or on the back if one was lucky. The fear of the inevitable cane created a status of haste and confusion and I took advantage of this by grabbing the rim of one of the garbage cans and walking out with the food detail as if I was one of them.

The members of the food detail soon realized that I was an intruder and began creating a disturbance, so I ran across the road and hid at the side of the barrack opposite, with a clear view of my barrack. Alerted by the disturbance made by the food detail, the kapo in my barrack soon realized that one person had left and had not returned. With the German obsession of keeping correct count, the kapo stepped out of the barrack and, seeing a young man passing by, he grabbed him and pulled him into the barrack. I saw the young man and witnessed his struggle to get away from the kapo's grip. A few minutes later, I watched as trucks arrived and backed into my barrack. The barrack was emptied. I wasn't there; I was not among them. I can see the face of that young man who was caught in the thicket of chance and died instead of me. It has haunted me ever since. I survived.

New people from a Hungarian transport came in to fill my now-empty barrack. My Uncle David Wieder was among them. Later that evening, when I snuck back into the barrack, I met up with him. We hugged and kissed. On seeing him, my emotions gave way. I reverted back to my childhood and started crying uncontrollably. Uncle David's wife was Aunt Valerie, my mother's sister. Aunt Valerie's twin was Aunt Giselle who had also lived in Budapest. Uncle David told me that Aunt Giselle had been caught on the street in front of the security building of the Swedish diplomat Raoul Wallenberg by the Hungarian fascist Arrow Cross party in Budapest and was taken at night to the Danube. Once there, the Nyilas guards performed their favorite forms of torture and execution for their own exclusive entertainment. In preparation for the night's excitement, they chopped a hole in the ice in the Danube. They shot Aunt Giselle and her body was thrown under the ice to float away. As the morning approached, they would scrape the bloody ice into the hole and by the morning there was no sign of any atrocities. The Nyilas were prowling the streets for Jews to be used in their Danube ritual.

The police had caught Uncle David about a month prior to that incident as he was going about his business. They had acted in a more conventional manner, turning Uncle David over to the Germans who sent him to Birkenau where he ultimately wound up in my barrack. Aunt Vali, his wife, went searching for him, was caught in the street and taken to Auschwitz. She survived. Uncle David told me that he had been imprisoned in Birkenau for some weeks. He said that he had been working in "Kanada" and gave me a bar of chocolate and some candy. He also instructed me to keep myself clean and not to get sick. The Kanada Kommando was a forced labor detail that worked in the barrack near the gas chambers and crematoria. These were the barracks that contained mountains of discarded personal belongings and were called the Kanada barracks, and thus, the workers were called the Kanada Kommando. Uncle David was one of them, sorting and packing the belongings of the unfortunates for shipment to Germany.[9]

In addition to the Kanada Kommando, there were also those who were forced to work hauling the dead and half-dead bodies from the gas chambers to the crematoria ovens or onto the pyres. These inmates were called the Sonderkommando (Special Detail).[10] What must have gone on in that gas chamber during the few minutes prior to suffocation can only be conjectured. It defies human imagination and would certainly defy description. To placate the victims, they were told that that they were going to take a shower. Once in, the door was hermetically sealed. An SS man would then throw in a canister of Zyklon-B poison gas through an opening in the roof. As the gas canister started to smoke and its poisonous fumes quickly spread, an unimaginable panic must have broken out. Lucky was the one who got a good whiff of it early and therefore suffered less. The nature of a human being's instinct for survival surmounts logic, therefore, they must have held their breath and prolonged their agony for as long as possible. My mother, grandfather and

9   The possessions and precious belongings of the Jews transported to Auschwitz-Birkenau were left in the train carriages and on the train platform as their owners were quickly put through the selection process. These possessions were taken by the "Kanada Kommando" to a sub-camp in Birkenau, nicknamed the "Kanada" warehouse, where the items were sorted and sent to Germany. The unit had the non-official name of "Kanada" since Canada was perceived as a country that symbolized wealth. The prisoners working in the "Kanada Kommando" usually lived in barracks that were inside the warehouse and provided them with better conditions than prisoners who were forced to work outside. They could also take extra food, shoes or extra clothing to protect themselves from the severe winter weather. Some smuggled valuables to use to bribe the kapos or guards. If they were caught, they were killed.

10   The Sonderkommando was one of the worst forced labor units. It consisted primarily of Jews who were forced to remove the dead bodies from the gas chambers, extract their gold teeth, cut their hair and transfer them to the crematorium. Since this company knew too much about the acts of murder, the Germans murdered them after a while and replaced them with others. The only armed uprising at Auschwitz was carried out by the Sonderkommando on October 7, 1944, with help from the Jewish women who worked in the munitions factory Weichsel-Union-Metallwerke.

many relatives were among the hundreds of thousands who suffered this Nazi bestiality in Birkenau Concentration Camp.

The system was that whoever worked in the Sonderkommando, worked a week or two and then they themselves were gassed or shot and cremated. Those who were selected to replace them never came back to the camp, but were replaced with new fodder. Thinking back, I am surprised that Uncle David was somehow able to make his way from the Kanada Kommando into my regular barrack. In any event, two or three days later, the whole group that came with Uncle David, including Uncle David, just never came back. He and they were gone. I never saw Uncle David again.

I was selected for a work detail in the women's camp, which was the best work as it gave me an opportunity to search for my mother. We were hitched to a wagon like donkeys, with a strap over our shoulders, and went to empty the commandant's cesspool. I spent all the time I could shouting, "Did anybody see my mother, Brandstein? Do you know anybody from Buština?" I kept on yelling relentlessly; perhaps someone would answer. Once, someone did answer, my cousins' aunt on the other side of the family. She did not live in our town but knew me well. There were electrified wires between us; therefore, we could only remain within shouting distance. She told me that she hadn't seen my mother, but had heard that some of her nephews, namely my cousins, Ervin and Victor, were alive and had been taken to a work camp.

I carefully calibrated how close I could approach the fence without inviting a burst of machine gun fire from the guard towers. On several occasions, I even managed to throw some food or other objects over the barbed wire to women on the other side. I felt they needed it more than I did. Years after the war, a woman approached my wife at an event and gushed about the fact that I had thrown to her a makeshift spoon that I had whittled using a stick and a rock.

The afflictions of the summer, which scarred our souls, went tediously by. Our misery increased as our strength diminished. The depressing days were peppered with beatings, selections and killings. New transports of people arrived that never made it to the camp, and those who did make it to the camp became fodder for the selections, which thinned out the ranks once again. It became a vicious circle of events. We were held like cattle awaiting our doomed inevitable fate. The crematoria chimneys were relentlessly belching flames and ashes.

As the summer turned to fall and the High Holy Days of *Rosh Hashanah* and *Yom Kippur* were approaching, the selections at roll call intensified. They were longer and on each occasion ever-larger groups of people were selected. Sometimes an entire section of five-abreast was marched off. Other times, all the inmates of an entire barrack were taken away. Often, the ferocious German SS no longer bothered to truck their victims to the gas chambers; they were beaten and rushed as they marched to their gloom. If there was such a thing as the worst time, it was the intensity of the selections and the brutality of the SS conducting them at that time, even when measured on the scale of Auschwitz-Birkenau. The bloodthirsty selections on *Rosh Hashanah* and *Yom Kippur* of September 1944 make them the highlight of the German bestiality. Surely, the fact that it was *Rosh Hashanah*, followed by *Yom Kippur*, was not lost on the German SS hierarchy. Large transports were still arriving as camp barrack after barrack was emptied and fed to the flames. It was also the quantity of people the Nazis were able to "process," which makes this time period stand out. In addition to the gas chambers operating at capacity, people were regularly burned on open pyres. Although the Germans doubled their efficiency, still, there was an added urgency because the Russian Army was barreling down their necks. The SS committed all resources into a single-minded rush to kill as many Jews as they possibly could in the shortest possible time.

During this period, the weather certainly contributed to the sense of doom. Like in a well-orchestrated show, the winds picked up and shivered our bodies and souls. The churning, dark, ominous clouds forebode our fate. The depression and gloom hovered over us. We looked pathetic with mud clinging to our bodies and sparse clothing. Our faces were death masks with bulging eyes and extended teeth. The guards called us derelicts and *Muselmänner* (inmates who were on the verge of death from starvation). I suppose I was too young to understand and was certainly unable to "read" the meaning of the heightened ferocity until I told someone that I had overheard a discussion among the Germans, saying, *"Der Krieg ist verloren."* (The war is lost.) From then on the "buzz" was that the Germans were losing the war. Like wild dogs devouring their prey, the Germans became increasingly more ferocious. The knowledge that they were losing the war gave me a new impetus to live and an escalating wish to see them suffer and die, which I awaited with all the patience I could muster.

The overheard comment of *"Der Krieg ist verloren"* was reinforced by the constant source of news and rumors from the new arrivals. Some of them drew maps on the ground to show the war situation. They lauded the deeds and heroism of the Serb Partisans who were successfully killing German soldiers and sabotaging their war effort, as well as tying down German troops who otherwise would have been available for front-line duty. Unfortunately, the arrivals also brought with them news of devastated Jewish communities. They told us about unimaginable atrocities and mass killings of Jews in open pits, perpetrated by the Germans as well as the Hungarians, Lithuanians, Ukrainians and Polish Nazis. We were lamenting the fate of our co-religious brethren, while we ourselves were condemned to unspeakable atrocities.

There were Jews who knew enough prayers by heart, who were constantly praying the *Viduy*, the last confessional rites and part of our Jewish liturgy. There were always some rabbis or religious men who kept track of the date and the day of the week, so we knew when it was the Sabbath.

During the High Holy Days I was selected for death during roll call. The entire section was cordoned off and marched out of the camp to a waiting truck. I could not find a way out. As we were marched out of the camp, my chances of getting away became virtually none. I found myself in a truck with strangers who had arrived that week. Among them I was the old-timer. They did not yet fully grasp our desperate situation, while I realized that we were going toward the gas chambers and crematoria. As the truck turned, I could see from the tailgate of the truck the chimney of the other crematoria. The realization that I was going towards the fire numbed me. I did not cry nor scream. I was numb with fear and the hopelessness of my situation. I remember thinking, "What will my father say?" I could not believe that I would never see my parents and brother again. I felt sorry for them, but not for myself.

The trucks carrying us to our deaths entered the gas chamber and crematoria compound. The trucks usually proceeded to the gas chamber and backed into the doors of the chamber, which would have virtually sealed off any possibility of escape. However, at the entrance, heavy construction machinery, materials and trucks impeded their progress. Instead, we were ordered out of the trucks, to assemble and then, at first, to trot, and subsequently, to run towards the gas chamber. Once again, and perhaps for the last time, everything was "*Los! Los!*" A person cannot think clearly when he is running to avoid a rifle butt or a bayonet. As we were running somebody yelled out, "This is the gas chamber, it is the crematoria! They are going to kill us!" Panic broke out and hundreds of us began to run in every possible direction. The German guards opened fire with their Schmeisser machine guns, firing indiscriminately from every imaginable angle. The dogs were barking and ripping into those whom they caught. I, too, was running and managed, somehow, to run into a relatively small cement sewage pipe. Bullets hit the cement pipe with a deafening crescendo. It felt as if I was inside a drum.

They killed hundreds of us. Those who they rounded up were put back into the trucks. I suppose that the guards did not consider a pipe as a possible hiding place, but, due to my small size, I fit in snugly. I stayed in that pipe until all the commotion had subsided. At dusk, I saw a work detail marching by and I attached myself and walked out of the crematoria compound back into E Camp, as if I were part of the labor detail. I survived being inside the crematoria compound. Since I was not familiar with the others who had been rounded up and put on the trucks, I was unable to ascertain whether any of them had survived. Knowing the German barbaric mentality, I am sure that they had not been allowed to return to the camp with their stories. Subsequently, I never met anyone who had experienced this episode.

We stood for roll call; they needed a new count as the Germans had no idea how many they shot and how many had come back. Also, some new people, mostly Hungarian Jews, had been brought into our camp. Subsequently, there were selections for transfers to work camps. Men with skills in bridge building, carpentry or engine repairs, etc., as well as those who were strong enough to clear rubble following an Allied air raid, were selected. After selection, they were sent to one of the sub-camps, where they were tattooed and transported to work camps in Germany or Austria. Despite E Camp being a holding pen for new arrivals awaiting selection to be killed or transferred to a work camp, I never left E Camp until January 1945.

Although the chimneys of the crematoria continued belching the smoke, fire and ashes of the new arrivals who fell victim to the evil deeds of the German "Master Race," the recent selections lulled us, once again, into a false sense of relative complacency, which did not last long. It was shattered by another round of vicious selections. They turned out to be the last in Auschwitz-Birkenau.

My life consisted of standing at roll call, avoiding selection and waiting in line for a crumb of bread or a little slop they called "soup." I tried to survive, I tried to retain my sanity and remembered my father's admonishment to preserve my dignity and not let them make an animal out of me. I was able to keep what little bread was issued and not spill my soup by someone grabbing it out of my hand, since the "newcomers" were not as hungry as the seasoned inmates. I tried to get allocated to labor details by hanging out where I would be most likely called upon. That is how I wound up on many of the labor details that got me onto the other side of our electrified fence, which was the women's camp, the purpose of which was to look for my mother.

People were encouraged daily to report sick. The loudspeakers repeatedly announced, "Anybody who is sick and wants to go to the infirmary or to the hospital should step out and they will be taken care of." Those who did, never came back. Although I tried to guard my health, as my father had instructed me, nevertheless I did get sick. I knew that I had a temperature and every bone in my body ached so badly I could hardly drag myself to roll call. I was burning up and coughing. Another inmate, a Jewish doctor, told me not to report sick and taught me how to suppress my cough. He warned me not to dare cough where anybody could hear me, that I should clamp my hand over my mouth so it would be completely closed, and then cough if I had to. He told me that I should never give the slightest inkling to anyone that I was sick. Even if I had to choke, I shouldn't cough where I could be heard. At night, I became delirious and began to moan. In the darkness of the night, a hand stroked my forehead and whispered to me to be quiet so that I would not come to the attention of the night kapo. In the morning, I woke up in a soaking sweat and was overcome with a general weakness. It worried me that I would not be able to stand for roll call that afternoon, certainly not undetected. The Jewish doctor came and instructed me to lie on the brick oven, which extended from one end of the barrack to the other. I was to press my chest to the oven for as long as I could stand it. He, once again, instructed me that under no condition was I to report sick or show any weakness at roll call. I scrupulously followed the doctor's orders;

I lay down on the oven on my stomach and pressed myself to it as strongly as I could while watching out for the kapo. By the middle of the afternoon, I felt miraculously well enough to pass undetected at roll call. I wished to stand at roll call next to the doctor with whom, I believed, I had developed a dependency kinship. I tried to find him but without success until I glimpsed him among those who had unfortunately been selected and he passed by me as they were marched off. I never saw him again. I do not remember his name, I doubt whether I ever knew it. Later that night, I cried for him. I remember thinking that I was crying for the first time since I had been separated from my father and brother. If he had not warned me, I would have reported sick and been killed.

Standing where I could come to the attention of the German kapo was not always beneficial to me. As it turned out, I had an unpleasant experience that nearly cost me my life. One late evening, the German day kapo gave me a chocolate bar and ordered me to come with him. I followed him, as ordered, to his barrack where he gave me a candy and ordered me to get undressed and get into his bunk. I thought, "How lucky can I get? I was wrong about him, he is really nice. Why did I ever fear him and try to avoid him? I know that he likes me, after all, he spoke to me nicely." Later, when he came to bed, I did not mind when he put his arms around me. But then he pressed himself against me in a way that I did not understand but knew instinctively was wrong. I began to fidget and moved away from him. He began to fondle me, which frightened and worried me. I was thinking of running away, but to where? And if I did, wouldn't he select me the next day and ship me off to the gas chamber? My predicament came to a head, when he forced himself on me and kissed me. I was pinned down and could hardly move. When he put his tongue in my mouth, I reacted with all my might. I was bewildered and managed to clear my face of his and begin to spit, inevitably, in his face. He reacted violently, by punching me in my face and kicking me off the bunk. The kapo bellowed and began to curse, yelling "*Ruhe*" (Quiet). My nose began to bleed and I was naked and sobbing. I found an empty bunk and cowered on the bare wooden planks, alert and listening to every sound. In the middle of the night, I stealthily retrieved my belongings. In the morning, I managed to get out of the barrack without being seen by "my" kapo. After that, I avoided him in every possible way. I no longer hung out in front of my barrack so as not to come to his attention.

It was a nearly daily occurrence that many inmates ran, whether consciously or not, towards the electrified wires, although it was suicidal. Some ran in a dazed condition, while others did so intentionally, trying to climb over it. All were electrocuted and needlessly machine-gunned by the watchtower guard. These poor souls remained on the barbed wire, mostly in a grotesque climbing-clinging position, until the power was shut off and they were removed. At night, when someone approached the wires, he would be greeted with a searchlight and a burst of machine gun fire. In order for me to get close to the wire and shout across to inquire about my mother, I made a study of it, calculating how close one could get before the guard in the tower would shoot to kill. Many times, bursts of machine gun fire landed at my feet, driving me back. One day, as I came close to the wire, a German SS guard, wearing a makeshift insignia (not the usual one), who was patrolling between the two electrified wires, approached me. He looked at me and said *"Ich bin kein Freiwilliger"* (I am not a volunteer). The SS were supposedly all volunteers. He looked at me, a child who was more dead than alive, just bones standing on bones, and felt the need to allay his conscience. He just wanted me to know that he was not one of them.

One early afternoon, the dreaded afternoon when roll calls culminating in selections were usually done, the clouds were the shapes of chariots racing through the sky. Remembering how much I enjoyed the sky and the clouds over my Carpathian hometown of Buština and how much I loved the shadows cast by the setting sun, I began to compare the sky and clouds over Birkenau to those which I knew so well and loved so much. As I daydreamed and longed for my home, an ominous cloud appeared that created turbulence in the sky. It proceeded to destroy my chariots, which fit perfectly well with me. After all, everything and everybody was being destroyed. Suddenly, loud, deafening sirens were heard and panicky guards ran into and occupied the entrance to our camp. Trucks with sirens blaring and loaded with armed guards were moving down the main road as well as outside the camp. The guards were agitated and began searching the barrack. Roll call was hastily called and we were repeatedly counted. The German officers spoke openly about "escaping Russians soldiers" and how "they don't have a chance of getting away."

According to the Geneva Convention, soldiers who were prisoners of war were not supposed to be in concentration camps, nor were they supposed to be starved, abused and used as slave laborers, but they were. There were barracks full of Russian soldiers in Birkenau. I don't know whether they were gassed and burned in crematoria as the Jews and the Gypsies were, but they were regularly marched or trucked out of the camp for forced labor.[11] A few hours later, as we were again standing at roll call, we were marched out from our camp to the main *Sammelplatz* (assembly point), which had water towers at each end. There were hundreds, perhaps thousands, of inmates gathered. The entire camp stood five abreast. Loudspeakers ordered, *"Ruhe!"* (Quiet!) and warned us not to leave the spot where we were standing, under the penalty of death, as usual; everything was always under the penalty of death.

They marched in the three recaptured Russian soldiers in their Russian uniforms and with their hands tied behind their backs. They were brought to the water towers and ropes were put around their necks. The three soldiers stood like that for approximately forty-five minutes while the loudspeakers announced, "This is what happens to anyone who even thinks of escaping. There is no such thing as 'out'." The Germans then ceremoniously proceeded to hang the soldiers by pulling them from the ground up, breaking their necks, one at a time. They hung them high enough for the whole assembly to see. The last to be hung appeared to be the youngest of the three, perhaps nineteen years old. As he was being pulled up, he lifted both of his feet and kicked the German soldier who was standing in front of him in the groin. Machine guns opened fire and kept on firing at him while his body was swinging back and forth. They kept firing until the lower part of his body literally fell off. There were some sounds of approval from the assembly for the heroic action that culminated in indiscriminate firing into our midst. Nevertheless, it was wonderful how this boy-soldier restored some pride to the entire assembly. The soldier was dead, but a point had been made. This was the first time I

---

11   The first Soviet prisoners of war were most likely sent to Auschwitz in July or August 1941 and were murdered almost immediately. In the beginning of September 1941, a group of 600 POWs, together with 250 Polish prisoners who were sick, were murdered in the basement of Block 11 with the use of Zyklon B. This was the first case of mass extermination by gassing in the camp. In October 1941, the SS built a sub-camp at Birkenau for some 10,000 Soviet POWs. The mortality among them was very high. Only several hundred were still alive in March 1942. In the subsequent years, smaller groups of Soviet POWs were sent to the camp. Most of the 900 who were in the camp in 1944 were sent in the autumn of that year to other camps in Germany. About 15,000 Soviet POWs were murdered in Auschwitz.

witnessed somebody kicking, hitting or resisting a German. I learned that they could be kicked, but only if one was willing to pay the price. It became the major topic of conversation throughout the camp.

Our miserable days began with the morning routine of fighting to get to the latrine drums before they got full. I never managed that, nor could I reach them to sit down even when I did get to them. Then there was the standing in line for our miserable rations and thinking about whether we would survive the upcoming roll call selections. Fights between inmates in the barracks were not unusual. The new arrivals knew each other and stuck together. They kept an eye out for the "stripers" — that was us, the ones who wore striped uniforms — the old-timers, who, as a pack, would start a fight while others in the pack robbed their food.

One particular morning, however, there was a special commotion at the rear of the barrack. Seemingly, one of the new arrivals had offered a wretched, starving "striper" food if he performed a sexual act of his choice. While I did not understand what was going on, nor did I have any clue why what was going on should create such a commotion, the situation got out of hand and it came to the attention of the kapo. The kapo got to the middle of the crowd by beating his way in with a walking cane. He hit the "striper" over the head so that his head broke open and his brains splattered, and the "newcomer" caught a few canes over his body and was then dragged to the front of the barrack for punishment. The method of punishment was not new to us; it had been used many times by this kapo, but never before to this extent.

The oven ran from the front all the way to the end of the barrack where it turned up as a chimney through the roof. At the front it had two doors; the upper one was for feeding the logs into the oven, while the other lower door was for cleaning out the ashes. The kapo ordered two inmates to put the object of the commotion into the oven up to his waist with his arms forward. It was a tight fit and it rendered him helpless. The kapo then usually applied five vicious hits with his cane on the protruding buttocks while the victim's cries were smothered. This time, however, the kapo did not stop at five; it went to ten, fifteen, twenty, etc. By now, blood was spattering with every hit and still it went on, until finally the poor guy fell out, mercifully dead.

Late in October 1944, as we were going through the usual routine of roll call, all indications were that a major selection was being prepared. I was numb with cold and was beginning to lose the will to get away. My spirits, however, were strengthened by thinking about going home to my family. I was always focused on my father's three last instructions before we were separated. So, once again, I began to assess the situation. This time, however, there was no selection in the usual manner; there was no clever way of standing at the front or back; no possible gimmicks could be applied. As we stood, the German officers, with their armed guards and soldiers, isolated the first three barracks on the left side of the camp, including my barrack that was the third from the front. Everyone from the first three barracks was totally cut off from any possibility of escape. Trucks were waiting at the gate, since the guards would not march such a large multitude the distance to the gas chambers and invite a possible riot, as had happened before. Although the direct distance was relatively short, that way was blocked with electric fences, so the walking distance was relatively longer than they believed they could safely handle. Accordingly, the trucks were there to drive us around the fence and through the various gates. I told myself that this was the end and there was no escape.

While we were standing and waiting, a German kapo with a red triangle on his jacket, which designated him as a Communist or socialist, seemed to be in command. With the aid of the SS guards, he began to orchestrate the specific groups to be marched toward the trucks. I had seen him before, he was a big shot, and I heard him arguing with the German guards whom he sometimes addressed as *Scheisskopf* (shithead). As my group was designated to be the next to be marched off to the trucks, this German kapo came over to me and said, "*Du Jüdisches lamm — du bist noch da?*" (You Jewish lamb, you are still here?) He could not believe that I was still alive. He followed this up with a well-aimed punch, hitting me under the chin with his open hand, which raised me off my feet and knocked me down. As a German guard ran over with his bayonet at the ready, the kapo kicked me in my ribs and yelled, "*Verschwinde, Du Schweinehund.*" (Get lost, you swine.) Nobody was expected to walk away, so I crawled on all fours as fast as I could, not thinking of anything else other than getting away from him. I finally managed to stand up on wobbly legs and ran. He had kicked me out of the assembly that was going to the gas chamber. Did he hit and kick me in anger? Was he venting his anger on a Jewish child when he called me a "pig," or, had he done it on purpose to rescue the little "lamb"? Unfortunately, I'm more inclined to believe that his behavior was not well intended. Either way, his action saved my life.

Enraged over the conduct of the war that they were losing, the Germans were processing the newcomers and emptying out the camp barracks with special haste, but somehow not me. One day after roll call, sometime in November 1944, they made us return to our barracks one at a time. Upon entry, they tattooed us and carefully recorded our names, addresses, etc. I was tattooed with the number "B-14611." The "B" was for "Birkenau." The grapevine had it that they would be sending us to a work camp. Why else would they tattoo and record us? Towards the end of November 1944, I overheard an SS officer reprimand two guards about their listless behavior. The closing statement of the reprimand was, "Perhaps you would prefer the Russian front." The guards recoiled from this threat and snapped to an animated attention. While it was the first time I had heard this particular threat, in the coming weeks it became common, convincing us that the Russian front was not a desirable place to be, and that the Germans were losing badly.

By then, I don't think I had any spiritual strength left. I was also emaciated. I wasn't conscious of the passing days; most of the time things just happened without my awareness. I suppose that there must have been a survival instinct that governed my actions although I wasn't aware of it. However, the realization that the Germans were losing the war and that our liberation might not be far away, gave me a new impetus to survive, which was a driving force in my survival over the months to come. I looked upon the days as a countdown to the day of liberation that to me meant going home. I looked at the faces of the SS officers and guards and thought to myself, "I will live and you will die."

In the beginning of December 1944, the roll calls were for counting and assigning work details. By then, the gas chambers and crematoria had not been active for a couple of weeks; the Nazis were not burning us anymore, but the shooting of us had now intensified. Mass shootings had been relatively rare in Birkenau, unless there was a riot or a problem with the new arrivals. The nights were no longer turned into infernos. The sky was dark. There were no longer the usual, eerie, hazy glows emanating from pyres in the fields behind F Camp.

I was selected for a work detail that was taken to F Camp. Once again, I found myself in the gas chambers and crematoria compound. We were commanded to remove carefully the tiles of the roofs of the crematoria.

We were given chalk to number each tile and ordered to layer them on skids with straw between the layers. Each lot was carefully recorded. The Germans knew that they were losing the war; all day and night the thunder of the Russian cannons and Katyusha rocket launchers could be heard ever louder. We overheard the guards saying that the skids of roof tiles were destined for Hamburg, Bremen, Cologne and Berlin to repair the damage the Allies had inflicted on Germany through aerial bombing them day and night. Nevertheless, we were ordered to count and carefully mark each tile. This was the German mentality. They were losing the war and running out of time to retreat. But each tile had to be separately marked and counted, and heaven help the poor soul who broke a single tile, it was considered sabotage and dealt with accordingly. The Germans made it clear with a catchy saying: "*Ein Bruch; Dein Tod*" (One break; your death). Besides the enormous time and effort wasted on persecuting the Jews, I believe the German mentality and doctrinaire obsession was a major contribution to their downfall.

One early morning, I was assigned to a work detail that took me out to the fields surrounding the camp. The work consisted of clearing drainage ditches. We were issued shovels, which I was not strong enough to lift. I had no choice but to pretend to work whenever a guard would look my way. At one point, I was closely watching a guard who was sitting on a rock eating sardines from a can. How I wished that I could have been "a man" and strong enough to hit him over the head with my shovel and run away. Although I knew that it was impossible, that I did not even have the strength to lift the shovel, I nevertheless looked around to see where I would go if I did have a chance to run. I am sure that I was not the only one who contemplated running away. After the guard threw the empty can into the ditch near me, I retrieved it and managed to scrape a few little pieces of sardine tail. In the process, I cut my finger and was bleeding badly. Attending to my bleeding finger, I neglected to notice that another prisoner had approached me. He grabbed the can from me and licked out the oil that was in the can. That person got dysentery from the oil and was moaning all night; I don't know whether he survived the night, but he saved me from the same fate, since I would have licked the oil if I had been given the chance.

I seemed to draw early-morning work details, perhaps because I was conveniently available. On one occasion, following a night of torrential rain, we were sent out of the camp once again to clear the drainage ditches. It was a foggy, cold morning with heavy dew on the grass. I loved the smell of the moist earth, which reminded me of the pleasing aroma of our earth at home. I saw little snails on blades of grass. Remembering that the French eat snails, I knew that they were edible, so I began to pick them as I marched. My teeth were loose and therefore, I could not crack the shells, even though they were only small and thin. Most of the tiny ones I ate with the shell. The others I put in my pocket and, with two stones that I found and managed to conceal in the cuff of my pants, I broke the shells and ate the snails back at the camp.

I was once assigned to a slave labor work detail to help the German war effort. Believe it or not, we were actually forced to pack parachutes for the German Air Force. At the risk of my life, I purposely sabotaged my efforts by packing some incorrectly. I hoped that the parachutes would never open.

Dysentery was a major killer in the camps. I knew that if I got it, I would not survive. I saw grown men who were stronger than me succumb to this wretchedness. Often, I would drink water by making a hole in the mud and waiting until water seeped in. Many times, the meager rations, if I got to keep and eat them, were enough for me. I didn't use to eat much at home either; I was a small, skinny boy who seemingly did not need much nourishment. I never got the "good stuff" — sugar beets, potato peels, etc. — in my soup; I was always pushed out of the line and could only get back in when the soup had become plain water. There was a partially filled barrel of rainwater outside the back of the barrack from which I could never drink. I wasn't strong enough to fight my way in.

Winter approached and it was getting colder by the day, and then it snowed for days. When the snow paused, the wind became brutally frigid; the cold was unbearable. People at roll call literally keeled over and froze. No clothing was issued other than half a blanket, which was given to us sometime late in November.

I was in the Auschwitz-Birkenau Concentration and Extermination Camp from June 2, 1944, until January 17, 1945.

THE DEATH MARCH

arly in January, the thunder and explosions of war were coming ever closer. The SS guards were augmented by additional SS guards who were not all German. There were guards with a variety of other nationalities. The nights were once again lit, not by the chimneys of the crematoria, but rather by the artillery and rocket fire that passed over our heads. There were days when roll call was skipped, the absolute well-greased, faultless machine of the SS seemed a little bit rusty and staggered at best. It had been snowing steadily for the past few days; sometimes it was even difficult to open the barrack doors. The sky was ominously gray, casting a gloomy atmosphere that matched our temperaments.

In the morning of January 18, 1945, we were hastily summoned to roll call and marched out of the camp. As we approached the electrified barbed-wire gates, we were ordered to pass in single file. As we did so, double rations of bread and pieces of margarine were dispensed. Someone grabbed the margarine from me. Many of those who "gorged" themselves on the margarine died of dysentery. It seems repetitious, but once again a mean or at least an unkind deed perpetrated against me, saved me from possible demise. We were reassembled, lined up in columns of five and ordered to march. We soon found ourselves on the road leaving Birkenau. When we came to a sharp curve, we saw that the road behind us was full of prisoners, as far as the eye could see. It was obvious that the entire camp was being evacuated. Our marching columns were joined at crossroads and feeder roads by hundreds, if not thousands, of prisoners from other Auschwitz satellite camps.

Those who conducted the march were mostly Ukrainian, Lithuanian and Croatian soldiers, who were in the service of the German Nazis. All too often they were more eager and brutal than the Germans. There were also some Poles, mostly civilians, who were conscripted into the service of the Germans. Prisoners were dying as we walked. As we passed villages, the Germans confiscated the Poles' horses, carts and their food and pressed them into forced labor collecting the dead and piling them onto the carts or shoving them under the snow to hide the bodies. The Nazis wished to hide their atrocities from the oncoming Russian Army. Artillery and rocket firing during the day and thunder and flashes of light during the night were both frightening and reassuring. Whispers of imminent liberation by the Russians were a tonic to our ears. "The Russians are near, surely they are advancing faster than we are walking," was the buzzword. Our destination was the rail station in the city of Gleiwitz. We marched through the city of Katowice and the town of Nikolai, among many others, to get there.

The weather was unbelievably cold. I wore only a pajama-like striped suit and cap with wooden shoes on my otherwise bare feet and I wrapped myself in my half blanket. I emulated the prisoner who was on my left and tore the edge of my blanket to gain a strip. Even though I could be killed for defacing German property, I tied the strip around my waist to keep the wind and snow out. My pants were so long that I managed to wrap my feet in my pants and squeeze them into the shoes. My wrapped feet filled the shoes better and kept most of the snow out.

The snow was powdery with significant accumulation. The ditches on the side of the road were almost level with the road, so that the snow in the ditches was substantially deeper. On top of the snow was a thin layer of ice that reflected the sun; its edges were sharp enough to inflict dangerous cuts. The beauty of the landscape was breathtaking — the stark, white snow contrasted by the bare trees with just their snow-topped branches. It reminded me of the winter landscape at home when I used to fall through the thin layer of ice into the powdery snow. The snow was so dry that it could not be made into a snowball. The thinly feathered edges of the ice reminded me of the sheets of ice that floated down the River Talabor from the surrounding mountains. In the summer, after the snow began to melt up in the Carpathian Mountains, sheets of ice broke off and floated downriver. Some older, but not necessarily brighter, brave kids would hitch a ride on the ice floats. Others like me, not as brave and not such good swimmers, avoided them and their games. The more villages and fields I passed, the more it looked like home. Sometimes, I felt that Buština, my home, was just around the next corner. Suddenly, I was snapped out of my daydream as I stumbled and fell on my face. The cold snow woke me out of my stupor and robbed me of my vision, while helping hands grabbed me and pulled me to my feet. I kept marching and began shivering uncontrollably.

The German forces used the main road for the evacuation of their wounded and for their general retreat; therefore, we no longer had the road to ourselves. Only three and sometimes only two of the five abreast could be on the road, while the others had to march in the ditch. Being on the road was a mixed blessing — the marching was easier, but the closer you were to the Germans the more likely you were to being shot or overrun. On the other hand, the survival rate of those marching in the ditch was much lower — due to the frequent deaths from exhaustion — compared to those who marched on the road. I happened to be on the road, either the first or second from the left (closest to the soldiers).

By the late afternoon, the beautiful powdery snow started to melt and became wet and heavy, clinging to our shoes. More people stumbled and had to contend with the likelihood of being trampled on by the closely packed marchers. Stumbling on the road was dangerous, as I found out. I stumbled because the snow was clinging to my shoes and immediately received a rifle butt in my ribs from a guard who happened to be next to me. As we reached the main road, our column merged with more columns of prisoners from other concentration camps. All marching five abreast, in columns that seemed endless. This was the infamous Death March.[12]

The retreating German Army overtook us. Convoys of trucks marked with red crosses and loaded with their wounded and dead preceded the main body of the German Army. Many of the wounded were transported in open trucks and horse-drawn wagons. They were bleeding through their bandages from their heads, bodies, arms and legs. We were marched alongside them as their hostages, as their "protectors." The German military used us to shield them and provide them with safe passage from air raids. Although we were considered to be their shield, nevertheless, many of the wounded German

---

12   Between January 17 and 21, 1945, the Germans marched approximately 56,000 prisoners (about 40,000 men and 16,000-18,000 women) out of Auschwitz and its sub-camps in evacuation columns. This was the last "Death March" to leave the camp.

Throughout March and April 1945, as the war drew to an end, the Nazis evacuated camp after camp, sending at least 250,000 of their 700,000 concentration camp prisoners on death marches. Some of those marches lasted for weeks, causing thousands of deaths along the highways of western Austria and central Germany. Often, the prisoners would be marched on foot part of the way, and then crowded onto trains — seventy people to a car — where they were denied food and water. In all, an estimated 200,000-250,000 concentration camp prisoners were murdered or died on these forced death marches that were conducted throughout the last ten months of World War II; between one-quarter and one-third of them were Jews.

soldiers were constantly firing their Luger pistols into our midst. Prisoners were shot; we were picked off like little wooden ducks in a shooting gallery. The man behind me was shot and fell forward, nearly knocking me down.

Once in a while, the wounded soldiers threw a grenade into our ranks, killing dozens of marchers. They apparently did this out of spite or purely for fun. Instead of human beings, just a large patch of horror was left behind. The snow was red, bright red, with bodies and body parts all over. Then, the guards ordered the remaining prisoners to cover the bloody mess with fresh snow, using their hands, until there was no sign of any bodies or blood. The wounded German officers were then ordered not to throw grenades, because the mess was difficult to cover with the wet snow. The Germans were careful not to leave behind any proof of their atrocities as they had mistakenly done when they retreated from Russia. The victorious Russian Army following them saw villages that had been completely wiped out, and Russian prisoners of war who had been executed and left behind. This crazed the Russian soldiers to fight harder and be harsher with the German prisoners.

There was nearly constant shooting, which caused panic in our midst. Three and sometimes four of the five abreast in the columns were now walking in freezing slush. It was physically impossible to march under these conditions even if we were not being shot. Some just sat down and gave up the struggle. It became impossible to continue to hide the dead in the snow banks without the chance that the advancing Russians would discover them. Therefore, the Germans confiscated from the local population any and all wagons with horses or oxen and pressed them into service, together with their Polish owners, to transport the dead. The terrain was mostly farmland with small clusters of farmhouses surrounding small villages. Once again, I dreamed of home and made believe that I was marching there. This hallucination sustained me and gave me little bursts of hope.

The Polish farmers put their crops of potatoes in mounds covered with straw to prevent them from freezing. Whenever the Germans came across the mounds in a field, they commandeered wagons and took a detail of prisoners to fill the wagons with the stolen produce. Since every horse and ox was already deployed, the prisoners were ordered to push and pull the potato-laden wagons. This became a new source of affliction. As the

Germans retreated from the Russian front, they robbed the Poles of their potatoes and anything else they could lay their hands on.

My feet were bleeding so much that my shoes were awash with blood and I could not feel my toes. The snow accumulated under my wooden shoes making it impossible to walk, and although I would fall I would try to get up before a guard got to me. Falling was tantamount to dying. During the night, the slush froze and became a new imperilment to us. I twisted my ankle and the resulting swelling nearly filled my shoe. It was excruciatingly painful just to take a step. However, I found a "remedy" for the pain — I made myself believe that the injured foot was not mine and that it did not hurt me. I mentally detached the foot from my body and was able to will the pain away. I used this form of self-hypnosis throughout the rest of my captivity and beyond.

The weather on the second day of our ordeal was clear and crisp. The retreating German Army continued their relentless sport of shooting into our midst. The snow was crackling under my feet. I was sweating and my body was steaming. I did not dare unwrap my tattered "clothing" in fear of pneumonia that would have meant death. All of a sudden, an ungodly roar like an oncoming doom permeated the miserable columns of marchers. Instantaneously, like lightning followed by a thunderbolt, Russian fighter planes with red stars on their fuselage, appeared two at a time behind us. Within that instant, we were in the midst of a massive air attack. The fighter planes flew sortie after sortie, machine-gunning the column of retreating Germans and thereby, inevitably, us. They flew so close to the ground that I could see the pilots' faces; sometimes I thought I could just reach up and catch a plane. The Germans were firing their rifles and machine guns at them to no avail. I never saw any of the planes shot down, but the Germans must have hit some of them.

Bodies flew up in the air as heavy-caliber bullets hit them. We cheered the Russians on by raising our arms in salute, ignoring the fact that we too were being killed. We were happy as long as the Germans were being massacred. It was a maddening pleasure. The slaughterhouse scene was unreal. Blood was leaking out of the German trucks; German blood as well as our own stained the snow red. The guards scattered and our columns disintegrated into total chaos. After the raid, which lasted approximately twenty minutes, the Germans reestablished our columns and increased their vicious behavior.

Our dead and wounded were abandoned and the rest of us were forced to continue to march. The Germans had the right to believe that the Allies would not attack them while they had their hostages as "shields." It had always worked for the Americans and the English. However, it did not always work against the Russians, as they were willing to sacrifice some of us for many of the Germans; perhaps rightly so. At least that was what we, the victims, felt at the time. In our minds, we were dead anyway and the Russian raid was killing the Germans. We were willing to pay any price to that end. It was an unimaginable carnage.

On the third day, I couldn't go on anymore. I often stumbled and instead of jumping up so as not to be noticed, I was content to remain down and I resisted being picked up. That was it; I could not go on. I felt that it was enough. I just couldn't get up on those sticks that were my legs; I could not go on and prolong the agony. Clotted blood glued my feet to my shoes. As a guard noticed and approached me with his rifle and bayonet at the ready, a fellow prisoner, approximately forty years of age, who had been walking next to me on my right, put his arm around my shoulder and picked me up. He hugged me and said, "Hold on, son, just a little longer." He pointed at a church steeple down the road and said, "Do you see that steeple? That's how far we are going. Just go to that steeple, just a little longer." In Poland, one was seldom out of sight of a church steeple. There were many, many more steeples to go and I collapsed on the way many times.

However, I learned a lesson that has served me faithfully ever since. I understood that the body and mind can endure the most brutal punishment when there is a goal to reach, when there is hope, when there is an end in sight. From that moment on, unconsciously, but then consciously, at fourteen and a half years old, I did not have to live for a year or a month, or even for a day or an hour, for that matter. All I had to do was live for one more moment, a moment at a time. I walked just one step at a time. I went to that tree and then I went to that marker and then to that steeple. When I fell, I got up, since I had only a few more steps to go...I no longer worried whether I would be shot or bayoneted in the future; all I cared about was that I was not being killed at that moment.

NIKOLAI, GLEIWITZ AND ČESKÝ TĚŠÍN

Russian rockets continued to light up the night and the thunder of artillery was our constant companion. Towards evening, a German command car stopped along the road near us and commanded the guards to divert a section of the marchers, perhaps fewer than a 100 persons, including me. We were marched off on a small, narrow road to a village that was to the right of the main road. A road sign identified the village as Nikolai. It was a clear, cold, starry night. We were taken to what appeared to be a mine; high mounds of earth with some sheds surrounded a clearing. All of a sudden, a roar of motorcycles could be heard and in a moment, a group of German personnel were upon us. As they came closer, we saw the insignia of the Sicherheitsdienst (SD — Security Service). Some were SS and we knew what that meant. We knew from those who had come to Birkenau from Poland that the SD and SS were the "*rotzchim,*" the killers, of Majdanek and Treblinka. There, Jews had been forced to dig large pits, were made to sit on the edges of the pits and were then shot in the head by these barbarians. The Germans always referred to Jews as "special" and killing Jews as "special handling." "Special" meant death to us.

They herded us like cattle with their devilish motorcycles towards one of the larger hills. The motorcycles had sidecars upon which machine guns were mounted. They surrounded and faced us in a semicircle with their glaring lights and machine guns at the ready. The sky was lit with streaks of fire emanating from the rockets that flew overhead. The deafening noise of artillery fire contributed to our gloom. Our death was imminent. We were shivering and scared. Some of us screamed, "*Shema Yisroel,*" Hear O Israel, most prayed fervently while others said the "*Viduy,*" the last confession. The terror, shrieking and crying are forever seared into my memory. While I myself was crying and yelling, "Mama!" I was also trying to move from the front of the group, to be as far at the back of the pack as I could, hoping that by being at the back I would have a chance to fall into the mound before being shot. In the camp, I had overheard others saying that when there is a burst of gunfire, the best thing to do is to fall first, but not before the firing begins. One thing I knew for sure, if I remained standing, I'd be more likely to get shot and killed.

Just as the command to commence firing was about to be given, a motorcycle with its horn blaring and wheels spinning in the mud and snow arrived. The driver was urgently shouting his need to see the commandant of the detail. He stopped in front of the commandant and, following an acrobatic dismount, he saluted and handed the commandant a piece of paper. Following a short exchange between the messenger and the commandant, the commandant shouted an order and all his devils started up their motorcycles and drove away in great haste, leaving us standing there by the hill. Whatever their new order was, they obviously had some more important killings to do somewhere else. We had been abandoned and began crying hysterically. Some of the group braved the deep snow and started to run through the fields toward the Russian front, the direction from where the artillery and rockets were coming. Some of us just sat there stunned by the foot of the hill. All I could think of was that I had better get moving to prevent myself from freezing to death, but where should we go? Someone said that it would be suicidal to go through the field, that there was no chance to avoid capture walking through the stark, white snow. There was no village within sight and it would have been sheer madness to believe that the native Poles would provide us shelter, especially with Germans all over the place. We could not think nor reason straight; the flashes and the noise of the bombardment drove any thoughts that we might have had out of our minds, we were shouting in each other's ears. There were perhaps fifty of us with fifty opinions as to what to do. I, as a child, had no opinion and I would certainly not stay behind. At dawn, we followed the road back to the main road and attached ourselves to the convoy of the death march that was still in progress, and started to walk.

I dragged myself along the road, replaying the night in my mind. I thought to myself, "Where could I have gone? I could hardly stand. Where could I have run?" I would not have survived long in waist-high snow. I had neither the strength, nor the will to run. All I had was the instinct to survive, but that instinct did not translate into running anywhere. Nobody really ran, some walked away and some of them were shot to death. Few actually got away. Our ranks were decimated. We were walking corpses. Most who perished, died of exhaustion, hunger, from the atrocities of the guards and the retreating German Army. The "special" forces of the German Army took its toll and, ironically, we were victims of the Russian raids. Those who could not go on stumbled and fell or just sat down and breathed their last gasp of breath. I remember the look on the faces of those who were at their end. Their skin was yellow and their eyes were bulging, their lips were tightly drawn over grotesquely large teeth and they seemed to have no feeling in their limbs. I was freezing and lost much of my ability to reason or even to make any sense of my situation. I remember passing frozen corpses and thinking that they must be cold; I felt sorry for them. We marched sporadically in somewhat organized columns, but mostly we just stumbled along. There were no rations of food or water other than what had been given to us at the time of departure, which had lasted about half a day. I was senseless and barely alive when we reached our destination of embarkment, the Gleiwitz railroad station. We had marched more than sixty kilometers in the freezing snow.

At the railroad station someone noticed the absence of the SD and the SS. The station and its vicinity seemed to have been in the hands of the Wehrmacht, the regular German Army, with relatively few SS officers and men. Nevertheless, our SS guards demonstrated their typical cavalier SS attitude and ran afoul of the Wehrmacht officers. The SS insisted that the Wehrmacht relinquish to them some of the freight trains at the station for the purpose of transporting the prisoners. The Wehrmacht, on the other hand, insisted on loading the trains with the mounds of potatoes that had been stolen from the Poles in order to send them to the starving Germans under siege as well as to the German Army. To the SS, killing and/or incarcerating Jews were of the highest priority. The impasse was obviously breached with a compromise. We were first made to load the potatoes into the railcars bound for Germany and then the SS would transport us.

Considering the physical shape we were in, the work was excruciating. We were provided with heavy wheelbarrows that we loaded with potatoes, which took four or five of us to push the considerable distance to the railcars. When we reached the freight car, we unloaded the wheelbarrows by hand, throwing the potatoes in. The SS relentlessly beat us and drove us to work faster. Nothing was ever fast enough for the Germans. An SS man noticed that a Jewish prisoner, who was pushing a wheelbarrow in front of me, put a potato under his jacket. The SS man grabbed the prisoner by the arm and threw him to the ground. He then proceeded to beat the prisoner with a cane until his lifeless body was a bloody mess, and then shot him three times. The punishment certainly did not fit the crime. To the SS, the life of a Jew was worth less than a potato.

There was something special about this incident. Not the incident itself, for it was a mundane, frequent occurrence that for one reason or another, one of us would be brutally murdered. By itself, this incident is hardly worth mentioning, except that a moment later, as I was unloading potatoes from my wheelbarrow, a German Wehrmacht soldier took a potato and, like a quarterback handing off a football, hit me with it in my stomach and said, "*Nimm es und verschwinde.*" (Take it and get lost.) Just a moment previously, a man had been brutally murdered for taking a potato. Now, a soldier was giving me a potato, the possession of which was punishable by death. Unfortunately, I did not possess the potato for long, as a few moments later, when I was out of sight of the soldier who had given it to me, another prisoner grabbed it from me and nearly broke my arm, to boot.

Eventually, the SS loaded us into the freight cars. I had been in cattle cars on the way to the ghetto and to Auschwitz-Birkenau. Those rides were unspeakably horrific, only to be surpassed by the horror of this ride. The Germans were packing us into the railcars like sardines. They packed us in as if they were using a loading shovel to push this mass of humanity into the cars. They just couldn't put enough of us in; they actually threw in bodies by swinging them by their hands and feet and flinging them over people that were already in. Many died in the cars and when they did, the others stacked them up in order to gain a little space. By the time we arrived at our destination, which was Mauthausen in Austria, we had plenty of room.

On the way to Mauthausen, I experienced two significant events that are forever embedded in my memory. One of them occurred as the train from Gleiwitz went through Czechoslovakia, en route to Mauthausen that is in Austria. The border between Poland and Czechoslovakia is a mountain pass. The twin city of Cieszyn straddles the border. On the Polish side, the town is called Cieszyn while on the Czech side it is called Český Těšín. Prior to crossing the border into Czechoslovakia, the Germans unloaded some of the prisoners from the closed cattle cars and put them into open freight cars and the tops of the closed cars were painted with the insignia of the International Red Cross, thereby identifying the train as a prisoner transport. Every third or fourth car of our train was open. Our train then proceeded to cross the border into Český Těšín in Czechoslovakia. The train station there was very large with many sidetracks for trains waiting for clearance upon leaving or entering Czechoslovakia. Our prisoner train was standing on one of the sidetracks second nearest to the town, adjacent to a large clearing. We waited for the better part of the day for a German military train loaded with war materials and military personnel destined for the front. Our train was to proceed side-by-side with the German military train, thereby providing the military train with cover. Once again, we were human shields for the German military. We were used as their protection against attack and strafing by the Allies. This was the usual modus operandi of the German Army. It had been many days since we had received any ration of food or water.

Our train had pulled into Český Těšín after midnight. In the morning, the Czech population of the town came to the station to demonstrate against the Nazis, bringing with them part of their meager rations, which they hoped to give us. The crowd consisted of mostly women, older folks and children. The SS guards prevented them from coming near the trains, causing the demonstration to spin out of control and become a riot. The commotion drew additional folks to the station. Although I was in a closed cattle car, I could clearly see what was taking place from the small barred window, which I had reached by standing on a pile of dead bodies that were placed near the window to air. The demonstrators were throwing potatoes, sugar cubes, vegetables and pieces of bread towards the trains. The prisoners in open cars were able to get most that reached and fell into their cars, even though German guards shot at anyone who stood up to catch anything thrown. One single packet tied in a handkerchief hit my window and I managed to grasp it. The packet contained sugar cubes and a piece of dried bread.

The rioters were screaming and crying as they rushed the barricades that separated them from our train. At first, the Nazis began to club them with their rifle butts and then set their dogs on them. Although the dogs eagerly complied by viciously attacking and biting the demonstrators, no amount of physical pain deterred the women from getting as close to the trains as they could, so that a few more packets of food could reach us prisoners. As the rioters broke through the cordon of guards, the SS started to shoot, first at the women's feet and then to kill. The demonstrators were hysterical; they threw themselves body and soul upon our train, just to throw another something. They did not have much, but they shared it with us. They were throwing toward us their clothing from their backs, ignoring the fact that it landed just a few feet ahead. The ground was littered with packets of sugar, walnuts, candy, socks, hats, gloves and scarves.

As the women came within shouting distance of our cars, they shouted questions and encouragements. "Where are you from? Hold out — don't give up! God will help you, you will survive!" It was an unbelievable experience. We were swept up by their encouragement. I felt my soul rising in my chest, which was expanding with hope. My racing heart was audibly beating with excitement and my pulse was beating in my temples. I felt faint to the extent that I had to sit down; otherwise, I felt that I might fall. My excitement culminated in a headache that I had not experienced before, or have ever experienced since. I lost my place at the window, but was still able to follow the action by listening.

The Czech women were wonderful. I had the feeling that this was not an isolated incident. I was born in democratic Czechoslovakia and felt proud of the Czech population. As Jews, the Czechs never gave us a day's grief. Our trouble started in 1939 when, following the Munich Conference, the Czechs left our town and the Hungarians came in.

By noontime, the long-awaited military train arrived, consisting of seemingly endless flatcars loaded with heavy armaments and covered with tarpaulins and camouflage. Many hundreds of soldiers occupied every possible space on the train that included open boxcars. It pulled in parallel to our train on the town side, thereby separating us from the town's people. Since there was now no way for the demonstrators to reach us or even see us, it effectively ended the riot. By the sound of things, the crowd was dispersed and kept away from the vicinity of the station. The proximity of the two trains was so close that one could imagine outstretched hands touching each other.

During the early afternoon, while we were still at the station, parallel to the military train, we heard a sound that was like rolling thunder approaching. Within a minute the sound and its origin was upon us. It is hard to imagine that man and/or machine can create sounds of this magnitude. It was the roar of a squadron of fighter planes that inflicted our ears. The noise might have been equal in magnitude to what I experienced during the air attack while marching, but this time it was amplified exponentially by the drum-like closed boxcar that we were now in. The Russian planes attacked the German military train with machine gun fire and this time with rocket fire as well. They strafed, bombing the Germans indiscriminately. The explosions created by the rockets sounded like thunderclaps. There would be a burst of flames when the bombs hit their targets, followed by the sound of exploding ordnance. Once again, just like when we were on the road with the retreating German Army, the fact that a prisoner train was in direct proximity did not deter the Russian Air Force from attacking the German armament train. It was carnage of biblical magnitude.

Standing once again by the barbed window of my closed freight car, I could see German soldiers running from the camouflage tarpaulins that they were under and jumping out of their closed personnel cars. They were running for cover under our cars for what they perceived was safety, but to no avail. They were scattering like rodents as they were being shot, maimed and killed. I saw the brave among them standing in their open armament flat cars, attempting to shoot at the planes, for which they inevitably paid with their lives. They were shot or killed by rocket fire or the secondary explosions. Soldiers were running like surprised rats with some of them being blown to pieces by the explosions. It dawned on me that the "master race" bleeds and dies just like we do; it was not a totally unpleasant revelation.

The raids gave me a hysterical euphoria of enjoyment that I was able to recall and relive whenever my faith, hope and belief in my eventual liberation needed a boost. I was crazed by the noise and the carnage that I saw. I wanted to get out of the car and be part of the action. I shouted encouragements and cheered on "my friends," the Russian pilots. I felt that "my friends" were doing the job for me. The possibility that I too might get killed in this Armageddon did not enter my mind. Oh sure, our car was strafed and some of us were killed. The roof of my car at the end, furthest from me, looked like a sieve made of bullet holes. Among us, the prisoners who were in the open cars suffered most of the casualties. Some of the cars were totally destroyed. I suppose that towards the end of the raid it was hard for the Russians to distinguish between the trains. Somehow our casualties just didn't matter to us; we took solace in the carnage inflicted on the Nazi troops and war material in the belief that this would hasten our redemption and thereby shorten our suffering.

When the raid ended, the Germans made haste to get the trains going. At sunset, under the cover of darkness, the trains pulled out, rolling side-by-side, parallel to each other. By that point, we were not aware of the passing of time. Hunger, thirst and the dying of the wounded totally engulfed our attention and awareness. The ride seemed to take forever.

Sometime in the morning, the trains parted ways and we wound up in the Austrian town of Mauthausen, which is near Hitler's birthplace, the city of Linz. We were marched from the rail station to waiting trucks that took us to the Mauthausen Concentration Camp. The camp, originally built as a prison, was situated on a large hill. The entire top of the hill was surrounded by enormous stone walls. On one side of the hill was the infamous stone quarry.

MAUTHAUSEN

We entered Mauthausen Concentration Camp through enormously high and large gates, which closed behind us with a thud that seemed to say, "You are entombed." We were in the *Sammelplatz* (assembly point), which was relatively narrow and surrounded by high stone walls. Standing on top of one wall that was level with the camp's barracks was the camp commandant. He was looking down and watching us with a jaundiced eye, examining his new victims. After being put through various roll calls, we were marched up a series of steps to the level of the camp. On our way, we passed multiple rows of well-built barracks. Our destination was the tent camp designated for the inmate "overflow" that was situated in a field on a higher plateau of the hill. The area consisted of large, mostly open tents that had been put up in a hurry to house the newcomers. Mauthausen was never intended to hold so many people, but it became designated as one of the recipients of the evacuated eastern camps. I was lucky that I was assigned to one of the few barracks situated on the edge of the tent camp. We had a German sub-kapo, who was marked as a criminal by his green triangle insignia. The head kapo, nicknamed the "Barber," was a German homosexual exhibitionist who preyed on some of the younger men in the barrack. I was wise to him and avoided any possibility of an encounter.

Relatively few men from the Death March were taken to Mauthausen. I believe most were dispersed and scattered in many different camps (Bergen-Belsen, Buchenwald, Gross-Rosen, Dachau and Ravensbrük, among others). The tent camp in Mauthausen was a very busy place with transports arriving daily. One transport contained a group of Hungarian Jews from slave labor camps. We envied them, because they had possessions and civilian clothing.

They were brought to Mauthausen and other western camps because their slave labor camps had been overrun by the Russian Army. They were generally younger, stronger and in relatively good health. They stuck together and organized themselves to protect their belongings from frequent raids by other prisoners. They called us in Hungarian the "*Csikosok*," the striped ones, on account of the striped prisoner's uniforms we wore; we were the seasoned Auschwitz-Birkenau, well-experienced prisoners. They sat in a circle facing outwards, with their belongings inside the circle. The "Stripers," who were mostly Polish Jews (I was a remnant — an oddity being a child and having survived the selections of the Hungarian Jews), soon organized themselves into raiding parties — while one group engaged the Hungarians in a fight; another group attacked the inner circle and grabbed whatever of their possessions they could. I did not reveal to the Hungarians the fact that I spoke Hungarian and therefore was able to understand them when they discussed their defense strategy. My information became a valuable commodity to my "friends," giving me certain advantages in my relationship with the "raiders," which was, alas, short-lived. My advantage ended when the Hungarians got wise to the "little runt" who was always hanging out near them and was the recipient of small handouts.

Prisoners of various nationalities who were not placed in assigned tents or barracks grouped themselves together. There were Hungarian, Dutch, Greek and other groups of different nationalities, among whom were some Christians. Each national group stuck together for security reasons. All of them were recent arrivals from forced labor camps or ghettos, or had been recent deportees from their native lands. They had in common the fact that they all wore civilian clothing, had some possessions and were new to concentration camp life. In our barrack, we had a diverse ethnic mix of Jews from Poland, Hungary, the Balkans and Holland as well as Christian Poles and Ukrainians, among others. Men with different cultures, backgrounds and religions were thrown together. We were all compatriots in our misery.

My barrack was situated on the edge of the *Feldlager* (encampment) with the tents, and had no bunks of any kind. We sat and slept on the wooden floor. One-quarter of the barrack, which was reserved for the kapo and the Barber, was furnished with two beds with nightstands, a small table and a washstand with a basin and a pitcher. The Barber exhibited himself daily by placing the washstand up front and ritually washing and flailing his penis in front of his "audience." While some laughed at this exhibition, it appalled and disgusted me. One other boy in the barrack, I believe a little older than me, was taken by the Barber every night. The boy would cry all day.

From the kapo's statements and actions, one could gather that he had complete disdain for the Nazis. At every opportunity, he would argue and eventually insult the guards. His favorite name for them was "*Scheisskopf*" (shithead). He also demonstrated his lack of love for us by being harsh and demanding. He had a deep slash on his forehead that ran from the hairline above his left eye to the bridge of his nose, and a deep slash on his left cheek from his ear to his mouth. Some prisoners among us said that these were fraternity marks of German universities. Whenever I saw his face or heard his voice, the thought that I would survive him crossed my mind and I actually caught myself saying it out loud. As kapos go, he was no worse and in many ways better than others. He was, however, the most German-looking and German-sounding man I had ever come across. I found that that alone was a reason enough to despise him.

One of the Dutch Jews kept singing a Hebrew-Yiddish song he had composed based on the prayer *Av Harachamim* (Father of Mercy). He sang it with a lamenting melody, while sitting on the floor and moving in a trance-like back-and-forth rocking motion. He sang a stanza of the original prayer in Hebrew followed by a rhyming stanza of Yiddish that he composed. This deeply moving song begged God for mercy and a speedy delivery from our tormentors. He pleaded with the Almighty to remember us for the merit of His servants, our Fathers, Abraham, Isaac and Jacob. He pleaded with our Creator to remember us for their sake and the innocent suffering orphans. Today, I unfortunately only recall one verse of the song. He sang the original first Hebrew verse, "*Av harachamim shochen miromim*" (Father of mercy who dwells in Heaven) and then rhymed "*Du bist der tata fin ale yisomim*" (You are the Father of all the orphans). Back and forth he went, alternating between the original and a rhyming commentary. I can hear the begging words beseeching Our Father in Heaven for mercy, as an appeal to the court of last resort. All those who heard and understood him were moved to tears. Some were swept up in a religious fervor that lightened their hearts. I too was moved to tears, but, unfortunately, to tears of sadness and despair. However, mercifully, I became distracted by the mesmerizing patterns on the barracks' windows etched by the winter frost and illuminated by the setting sun. Looking through some clear spots in the frost, I could see neighboring barracks encircled by icicles hanging from their low roofs that were enveloped in brilliant white snow. Yes, I thought, just like at home. The thought eased my despair. Unfortunately, the Barber did not appreciate the Dutch Jew's chanting. When the chanting did not stop, the Barber clubbed the Jew to death. His blood splattered all over me. Today, when I say this prayer each Sabbath, I get shudders running up and down my spine.

The tent camp became notorious for being lice-infested. We soon learned that any object of clothing that we "acquired" from the others was teeming with lice, so much so that it came to the attention of the camp authorities. Fearing an outbreak of typhus, they instituted a crash remedy spanning three consecutive days of delousing, which was presided over by the Barber. Everyone had to undress and search his clothing for lice. Being informed by a doctor among us of the dire consequences of disease-bearing lice, I became very proficient at the "search and destroy mission" I set for myself. I searched my clothing systematically, especially in the crevices and folds, where I learned from experience that that is where lice hide. When I found some, which was often, I squashed their hard shells between my thumbnails.

There were no systematic exterminations taking place in Mauthausen, but there were sporadic killings at the "execution wall." It had iron rings attached to the stones to which prisoners were tied before being shot and the wall was pockmarked with bullet holes. I gather that prior to our arrival, there were many German prisoners who were classified as traitors and executed at this wall. Our fate was essentially slow death from hunger, thirst and disease. Mauthausen had a gas chamber, disguised as showers, with a capacity of perhaps fifty and a crematorium that was double ended with a capacity of only two bodies at a time. It wasn't a *Vernichtungslager*, a mass killing exterminating camp. Nevertheless, infamous atrocities were committed there. Some days, sometimes twice a day, a group of ten to twenty prisoners were marched out of the camp. Approximately half an hour later, shots were heard from the direction of an empty field. None of these prisoners ever came back.

In Mauthausen, there were many days when rations were skipped. Even in Birkenau there was soup that was dispensed from garbage cans. In Mauthausen, there was no systematic feeding. Rather, once in a while, perhaps every second or third day, we would be made to line up for a piece of bread and margarine. One never knew when or if there would ever be any more bread. Therefore, I rationed myself by eating just pinches of it, thereby making the bread last as long as I could. I had a shirt that was down to my knees and I tied my bread into it. It made a security pack that I kept dangling between my legs. I was able to untie just a part of my parcel, which allowed me to pinch off a few morsels without exposing my whole ration to the risk of being stolen. When I slept, I also kept it between my legs.

Hunger was so intense that prisoners would attack each other for a bite of bread. I witnessed once, and only once, cannibalism in Mauthausen. I saw two inmates cut a piece of flesh from a dead person with the sharp edge of a stone and eat it. Other fellow prisoners who witnessed this episode pounced on them. One of those who participated was dead within two hours. He was dying of hunger and this was a desperate, terrible and, perhaps, unconscious deed. Seeing this, I fell on my knees and threw up so violently that I had a bellyache for days. In the following weeks I threw up just at the thought of it. There seemed to be no limit to how low a man could sink in desperation. I shall not elaborate further on this subject.

Another day, I saw one young man, who was perhaps twenty years old, being caught stealing bread from the man sitting next to him. The man whose bread was stolen started a commotion and fell upon the thief, wrestling his bread back from him. The young thief was warned by his intended victim that if he ever attempted thievery again, there would be dire consequences. There was no next time. Within the hour, the young man who was still sitting propped up against the tent, fell over onto his side and with terrible gurgling noises coming from his mouth, simply died. It turned out that he had been too weak to stand in line for his ration. His action had been a last, desperate act to survive. That was not my first time to notice that big, strong men had a lower tolerance to hunger than smaller, thinner and weaker men. I saw this in the ghetto, in Birkenau and witnessed it there in Mauthausen, and later in the Gunskirchen camp as well.

What made a greater, lasting impression on me as a child was when I saw a son ripping bread out of his own father's mouth. The father was so weak that he could not resist, and was dead by nightfall. I could not get over this callous act. The question of how anybody could do anything bad to his father kept reverberating in my head. The answer perhaps was that many prisoners by that time were dehumanized. In my ears, rang the words of one of my father's three commands, "Be a *mensch* [a person of integrity] and don't let them make an animal out of you."

I did everything possible to live up to my father's instructions, including his expectation that I would meet the family back home. I had trust, belief and hope that I would go home, if for no other reason than because my father had told me to do so.

The barrack that contained the latrines and washbasins with running water was situated on top of the hill, of all places. There, in that barrack, I saw bars of soap with the initials "RJF" pressed on them. The rumors were that it stood for "*Reines jüdisches Fett*," pure Jewish fat.[13] From the high point of the latrine barrack, I could look over the prison wall and see the town of Mauthausen below. I could see women pushing baby carriages, enjoying a stroll on a warm and sunny early spring day in late March. My spirits were decimated by the contrast to my situation. But it did help me realize that there was still life, a mother and a child, in this bleak, cruel world. I liked the advantage of being on the hill and overlooking the wall. I found a spot of solitude out of direct sight of the guards. There, I watched the sky and daydreamed of home.

One morning, someone said it was Friday and therefore that night would be the Sabbath. I was overtaken by envy and a queasy feeling of homesickness that was soon replaced by a vision of home. I thought, "What would I be doing right now if I were home? The whole family would be getting ready for the Sabbath. ...'Andi! Let's go, we will be late.' Papa would be standing in the doorway with my brother, Tibi. 'Why are you always late? Matu, could you please get your son out? We will be late for the Sabbath prayer.' Our father would not think of foregoing the pleasure of going to the synagogue without both of his sons."

---

13 Jews read the initials as "RJF" and interpreted them to mean "*Reines Jüdisches Fett*" (pure Jewish fat), and the rumor that the soap was indeed made from human fat was widespread. However, the rumor was incorrect. The acronym was actually "RIF" and signified "*Reichsstelle fuer industrielle Fette*" (the Reich Department of Industrial Fats).

Looking up at the brilliant sky with a few white clouds floating around, I could clearly see the scene of the Sabbath table at home: My mother is ushering in the Sabbath by lighting the Sabbath candles, the glow of which gives her an angelic look, and a taste of heaven to the entire home. At the opposite end of the Sabbath table are the two freshly baked Sabbath *challot* (braided loaves). At the head of the table is our papa's silver Sabbath goblet for the benediction that precedes the meal. We are dressed in our finest Sabbath clothing. We kiss Mother, wish her a good Sabbath and leave for the Sabbath eve services at the synagogue next door.

I found myself crying with tears running down my cheeks. Looking around, I saw the reality that surrounded me. I thought, "Where is my family? Is it true what the kapo told me when we arrived in Auschwitz — that my mama went to heaven through the flames that rose from the chimney of the crematoria? Is that what the SS referred to as '*Himmelmensch*?' [Sky Person]. Are Papa and Tibi alive? If they are, do they know that I am alive? Where is Grandfather? How and when will I get home?" I decided then that my ultimate priority was to do everything I could to survive. Surely my loved ones were doing everything they could, and soon I would know what to do next in order to go home and be together with them once again.

On another day, while overlooking the wall, I saw a woman, a mother, running after two boisterous children. As I began to enjoy the sight, I noticed on the horizon little silver birds approaching. As they came a little closer, I realized that they were planes flying in groups like migrating birds. I was hoping that they were on their way to do what I had heard the sub-kapo of our barrack saying to the Barber — that the Americans were bombing German cities by day and the English were bombing them by night. My hopes were confirmed when I heard some guards talking to each other, saying, "I wonder which of our cities will be destroyed?" From then on, seeing the "silver birds" brought joy to my heart. I began to count them and compared the count when they returned. It saddened me when there were fewer returning. Sometimes on their return trip, after the main groups of planes had passed overhead, one or more planes came a few minutes later. Such an event provided us with a sad spectacle in the sky, as German fighters attacked and usually shot them down. Many times the stragglers were able to fight off the fighters, and even to our great joy, shoot some of the fighters down, only to be shot down by the anti-aircraft batteries. The Germans had installed anti-aircraft gun batteries inside the camp and were shooting at the planes almost straight up, so that hot pieces of jagged, blue-steel shrapnel came raining down on us like hailstones. One such piece wounded me in the groin. Once in a while, a German fighter plane or one of the anti-aircraft batteries managed to shoot down one of the "stragglers" and a descending parachute could be seen clearly. Despite the Geneva convention, I saw parachutists being shot at as they were descending. I saw the body of one parachutist swinging wildly as he was hit. I pitied and cried for the American airmen who were killed and did not envy those who made it down. None of them landed in the camp.

During the last week of March, we heard rumors that to ease the overcrowding, some prisoners were being transferred to other camps. Over time, there was also less and less resistance and pursuit from the German Luftwaffe in the sky. The little silver birds seemed to have the whole sky to themselves and seemed immune to the anti-aircraft shells that could not reach their height. I remember admiring the American planes with two tails that flew over us and made a white circular mark, like skywriters, over the camp. This way, the returning wounded stragglers knew to avoid flying over us and thereby avoid the heavy anti-aircraft fire from our camp. We looked forward to seeing the white circle over us, knowing that it meant that Allied planes would soon be returning from their strike in the Nazi heartland. They delighted my heart and I considered them as God's revenge against the bestial Nazis for what they were doing to His people.

Just outside the rear gate of the plateau upon which was the Mauthausen camp was a clearing, which culminated in a sheer cliff of an infamous stone quarry. At the edge of the cliff, a derrick crane was used when the quarry was in commercial operation, to raise the quarried stones to the top. The crane was now equipped with a cable that had a noose at the bottom to accommodate an SS guard who stood with a foot in the noose, and held onto the cable with one hand while brandishing a long stick with the other. He had a machine gun slung over his neck. The manipulation of the crane operator, another SS man, allowed the guard to reach any height or part of the quarry. There were steps cut into the stone that allowed one to descend into or to reach the top of the quarry. This quarry was the scene of horrific atrocities. Although I did not witness this myself, I was told by the other prisoners about the common occurrence of the guards assembling a group of prisoners at the rear gate, perhaps twenty-five or thirty of them, lining them up five across and then marching them off toward the sheer cliff with a precise military drill. The group was force-marched right over the edge of the cliff to their deaths. This was simply a form of execution. At the bottom of the quarry I personally saw mounds of broken, dead bodies, which other prisoners were forced to remove by carrying the corpses up the steep, stone steps. Judging from the laughter of the SS, this atrocity was considered a fun thing to do. It was performed at the command and for the entertainment of the commandant who enjoyed a hardy belly laugh every time he witnessed it, only to be outdone by an atrocity that he himself performed.

The stone quarry was also the scene of deliberate torture and the degrading of the human soul. I was a potential victim of one of these forms of torture. I gather it was a modus operandi at the quarry. Our work detail was ordered to descend using the steps to the bottom of the quarry. The steps were so narrow and steep that often one man would fall and wipe out the entire row of men in front of him. We were commanded to carry the stones from the bottom of the pit to the top. I, for one, could not possibly have walked up the steep steps carrying a rock, even a small one. It was out of the question, even though my life depended on it. I, therefore, made use of a trick I learned on other work details, whereby I could avoid the attention of the guards by making myself look busy. There was so much action for the guard on the cable supervising the steps and the two guards at the bottom of the pit, that they had their hands full and did not notice that some of their victims were not playing their game. If I was unable to elude their attention, it would have undoubtedly meant my death on the steps. Certainly, being the smallest and the youngest in the group contributed to my survival. Many a stone was dropped on the way up and, once again, it would wipe out a line of prisoners laboring on the steps below. After this great sacrifice and effort, the stones that did make it to the top were then immediately kicked over the edge of the cliff by the guards, once again, killing or injuring the poor wretches below. Clearly, there was no other purpose to this exercise other than death by torture. The guards were laughing; they called out to each other, "Look at this!" as they kicked one poor victim off his feet as he approached the top. It was a game, a thrill, and they enjoyed it.

One particular atrocity that I witnessed was perpetrated by the camp commandant himself, despite (of course) the Geneva Convention. The commandant came to the edge of the quarry cliff with a bottle of champagne and two glasses. He was accompanied by an Allied officer prisoner of war who was cleaned up for the occasion. The commandant filled the glasses with champagne and handed one to the Allied officer. He then proceeded to toast and congratulate the prisoner for his impending victory. The commandant followed that up with a salute and then, with a little encouragement, they both drank the toast. At the conclusion of this ritual, the commandant clicked his heels, raised his hand in the Nazi salute, and shouted "Heil Hitler," as he kicked the Allied officer over the cliff to his death. The commandant then drank another glass of champagne, threw his glass down the cliff and triumphantly went back to his den.

It is hard to imagine that all of these atrocities continued even to the last day of our stay in Mauthausen, up to the first week of April 1945, five weeks before Germany surrendered.

GUNSKIRCHEN

Early on a rainy Sunday morning in April, about 450 of us were selected for transport at roll call and marched down the steps to the *Sammelplatz*, the assembly point, which was surrounded by the highest walls of the camp. It was the area just inside the enormous camp gates, the place where we had first arrived in Mauthausen. The massive walls still intimidated me and emphasized the reality of my captivity. Some of those among us created a panic by saying that we had been selected for the purpose of being executed, while others reasoned that they had no reason to take us out, when they could shoot us in the field on the other side of the camp, or by the execution wall. This reasoning had a calming effect on us. My emotions and my level of fear rose and fell with every utterance within earshot or glimpse of a new development. I was deeply troubled by the thought that, although I had come this far, I might not go home to my parents and brother after all. After an excruciating wait, which afforded us the time to oscillate between different levels of panic, the camp gates opened and two large trucks entered and were positioned on each side of the gate.

One of the commanders said to an officer, "It's 10 o'clock, let's get moving, out with this filth!" We were ordered to march out of the camp. On our way out, as we passed between the trucks, we were given a ration of half a small bread loaf and one-third of a stick of margarine. This receipt of rations lifted our spirits, foremost of course, because of the food, but in addition it gave us a psychological peg to hang our hopes on. The optimists were saying that if they were going to kill us, they wouldn't be feeding us. And so we marched down the hill to the town of Mauthausen.

We were marched five abreast, through the streets of the town. An SS staff car preceded the convoy, and armored vehicles with SS personnel followed the procession, while SS staff cars drove up and down the length of the convoy. Armed soldier guards marched on either side of us. The first street we marched through was the very street I had looked at from the latrine on the hill. The townspeople we encountered gave us furtive glances and stayed at a safe distance. Most of them made not the slightest attempt to express their pity and certainly, none of them attempted to give us anything. A few, however, threw a few well-chosen epithets at us, such as "*verdammte Juden*" (damned Jews), and some women spat at us and then followed it up with a string of curses.

The guards did not forcefully discourage either action — neither the name-calling, nor the spitting. Nevertheless, the behavior of the guards was remarkably subdued in the presence of the townspeople, an example of which can be illustrated by their action following an escape incident. As we passed a particularly narrow street that was relatively full of spectators, mostly women and children, four inmates broke ranks and ran into the crowd. Two of them wore civilian clothes, which gave them a distinct advantage; the other two wore striped camp uniforms. As some of the guards took off to retrieve the escapees, the other guards were shouting at each other to tighten up our ranks. Moments later, the escapees with their hands up and at bayonet point were escorted back into our ranks. The retrieval by the guards of the escapees was facilitated by the anxious cooperation of the "spectators," who were most cooperative in pointing out the buildings and hallways in which they hid. We were astonished to see that the escapees were not punished; all that happened to them was that they were caught and returned. Some inmates made repeated unsuccessful attempts to escape, all without punishment. Normally, in situations like this, they would have been summarily shot. I assume that it was because we were in town and in front of witnesses that the SS behaved in an uncharacteristic manner.

It was quite a show and we must have delighted the crowd. It wasn't every day that the good citizens of Mauthausen got to see the cream of the Third Reich at work, herding dangerous criminals disguised as walking corpses. Wretched prisoners being marched through the town with their ghastly corpse-like fingers curled around a piece of bread and a small cube of margarine. The crowd scrutinized us with easily surmised thoughts, "I can't believe we feed these people...yeah...and look at our debonair SS...isn't it a shame that they have to waste their time with this filth and get their beautiful uniforms wet in the rain doing it? Look at our boys...aren't they great? They are doing a yeoman's job keeping these dangerous enemies of the State at bay.... If it weren't for the SS, these bloodsuckers would devour us.... Just look at them...look at their faces...you can see that they are dangerous and filthy villains.... The Fuehrer is right...they are the dregs of the earth.... We must erase them...we must be vigilant...none of us can sleep as long as they are around.... I am lucky that my Greta is in the army servicing the soldiers and thereby propagating the master race, otherwise, these wretches would certainly cast their evil spell on her.... I am sure that our son Hans is doing just as an important job in the Luftwaffe.... I haven't heard from Hans since he wrote that he would single-handedly capture England and slit Churchill's throat...I am sure that his father is doing no less to Stalin...let me get closer so that I can spit at and curse them..."

The spectacle was over soon enough, as we left the town and were marching into the countryside. It was a warm spring day, the rain stopped and the sun began to shine, which in turn made our rags steam. The guards became appreciably harsher; no one would dare to escape. Escape? Escape to where? What would be the purpose? Where are we going? As the rain clouds were driven away by the wind, patches of beautiful blue sky replaced them. The smell of the steaming earth and grass, once again, turned my mind towards home. I became terribly homesick and yearned for my mother. I found refuge in my thoughts of home:

...It is Sabbath morning; Mama is preparing Tibi and me for the synagogue. We quickly eat a small, hurried breakfast and are off with Papa. The synagogue has the mellow smell of age-old oiled mahogany mixed with the savory sweet smell acquired from the burning of beeswax candles. Papa takes his seat, which is situated in front of the synagogue facing the Ark and I sit on his knee as we solemnly join the congregation in prayer.

Trucks with wood- or coal-burning stoves attached to their sides are passing us. Someone said that these stoves provide the fuel for the trucks; gas must be a military priority. One of the drivers spits at us and another curses us as he passes. I know that they are losing the war; I just can't figure out how the war was my fault to begin with and how it is my fault that they are losing it. I think, "What is it that I have done to turn their fortune? If I only knew, I would do some more."

...It is December 1943, it is my *Bar Mitzvah*. I'm being called up to make the opening and closing prayer for the reading of the weekly portion of the Torah, followed by my reading of the *Haftorah*, after which I gain the honor of being declared a man.

...We are walking home from the synagogue. Our entire family, as well as our revered rabbi, are coming to our house for a festive celebratory lunch. The meal is elaborate as usual. The rabbi's eloquent speech followed by that of Grandfather and Papa amplify the solemnity of the occasion. The congratulations are followed by benedictions and well wishes. I know that I will be receiving my gifts the following day in respect for the sanctity of the Sabbath. Alas, as I look around the festive table in order to commit it to my memory, tears come to my eyes as I see that there is an ominous cloud over us. The festivities are visibly marred by the display of the shameful, degrading yellow star and what it stands for on everybody's breast, including mine. Only my brother, Tibi, seems to reflect the joy of the day. The joy of the day is forced and accompanied by the attitude of "let's make the best of it; let's not *farshter* the *Simcha* [disturb the festivity]..."

At this point, my thoughts were interrupted by the jolt of realization that I was there marching, and to who knew where. Tears were running down my cheeks and my fellow prisoner next to me was concerned. I was sobbing uncontrollably with the thought of how I was robbed of the joy of my *Bar Mitzvah* and of being a man. I cannot overemphasize the impact my *Bar Mitzvah* had on me; it was to be the highlight of my life, the greatest thing that happened to me up to that time. Alas, it was not what I had hoped for.

While reminiscing, I must have stepped or stumbled out of line as an abrupt, forceful shove scared me out of my daydream. I almost yelled out, "Mama! Papa! Where are you? Where am I? Why am I alone?" We were still walking, and judging by the sun, it was probably late in the afternoon.

The blisters on my feet had burst and they were now killing me. Each step was pure agony. Everyone was complaining of thirst. My lips were parched and my tongue was swelling in my mouth. By dusk, we were mercifully being herded into a field for the purpose of relieving ourselves. It was not a pretty scene. We rushed, as within minutes we were expecting to be ordered back on the road to resume our march. However, instead, we were ordered to sit down and were told we would be staying there for the night. We all wondered, "Where are we going that takes overnight?" No one knew, but everyone seemed to have an opinion.

The grass felt like the grass at home. The earth smelled wonderful. I looked for some berries or at least some edible grass but could not find any. Nevertheless, I found a thick patch of grass and put my head down on it. The sky was clear and I imagined it to be a star-studded blanket. I could make out the Big Dipper and the Little Dipper. I lined up the Big Dipper's two vertical stars and found the North Star. It was the same star I used to look at back at home. The moon, too, looked familiar. While thinking, "If I could only catch a ride on them and go home," I fell asleep.

At the crack of dawn, we were ordered to stand five abreast for roll call on the road, following which the command to march was given. After two or three hours, my feet were raw and bleeding. My wooden shoes were not a matching pair nor were they of the same color, style or size. They had stripped the skin off my heels. I decided to remove my shoes and tuck them halfway into my pants. After an hour of being barefoot my feet were throbbing with pain and my ankles felt broken. I was sure that my feet had become infected, and the notion entered my mind — and scared me — that they would need to be cut off. Once again, I relied on a form of self-hypnosis. I told myself, "No! I will not lose my feet! I will not die! Look, my feet no longer hurt me! You see, I can press, scratch and twist the toes…I don't feel anything…. What bleeding feet? These feet are not mine. My feet are all right, nothing is wrong with them. Look! I'm walking and they do not hurt me." I, again, discovered that I was able to separate myself from the reality of my painful feet to such an extent that they really did not hurt, or at least I did not feel the pain. Although I was able to will the pain away by this method of self-hypnosis, in reality, my feet became dark purple and swollen.

The second day of the march was quickly coming to a close. Once again, we were ordered to march off the road into the fields for the night. My exhaustion was so great that I ignored the stench of human waste that was all around me. I could hardly eat my last few morsels of bread and a few licks of margarine before I involuntarily collapsed and fell sleep. Once again, we were ordered to resume our march very early in the morning. By the early afternoon, we noticed that the front of our column was turning right into the woods. No one around me knew what time it was, but it seemed that there were approximately two hours before sunset. The SS stopped the march and ordered us to tidy up the lines for roll call. We stood there on the road for at least two hours. Thoughts ran through my head, "Why the march? Why haven't we been trucked? There is something fishy! It just does not make sense. Unless, maybe we were destined to go somewhere near, perhaps for forced slave labor in a field or a factory or somewhere, and the German staff car that encountered us changed our destination and we are marching on new orders. If so, is that good? Why are we stopping here? What are we waiting for? What is going on in the woods? The first group went in, and we haven't heard any shots fired, that's good."

We resumed the march and then turned off to the right onto a muddy road leading into very dense woods. Dense forsaken woods bode us great apprehension that escalated into acute anxiety with every step. The darkness was so intense that we could hardly see in front of us. The ruts in the mud were so deep and the mud itself was so sticky that it became peppered with stuck and abandoned shoes. The mud felt good to my bare feet but moving in the stickiness exhausted me. We had difficulty making headway, which brought on the ire of the guards, heightening our fear. Our panic was fed by those among us who knew or had heard about the killings in the woods of Treblinka and other infamous godforsaken places. Even the optimists among us, while still insisting that they could have killed us in Mauthausen, were gripped by fear of our imminent execution. The pessimism of the optimists, the men whom I looked up to and identified with, gripped me with an uncontrollable fear. I felt pain in my heart and I began to shiver and cry. I was unable to stop crying until some concerned "friends" convinced me that we would be safe. The fear continued until, mercifully, we arrived at a clearing and were ordered to stop. There, we saw prisoners milling around. A guard told another that it was 10 o'clock; we had been on the road for three whole days, including the waiting time. We had marched nearly sixty kilometers.

The camp was in Gunskirchen, one of the satellite camps of Mauthausen, near the large Austrian city of Linz, and was primarily an SS Panzer (tank) group encampment. We were hostages, once again; only this time we were joining those who were being used as shields to protect the Panzer group from Allied air attacks. The camp consisted of a collection of large, green barracks, which were to be our "homes." They were more like sheds, with wide barn-type doors. There were bare earth floors that had been chewed up by tank treads, creating deep, muddy ruts that were filled with rainwater. Prior to our arrival, these barracks had been used as sheds for the tanks. The air was perpetually humid and rancid from the lingering diesel fumes. The rafters were barn-type with beams running across and lesser beams supporting the roof. The barracks were situated in a half-moon fashion around a clearing; one of the barracks had a large red cross newly painted on its roof. There were no barbed wires or any walls surrounding the camp. The guards were in sentry booths within sight of each other and were armed with rifles and side arms. The camp's security was controlled by a simple rule that was prominently posted and broadcast twice daily on the loudspeaker and was soon demonstrated. The rule was: An escape attempt will be punished by death.

Over the loudspeakers, we were ordered to roll call. I stood barefoot while clutching my muddy wooden shoes to my chest. Before we were dismissed, we were given approximately six ounces of bread, half a stick of margarine and a quarter of a sugar beet. All these provisions were dispensed from a truck. Some parts of the barrack were uninhabitable because of the mud, while the drier parts were most desirable and highly congested. Once again, because I was one of the youngest, I was at the bottom of the totem pole when it came to occupying and preserving a choice place. Thus, I emulated some of the other prisoners in my predicament and joined them on the crossbeams of the rafters. Due to developing circumstances, this solution turned out to be a temporary one.

At sunset, we were herded into the barrack. Soon the earth shook and the ungodly roar of engines was heard, followed by the distinctive smell of kerosene. Within minutes, the source of the smell — a cloud of thick, choking, diesel exhaust fumes — permeated the whole clearing and penetrated our barrack. Those among us who were close to the road, saw through the cloud of smoke, black-painted tanks heading towards the main road. I personally only saw a few of the tanks, while others reported that there were many. Judging from their departure at sundown and return before dawn, it was determined that they were part of a night-raiding tank group. This was confirmed when we overheard the Panzer SS referring to their part of the camp as a "wolf's lair." During the following weeks, when I ventured to the edge of the camp, I could clearly follow the tank tracks and observe them leading to earthen bunkers dug into the ground. Their camouflage was so perfect that even a casual observer on the ground would have difficulty discerning their presence. Therefore, they were practically immune from air attacks. From the air it looked like a prison camp that included a hospital barrack. Not only was our barrack in the open, but during the day all prisoners had to remain in the clearing or in the sparsely wooded areas while the SS barrack was well hidden deeper in the woods.

At the far end of the clearing was a long trench that served as an open latrine. New trenches were dug and the old ones filled as required. The best way to know what was going on was to go on a work detail that would span the entire camp and perhaps even outside the camp. A work detail outside the camp consisted of shoring up the "lairs," the earth bunkers that the tanks were in and sanitation or maintenance work in the SS barrack. The sanitation work (i.e., collecting the dead) involved six prisoners and a horse with a harness that had a long iron chain attached to it. As was customary in garbage collection, those who died during the previous day and night had to be put outside the barrack for collection. The sanitation detail had S-hooks, like meat hooks, which were counted when issued and returned. A lost S-hook could cost you your life. One prisoner held the horse by the bridle, while the other five dragged the corpses to the chain. A corpse was then hooked and attached by means of the S-hook. In this manner, the bodies were dragged to the latrines, into which the bodies were then dumped. Some days, more than one round trip was necessary. Once, and only once, was I put on the morning sanitation detail. Mercifully, the others judged me as too young or incompetent for the work and I was therefore able to avoid hooking anybody or even having an S-hook in my hand. Nevertheless, regardless of the terrible toll on my conscience and my inability to suppress the sickness of my stomach, I did have to help with the dragging and dumping. I avoided any possibility of being part of this detail ever again and had a particular disdain for those who were part of it more than once. The experience became a lingering, harrowing experience. I began to have terrible hallucinations and bouts of bad conscience that I had never before experienced. The incident triggered in my mind other events that replayed on the inside of my closed eyelids like a horror movie on a screen; incidents that terrified me. At night, I would wake up in a pool of sweat, shivering uncontrollably. These bouts of horror lasted well past liberation and, to some extent, have remained to this day.

I embarked upon the task of inspecting and familiarizing myself with the outlay of the entire camp. I spent my time observing and studying the sentries in their boxes. I noted when and how they changed. I noticed that the sentries had clear sight of each other and I caught myself unconsciously searching for blind spots in the sentry system for the purpose of escaping; although I never attempted to do so, nor did I even come close to consciously consider escaping. I saw pillboxes with machine guns in them and overheard the conversations between guards, conversations concerning the status of the war, which they considered lost. They expected the surrender of Germany to be imminent. Within a few days, as others overheard and disseminated the news, the entire camp was buzzing with our impending liberation.

I am reluctant to recount one incident that took place in Gunskirchen and I tell it with caution as it is not complimentary to a popular nonprofit international institution. Nevertheless, I wish to emphasize the fact that the following is not something that I merely heard about or observed. Rather, I am recounting events in which I personally participated.

One day, the SS selected from the camp a group of approximately twenty prisoners. The SS officer saw me after his quota was filled and exchanged me for another prisoner, so I became part of the group that was hoisted onto a waiting truck. Our natural fears got the better of us until we clearly heard the SS officer remark to a guard, as he was pointing to me, "This child will make a good impression." I, of course, was the youngest in the group. We were driven to the SS compound, where we pulled up in front of a barrack, which was the SS washroom. There, we were ordered to strip and place our belongings into individual piles. I don't need to elaborate upon the condition of my "clothing." The reader can extrapolate its condition when I say that I was in the same striped "uniform," the same pieces of rope were holding up my pants and my feet were wrapped in the same rags that I came with from Birkenau and Mauthausen. I was in rags that were stiff with caked-on mud. We were given haircuts and the older men were shaved clean, after which we were ordered to wash up. We were then given clean clothing, including shirts and shoes! Back on the truck, we were taken to a clearing in the SS camp where we found another truckload of prisoners all clean and dressed, making us a group of approximately fifty.

At one end of the clearing were a few khaki-colored trucks. We quickly noticed that they were unlike the German military trucks. They were rather like large jeeps with red crosses prominently displayed and marked "Schweizerisches Internationales Rotes Kreuz," Swiss International Red Cross. The personnel were Swiss; there were approximately fifteen of them, including some women. They were all tall and blond and wore smart, semi-military, khaki-brown uniforms with Red Cross armbands and were accompanied by a group that was filming the entire scene. They spoke German as they bantered and jostled with a group of SS officers. They were joking, laughing and slapping each other on their backs like good friends do.

We were lined up in small groups as the Swiss set up additional movie cameras. I remember that the cameras were marked "Pathé," the well-regarded European producer of newsreels, with a rooster for a logo. They began to film us while the SS were in our midst shaking our hands and patting us on our backs. We were then lined up in single file and marched towards the Swiss trucks. As each one of us approached a truck, an SS man and an International Red Cross person took a package off the truck and handed it to us with one hand, while positioning us to face the cameras with the other hand. We were filmed and made to linger in the company of an SS officer and Red Cross representative for an appreciable time, while all three of us held onto the box as if it were a plaque given to us at a testimonial dinner. Then an SS officer alone was filmed handing me a package while he patted me on the head and hugged me. One of the female Red Cross representatives bent down to me and put her cheek to mine while she squeezed my shoulders. I remember the wonderful smell of her perfume and that her hair felt like silk. This realization made me instantaneously homesick for my mother. For reasons that suited their purpose, I was something of a celebrity. I was made to linger with them longer than the others. Then the woman called one of the SS officers by name, saying, "Let's go," and disappeared with him for the entire duration, returning at the end happy and singing. The packages that were all alike were boxes of approximately a foot square and were tightly wrapped in wax paper. The filming continued as we were marched off carrying the packages back to the trucks. Once on the truck, we tried to open the packages but to no avail; they were so tightly taped that we could not penetrate the wrappings. The short ride took us back to the SS wash barrack where we were ordered to get off the truck and leave the packages behind. We never saw the packages again, nor did we ever know what was in them.

This was my encounter with the International Red Cross. They never entered the prison camp that was just across the thick woods at the next clearing. All this took place in the SS military camp in front of the commandant's house with a manicured lawn. It was a charade, a propaganda stunt, a show and a farce at that. The Red Cross representatives all seemed to be buddies with the Germans. Surely the Germans made good use of the newsreel film that was witnessed, participated in and endorsed by the International Red Cross, showing the wonderful, jovial, benevolent SS and the well-cared-for political prisoners in their charge, wearing clean clothing. The child, namely me, must have been a real hit. I have no reason to believe that this was an isolated incident.

Late in April 1945, the camp commandant made an announcement over the loudspeakers, which was not an unusual occurrence. Frequently, just before an air raid, the commandant would order us out of our barrack into the clearing, to be visible to the Allied pilots, thereby preventing them from attacking the place. This time, however, the commandant announced that the war would soon be over, but we should not rejoice, because he said all of the barracks were mined. He assured us that there was no way we were going to survive and be liberated, and promised us that his last act would be to blow us all up. Although I was unquestionably sure that I would survive him, I took the commandant's words literally and did not spend another moment in the barrack. In order to have better control over us and prevent the possibility of escapees, the guards drove as many of us into the barrack as they could, especially for the night. It was like a leaking dam; some were driven in while others snuck out. Nevertheless, I, for one, managed not to spend any time in the barrack; I hung about outside during the day and slept outdoors wherever I could, usually behind the latrine where there was always some commotion.

The ethnic composition of the Gunskirchen camp consisted mostly of Hungarian Jews, with some Polish and Dutch. It mostly held prisoners who came through Mauthausen, like I did, or some other satellite camp. There were a few Christian Polish slave laborers who had either originally been there or had come from a nearby camp. The camp was way over its capacity and cramped. The temperament was intense; few of us knew each other.

In early May 1945, we were experiencing torrential rain that lasted for three days, during which the tanks did not leave the camp. Our camp clearing became a lake. The mud was so deep and sticky that it was difficult to negotiate. Not sleeping in the barrack took its toll on me. On the second day of the rain, I spent the night shivering from the wet and cold and became fearful of the thunderclaps and ominous streaks of lightning that were of an intensity that I had last experienced at home, well tucked into bed or held in Mother's arms. It stopped raining on the morning of the third day. As I approached the latrine, I noticed that the sentry box was empty. I did not know what to make of it. I decided to check on some other sentry stations. As I approached the next sentry box, I saw the sentry take off his uniform and throw down his rifle; he then proceeded to run towards me into the camp. I ran back excitedly to report, to no one in particular, what I had seen. I discovered that my news was no longer news, as everyone was yelling, "The guards are running away." Some yelled, "Don't go near the barracks, they will be blown up." Others were shouting, "We are free." I was bewildered to such a degree that all I did was sit down and cry. On May 4, 1945, the 71ˢᵗ Infantry Division of the US Army liberated Gunskirchen.

PART IV

LIBERATION

MY JOURNEY HOME

Perhaps an hour or two after I had seen the Nazi guard flee, a military jeep with a white five-pointed star on it and carrying two African American soldiers arrived in the clearing of the camp.[1] I was startled and afraid. I had only seen a black person once before, back in Buština. At the age of perhaps ten, my mother had taken me to the circus that came to town. One of the featured performances was a large black man wearing a red fez who wrestled a brown bear. I remember rooting for the bear because, having just read the book of Robinson Crusoe, I was thinking of Friday. Although my mother assured me of the contrary, I was sure that if the black man won, he would eat us.

The American soldiers in the jeep accidentally discovered the camp while on a scouting mission. I watched the driver forcefully apply his brakes and, while skidding in the mud, manage to make a U-turn. With spinning wheels, the American soldiers hightailed it out of there to report their discovery. Soon after, an American armed convoy entered our camp. We

---

1   For accounts of the US Army's liberation of Gunskirchen, of whom African Americans were among the soldiers, see https://www.jewishvirtuallibrary.org/jsource/Holocaust/Gunskirchen.html (accessed, March 17, 2016).

greeted them by yelling in our native tongues, "*Amerikaiak! Amerikanski! Amerikaner!*" This was liberation; two black American soldiers in a jeep liberated us. I was going home!

My mind immediately searched for a way for me to get home. From the moment of liberation, I could think of nothing else. That had been my father's instructions. I was obsessed with the idea that I was going home to be with my family. Now, everything would be right, with no more suffering. I deeply believed — actually refused throughout the war to let myself not believe — that we would all survive and meet back at home. I imagined that I would soon feel the strong embrace of my mother. I could feel her warmth and smell the scent of her body. Father would once again take care of everything. All I had to do was follow my father's instructions and return home. Everyone would be waiting for me. It was May 4, 1945, at approximately one o'clock in the afternoon. I knew because the sun was past its highest point.

The adult liberated inmates, who, unlike me, were obviously conscious of things such as the location of the various food storages, stampeded and attacked the food storage facilities of the SS. There were stores of sugar beets and margarine as well as other foods. Some inmates were trampled to death. I did not participate in this frenzy. It would be untrue to say that my lack of participation was due to cautionary considerations, that I consciously judged it to be unsafe to participate, that I said to myself, "Hey, wait a minute, I am not going. I don't want to get trampled." However, nothing can be further from the truth. I wanted and would have participated; I even made an effort to participate but failed. I took a few steps to join the crowd and somebody mercifully knocked me down. Luckily, I was the first casualty. Had I succeeded to be in the thick of it, I surely would have been among those who were trampled to death. Once again, my survival depended on what seems like happenstance, just haphazard circumstances. Was it dumb luck or was someone watching over me?

That very evening, I began my journey home. To that end, I attached myself to a small group of newly acquired "friends" who also professed their desire to go home. We started walking on the road in the direction that the German Panzer tanks used to go, hoping that it would lead us out, and so it did. Once on the main road, we could see some city lights in the distance and we decided to head towards them. There were six of us and we shared the food we found. Being the youngest by far in the group, I was taken care of and looked after by the others. This became my luck; from then on, wherever I went, I was treated like a mascot.

On the way, we found a group of dead and mangled German soldiers. We took their possessions, including their rifles, ammunition, grenades, a few cigarettes and some food but not their uniforms, which we felt was dangerous. We were afraid that the uniforms might cause mistaken identity. Since carrying the rifle for any appreciable distance was way too heavy for me, I decided to abandon the rifle and carry a pistol, which was part of the loot. My "friends" offered to help carry my rifle so that I would not have to abandon it. We walked and rested a lot in the ditches on the side of the road. By daybreak, we arrived on the outskirts of the city of Linz.

Everyone test-fired their rifle, but being too weak to lift a rifle to my shoulder, aim and shoot, I lay in the ditch and rested the barrel on the edge in order to aim and fire it, which I successfully achieved. I was familiar with rifles, since my friend Pepik's father, who was an officer in the Czech police, had taught Pepik and me how to handle one. We had learned well and were able to accompany him on bird-hunting excursions in our fields. That had been a .22-caliber light rifle, but this German military rifle was exponentially heavier, with a kickback that hurt my jaw. On one occasion, as we were resting in a ditch, we saw a youthful adult in civilian clothing cycling toward us. One fellow resting next to me said, "Kid, hurry, get him, shoot him." Without thinking of the morality or the irreversible consequences, I shot him once and brought him down. I did not go over to see whether or not I had killed him, although I was urged to do so. Even though I became an instant celebrity among my peers, I found no joy in it. Within minutes, I had taken to brooding over my deed. Although I was convinced that everybody but us was a Nazi murderer or accomplice and deserved to die, I wondered what my father would say when I told him about it. However, I knew darn well what he would say and I was troubled by it. This sorry episode had a lingering effect on my attitude towards my "friends," while also leaving my conscience scarred.

We walked through the streets of Linz like a marauding gang. Walking near the fellow with whom I felt the most comfortable, I voiced to him my concerns regarding my shooting of the man. He conveyed to me his attitude, saying, "All that has happened to us could not have happened without the people agreeing, or at least not disagreeing, with the perpetrators." He added, "Notice that all the men were away in the army. Doing what? Shooting, beating, torturing and killing us! That's what!" My belief in this argument was strengthened when we made our uninvited presence felt by bursting into a Linz home; there we encountered only women. The men were only in photographs, dressed in military uniform and prominently displayed on the mantelpiece.

We asked the women for food, which they seemed anxious to provide and rushed to do so. They offered us some trinkets in the hope of befriending us. On the way out of the house, some of those in my group, including the man whom I accepted as my mentor, kept on referring to the photographs on the mantelpiece. They screamed "Nazi bastards" and threw grenades through the windows of the room where the women were huddled together in fear. My "friends" proceeded to repeat their deed on at least two other occasions, calling it revenge. I did not know the exact meaning of the word, but knew the consequences of revenge and it made me sick. Although, prior to this incident, I had thrown a grenade or two and fired my pistol at, or in the general direction of houses, I did not actually see anyone being killed by me, except for the cyclist. Thereafter, I did not enter another home, nor did I participate in any other revengeful acts. Following this incident, I broke away from my newly acquired "friends" and decided to get back on the road from which we had come in the hope that I would encounter some other, more appropriate, fellow prisoners and continue my quest to go home.

The incident in Linz has been reverberating in my mind all these years. I do not buy into the "*C'est la guerre*" (This is war) philosophy. I kept on asking myself, "Am I guilty?" If the answer is yes, then what exactly am I guilty of? Being present and not making even a futile attempt to stop it or to protest the deed while it was being perpetrated, I suppose, is guilt in itself, and therefore, I am equally guilty. While I vehemently support the punishment of the guilty, I do not subscribe to communal guilt. Sometimes, I catch myself wondering whether I would have been as upset if the victims had been men. And, sometimes, I conclude that I would not, which puts a completely different aspect on the problem.

In addition to the brazen actions of my fellow prisoners, of which I increasingly disapproved, they seemed to have lost interest or at least lost focus on going home, which had been their previous stated goal and the primary reason for my association with them. If their goal was still to go home the quickest way, they were certainly not making haste to do so. It did not dawn on me then that, perhaps, unlike me who was motivated, they had nowhere to go and nobody to whom to go home.

The road I was walking on looked very much like the road back home; it felt like the road on which I had often walked to my high school in Técső. I could even smell the fresh earth alongside the road. I looked for the ever-present young corn and sunflowers that I had usually encountered and had often eaten. I remembered playing tag with my cousins on the way; a game that required a lot of running, so that it doubled the distance of the walk. I was enjoying the early summer sun. There were moments when I felt that home was just around the next bend.

I met up with groups of liberated prisoners who warned me to look out for Americans. They said that the Americans riding in small open jeeps were grabbing and arresting any prisoner they could find and taking them to their concentration camp in Linz. They told me that they weren't shooting and, therefore, I could run from them without the fear of being shot. Heeding their advice, I ran and jumped into a ditch whenever I saw a military vehicle or truck. On one occasion, an American soldier jumped off his jeep, outran me and grabbed me. He kept repeating the word "*kamarád*" (comrade). He then forcefully disarmed me, picked me up and carried me to the jeep while I kicked and screamed. He deposited me in the jeep and got in next to me. Reaching into his pocket, he pulled out a chocolate bar, and on seeing my eyes almost fall out of their sockets, he gave me the bar, which I made quite a mess of as I devoured it. He held on to me the entire trip as the jeep continued toward Linz. He spoke with the driver of the jeep in English, which sounded to me as if his mouth was full of potatoes. Although the chocolate bar tasted funny, somewhat salty and so hard that I could hardly bite it, it went a long way in my establishing a psychological bond with him.

Our destination turned out to be the city's soccer field. I noticed, much to my relief, that this was no concentration camp, rather, it was a collection station set up and run by the occupying American Army. At this point, just a few days into liberation, there were a few hundred people, all of them men, milling around outside various tents. Some American soldiers were busy putting up additional tents, while others were riding around in jeeps organizing and gently herding people, including me, to the tent that contained the showers at one end and where good and relatively nice clothing was dispensed at the other end. Once again, because of my age and size I had trouble finding suitable clothing. I was unable to wear the clothing that I was originally issued. The soldier who was distributing the clothing saw my dilemma and walked me over to a section where another soldier fit me with something reasonable. The clothing that I eventually received proved to be good enough to last me for the next two years.

The United States Army was a fantastic organization; they anticipated the needs of the liberated prisoners and acted to fulfill them. The United States has a mosaic of ethnic populations; it is a country of immigrants, all with different native languages. The US Army took advantage of this unique, rich resource and put it to good use. There was a large open interpreter's tent, which was set up with tables and chairs. Each table had a sign saying which language the interpreter spoke. The interpreters were available to give out orientation information and advice, and told us what we could anticipate from the US Army. They answered a torrent of questions on any related subject. Access to someone with whom to speak was singularly the most calming influence upon an anxious, apprehensive, clientele.

We were then escorted toward the medical tents that were marked with the insignia of a red cross. Inside the medical tent there were various examining stations manned by doctors and nurses. I went through a bevy of medical examinations. I was examined from head to toe, including my ears, nose and throat and every crevice of my body. They hung tags around our necks that the doctors wrote on as we went through the examinations. In addition to their tags, those who had tuberculosis or some other infectious disease had their bodies marked up by the doctors and were separated and taken to the hospital tent. The most common problems — other than emotional and psychiatric — were malnutrition and diarrhea. The doctors looked at the skin of my entire body. At the dental station, they checked my teeth, which were literally falling out. Following my oral examination, some foul-tasting substance was applied to my teeth and gums. I was given prescriptions that I was to take to another tent to fill. There I was given various injections, medications and vitamins, as well as water purification tablets.

From there, we were asked to go to the canteen in another section of the field, where we were given bowls of hot soup and sealed boxes containing food. I sat on the grass and ate the soup that I found to be delicious and then I set about to examine the contents of the food box, which had a large letter "K" on it. My box, and I assume they all did, contained a bar of Fig Newtons. I did not know what Newton meant but was familiar with the word "fig" and I liked figs. Much to my surprise, I was disappointed in its taste. I remember eating it and thinking, "What kind of people are these Americans? The figs are salty and the chocolate was like a rock!" I had to use a bayonet to break off a piece of chocolate. It was also salty. An interpreter explained that all foods that we were given were laced with vitamins and nutrients. Much to my surprise, I found a little packet of toilet paper and four cigarettes in the box. I thought that America must be some country to treat their soldiers like this. The box also contained canned meats, puddings, canned potatoes and vegetables. Even the "ordinary" food tasted odd.

I went out of the stadium on an average of twice a day to wander the streets of the city. I wanted to see what was going on, and perhaps I could meet someone who had seen someone from my family. The authorities in the stadium did not mind, they made no effort to keep us in against our will. The first few days of liberation were crucial to them in order to prevent diseases and to disarm us. They also figured, rightly, that we were hooked on the good care that was provided to us.

American military police, MPs, were stationed at major intersections of the city to direct the passing American truck convoys. They were impeccably dressed in their clean pressed uniforms, white helmets and scarves and MP armbands. I learned that it was profitable to hang out at the intersections watching the MPs at lunchtime as, inevitably, an MP would sit down under a tree or some other shady spot, with his helmet off and his gun next to him. I would sit down opposite him and look at him as he was opening his lunch ration and say, "Johnny — *chokolat*." This appeal never failed. He would toss me a chocolate bar or some other goodie. I would then rush to another intersection and do it all over again. Usually, there were others who played the same game but I, being the youngest and smallest, got more than my share of the loot. The MPs learned to be careful with their possessions. There were groups of liberated prisoners who took advantage of their compassion and goodness and preyed on them. While one of them stood close to a soldier, another would grab the MP's helmet or any other possession left unprotected. What could the MP possibly do about it? He would not shoot them, even if he could, so the MPs learned to hold on to their possessions whenever any one of us came near. They seemed to have no such troubles from the conquered Austrian natives whom the MPs did not befriend. The American soldiers did not seem to have any relationship with the Austrians, who feared and respected the soldiers.

The same scenario was repeated wherever American soldiers congregated. If a group of soldiers sat down at the side of the road to have their lunch, inevitably they would be joined by some of us looking into their mouths. The soldiers wound up first sharing and then giving their lunch away. I once indicated to a soldier that I would like to have the penknife that he had in his hand and he just gave it to me. (I still have it today.) They gave us articles of clothing. One soldier put his helmet on my head and pointed to me and said, "Soldier," and then he laughed and hugged me tight.

Before going back to the stadium, I would barter my goodies for some other valuables such as a watch, a piece of jewelry or some American money. If I was going to be successful in getting home without the slow and tedious help from the organizations that were springing up like mushrooms, I had to have lots of money or its equivalent.

When we had still been at home and had listened to our clandestine radio, the Nazis had always referred to the US Army as "a bunch of misguided boy scouts and the sons of gangsters who were fodder for the German Army." In contrast, I found them to be overwhelmingly kind, congenial, happy-go-lucky, friendly, compassionate, good-hearted and highly motivated. They were an efficient bunch of guys delighted with their role as liberators.

Every American was "Johnny" to us; they were friendly and compassionate to a fault. I liked, respected and admired them to no end. Some of them were eager to display even their minimal knowledge of their ethnic backgrounds and tried to engage us in our native tongues. As far as I knew, America was a far forbidden land, a country that I had learned about in geography class. I thought that it was a country full of forlorn cowboys and savage Indians. It was a country where the man with a white hat always triumphed over the guy wearing a black hat. This stereotype was fostered by the movies I had seen and the books I had read. We heard that people got to America by running away from a restrictive home. Back home I had heard mentioned that America was a materialistic, cultural and religious wasteland populated by the disaffected dregs of humanity. It was a land to which a man would run if he wanted to abandon his wife and children. It was a place where deserters from the Tsar's army and fugitives from justice made their destination.

In the morning of the third day, as I lay sleeping on my cot in my tent, I was awakened by the blaring loudspeakers announcing in different languages, "Attention! Attention! Everybody is requested to assemble with all personal possessions and stand in line in front of the tables that are at the clearing." Not being the fastest to respond to any command, by the time I got there, there were a couple of hundred people lined up in front of different tables. Unlike some others, all my meager possessions were in a single rucksack. I did not want or need anything that I could not take along. When my backpack overflowed, I eliminated items that were less important. Therefore, I had no trouble taking all my possessions along.

The army interpreters were busy expediting the crowd. As the line got too long at one set of tables, they directed us to another set. The tables were abutting each other end to end, and had maps of Europe spread out on them. The maps had markings on them indicating the American, British and Russian occupation zones of the conquered and liberated countries. In order to relieve the congestion in the camp and set the desired repatriation process in motion, the American military command decided to dispatch us to other military authorities that were the occupying or liberating powers of our native countries.

As I got closer to the tables and it would soon be my turn, two soldiers approached me and asked me to follow them. I was put in front of a high-ranking officer in the company of other officers. They were standing at a table laden with communication equipment. According to my request, a Yiddish-speaking interpreter was assigned to me, who asked me to wait for the colonel who wanted to meet and speak to me. He actually said, "*Du wait for Colonel, er will ret mit du.*" (You wait for the colonel, and he will talk with you.) This was the first time that I was exposed to "American Yiddish," or what I call "Yinglish," half Yiddish, half English.

We waited there as a newsreel camera was set up and then the colonel put on white gloves and, while the camera was grinding away, shook my hand. The cameraman kept changing his position, looking for different angles. I was maneuvered into different positions while the officer kept on shaking my hand, slapping me on my back and saying things to me that I could not understand. I was not in the best of moods; I did not like him and was not very cooperative. Where I came from, one took his gloves off before shaking someone's hand. Shaking hands with gloves on was, to me, a boorish insult. Later, I understood that it was actually a prudent, preventive measure, against the possibility of contacting a contagious disease; it might even have been part of a regulation. Come to think of it, nobody touched us without wearing gloves. At the time, I concluded that it might be an American custom. Later, after I arrived in the United States, I saw a documentary depicting the American Army's liberation of the Nazi concentration camps and I actually saw myself. There I was, standing in front of a table shaking hands with an American officer, while the narrator said that I was among the youngest of the liberated prisoners.

I was then escorted back to the long tables, feeling like a celebrity because I did not have to stand in line again. I was asked, once again, what language I spoke and I answered Yiddish, Czech, Hungarian, Ruthenian-Ukrainian and German. They assigned to me the same Yiddish interpreter. He, in his "Yinglish," managed to get across that I was to point out my hometown on the map. One of the heavy red lines that was drawn on the map, which indicated the extent of the Russian and American zones of the conquered countries, ran along the River Elbe, right across the city of Linz from where we were. When I pointed to my hometown of Buština in the Carpathian section of Czechoslovakia, the interpreter turned to the attendant and I believe said "Russian zone." I was asked to proceed and join a group that was pointed out to me; a group that was standing by a formation of trucks to the left of the tables.

As soon as there were enough of us to fill a convoy of trucks, a bench was brought, and, with the help of a few soldiers, we climbed into the trucks. The trucks then proceeded out of the camp and drove through the city of Linz. I thought about the contrast of this ride to other truck rides. Here, under the auspices of the American Army, I felt protected and well taken care of. Everyone was in a jovial mood and someone started to sing. We were sure that we were being taken to some private housing, but we became apprehensive when the trucks stopped at a sentry checkpoint on a bridge. Our apprehension heightened when we were asked to get out of the truck. We were gently encouraged at first, but when we showed reluctance, they slightly nudged us to proceed across the bridge that turned out to be the border of the Russian zone.

On the other side of the bridge the Russian soldiers greeted us with great enthusiasm, especially me, the youngest in the group. Since some of the Russian soldiers were kids themselves, I shared their affinity. They were overwhelmingly emotional, warm-hearted and happy-go-lucky, wonderful guys. I felt good in their presence for three reasons: First, I understood their language to the extent that the Slavic language was familiar to me; second, I admired their great sacrifice and heroic resistance and eventual victory over the Nazis; and third, they were overly emotional with me, treating me like a hero. They admired me for being a child who had gone through the hell of the Holocaust and survived. In contrast to the Americans, who I thought did not act as conquerors, most of the time, to a point of leniency toward their formal enemies, the Russian soldiers were rightfully very much impressed with themselves as conquerors and dealt harshly with their conquered former enemies. By their behavior and actions, the shabbiness of their uniforms notwithstanding, they gave off an aura of invincibility that was contagious; it swept me into their sphere. I began to feel and share their bravado, becoming proud of persevering over the Nazi hell. Being the Nazis' victim and triumphing over them by surviving was my contribution to the cause of defeating the forces of evil.

They put us in trucks and took us to their nearby camp, which — it quickly became obvious — was nothing like the American camp we had just come from. There was no particular organized reception to receive us and it was functional but relatively shabby. The very day I arrived in the camp, I was taken in their version of a jeep on a hunt for food. There were two soldiers and I in a truck. One soldier was the driver, while the other was armed with their standard-issue automatic assault rifle they called an "Automat," equipped with a round magazine of seventy-two bullets. The soldiers were smoking foul-smelling tobacco they called *makhorka*. Using newspaper, they rolled the *makhorka* into cigarettes. The heavy, blue pungent smoke burned my throat and eyes so that I could hardly breathe. I carried on complaining to such an extent that my conduct provided them with comic relief.

We drove off the road through farms. To this day, I have no idea how this vehicle stayed upright. It bounced through the ruts, logs, rocks and tree stumps so hard that I hurt myself and began to cry. Although my companions thought that it was silly and unmanly of me, nevertheless, the armed soldier took me in his lap and held on to me while he told the driver to slow down and derided him for ridiculing and making me cry. "After all," he said, "he is just a boy." We drove through closed barn doors into the barns looking for livestock.

Soon the "barn-busting" technique paid off. A couple of pigs ran out of the barn and we took off after them. We chased the pigs with the truck, a bone-jarring experience. When we came close to the pigs, the soldier with the gun emptied his clip of bullets in the direction of the fleeing animals. When the pigs dropped dead, the soldiers loaded the bleeding pigs into the truck and we headed triumphantly back to the camp. When I finally got out of the truck, my legs collapsed under me. The driver helped me up, and, slapping my back, he called me his hero and a good sport, while the other soldier asked him to cut it out and told me to leave. I did not feel like a good sport, I ached all over and felt sorry for the pigs. Due to my "excursion" I had not been present when bunks were assigned. Therefore, I was assigned to a soldiers' tent that provided me an opportunity to observe the Russians more closely. Unknowingly, as Providence would have it, the fact that I was assigned to this particular tent saved my life that very night.

The pigs were roasted on a fire in open pits. I then sat with the soldiers around the fire and ate. The Russian soldiers literally spat out the bullets as they ate their share. They washed the food down with any liquid, preferably alcoholic. Some of the soldiers drank antiseptic alcohol that they had obtained from raided barbershops. Most of the Russian soldiers, at least in this particular group, were relatively primitive. They were young; some of them were just kids. They chased the Germans from the steppes of Russia to Linz in Austria. To me, they were wonderful; they treated me like a member of their gang and I admired their courage and was thankful to them. I looked upon them as the scourge of the Nazis.

Had there been a choice, I would have preferred to eat only kosher food and pig is considered particularly abominable. Nevertheless, it was just a few days after liberation and I did not give it as much thought as it deserved. Anyway, since I did not have a choice I ate what I was given. That night, as if I was punished by the wrath of God, I paid for it dearly. My bowels were churning and growling so loudly that I thought they would rip out of me. I was sure that this would kill me and I would be dead by morning. I had water running out of me from both ends of my body at an alarming rate. By the middle of the night, I almost choked on my vomit and I became so weak that I could no longer make it to the latrine, which resulted in soiling my cot, which, in turn, disturbed me no end. I was ashamed, and could not imagine facing my soldier friends. My heart was racing with the fear of dying and my mind was totally engulfed with begging the Almighty for help. I begged Him not to let me die now after all the suffering I had been through and before I could see my parents and brother. I was sweating profusely, and began moaning audibly.

The ranking Russian officer of the group, whose cot was at the front of the tent, came over to my bunk and asked me in Russian, "What hurts you, kid?" I told him that my belly hurt and that I was dying. He felt my head with his hand and said, "You ate pig, yes?" and then he looked at my soiled cot, which embarrassed me. He said that he would be right back and left. Minutes later, he returned with a cup containing some kind of a brown liquid and said, "Drink, kid, it will be good for your stomach, drink, drink it all." It was the bitterest thing I had ever tasted in my life, and pushed away his hand with the cup. "You have to drink," he insisted, as he lifted my head with his other hand and pushed the liquid into my mouth. I managed to swallow it in two gulps. Soon, I was asleep and in the morning I woke up feeling much better and awash with sweat. I felt an unfamiliar sense of relief and euphoria, as if someone had relieved me of a great burden. The officer who gave me the medicine, noticing that I was awake, came over to me and asked, "How do you feel, kid? I looked at you a few times during the night and you were always sleeping. Do you feel good, kid?" I told him that I felt very different and asked him what medicine he had given me. "Opium," he said. "It is good for the stomach, yes?" "Yes, it is good," I said. Then I asked him if he was a doctor. His answer was, "Yes, I am a doctor." He then told me to wash up well and throw away everything on my cot. I found out later that many liberated prisoners died from dysentery because their stomachs could not digest the foods that became available to them. The Americans were aware of this and fed us food that was "good" for us, but others who were in the Russian zone under Russian supervision, or those who were on their own, were inflicted with the scourge of dysentery. Many died, while I, once again, was saved through the grace of the Almighty.

I looked for the opportunity to thank privately my savior. Later in the day, I found him alone on his cot and thanked him profusely. He asked me to sit down and engaged me in a conversation by asking me my name, where I came from, and where and in which concentration camp I had been. I told him my name, my town in the Carpathians and that I had been in a ghetto, and then in Auschwitz-Birkenau, Mauthausen and Gunskirchen. I told him that the Americans liberated me from the Gunskirchen camp, near Linz. He kept interjecting my words with curses directed at the Germans and then took my head into his hands and held me close to his heart. He asked me about the Americans; he was interested to know whether the Americans were rich and I told him that they were. He was impressed when I told him about their organization and that they helped us with many doctors. As we became friendlier, he told me that he did not believe that any of his family was alive. He then told me that he was a captain, a doctor and a Jew from the city of Kiev in the Ukraine. He had joined the Russian Army right out of university and had not heard anything about his family, and whatever news he had received, was not good. I was, and am, convinced that he saved my life that night. He told me to pay attention to what I ate; especially, he said, I should avoid fat, like pig. He asked me where I was going from there, and I told him that the last time I saw my father he had instructed me to return home to meet the family. The captain took out a map and looked at it. He then said to me, "Stay here for a few days. I might be able to help you go home." I was elated and thanked him.

VIENNA AND BUDAPEST

In the morning, two days later, the captain came over to my cot and told me to get up and take everything I had with me. He told me to hurry, that we were going to Vienna, which was on my way home. I could not believe my ears. I was not able to concentrate nor could I think of a single question such as how I would get home from there. His parting words as he left the tent were, "Let's go, kid, hurry."

So I found myself sitting between the driver and the captain in a truck going to Vienna. On the way, I ate from their rations. The captain gave me a map marked up with the best route to get home. He told me that from Vienna I should have no difficulty finding a Russian military truck going to Budapest, from there to Prague, and then home. When we arrived in Vienna, he unceremoniously wished me good luck, gave me a piece of bread and, without further ado, let me loose in the city.

I walked aimlessly through Vienna wondering where I was going to eat. I had eaten the bread the captain had given me hours before. I also had no idea where I was going to sleep. I had wasted many hours wandering around the city looking at places and things that fascinated me, instead of trying to approach some Russian soldiers for the possibility of a connection that could help me. I ultimately stopped a person who I thought was Jewish. He was not, but he advised me to go to the Red Cross and proceeded to give me directions. I thanked him courteously, but resisted the advice because of my previous experience with the International Red Cross. On further inquiries, I was told that many refugees went to soup kitchens in churches. Actually, I saw priests standing outside their churches trying to persuade passing refugees, especially if they were Jewish, to come in and receive a good meal and a clean bed in which to sleep. I did so and while the food was good and plentiful and the bed was clean, the price was to sleep with a cross over the head of the bed. In the morning, the priest woke me and asked me to accompany him to church. The meal, the bed and the request were done with the greatest kindness and personal concern. I did take advantage of the fine meal and a bed, but the rest of it was too foreign to me and I decided to leave. However, towards the evening of the next day, I was looking for another church to repeat the previous night's experience, but I could not find one that had an available place. It was too late in the day, I suppose. In desperation, I eventually wound up at the Red Cross for a single night, but I was very uncomfortable and had trouble swallowing the food they gave me. My prior experience with the Red Cross bothered me to a point that I could not stay there or in any other Red Cross facility again. On subsequent nights, I slept in other refugee houses.

After four days of trying to find a ride to Budapest, the vigorous effort paid off. I managed to make contact with some Russians who promised to take me there. From Budapest, I intended to go to Prague, and from there, I intended to weave through various cities in the direction of home. I realized that it was essential to go through the big capital cities if possible. Every large city had a concentration of literally thousands of refugees from all corners of the earth. All the relief organizations were based in the major cities, which were also safer and where refugees were most likely get sorely needed help.

The American Jewish humanitarian relief organizations that sprouted up throughout Europe were absolutely and incalculably essential. They provided funds and services that were beyond generous, even when measured on the American scale. They employed selfless, dedicated, compassionate and caring professionals. One cannot overstate their contribution to alleviating the suffering of the wretched souls that they were aiding. The relief organizations literally saved countless lives. In the vacuum of authority and the confusion following liberation, they detected the needs for services, and rushed to fill them. There was no problem that they could not surpass; they were the beacons for the lost, but hopeful, souls.

Jewish refugees were drawn to the large cities to seek each other out, to commiserate and to exchange information about family and friends. Wherever one went, one could hear questions such as, "Did you see Moshe of Chust? What about Haim from Sighet? Who were you with?" I kept asking if anyone had been with anybody from Buština of Czech Carpathia, but never received any response. People posted notes on the walls of relief organizations, such as, "Abraham ... from ... is alive." I posted, "Moshe (Andi) Brandstein, the son of Mordechai, the grandson of Eliezer Brandstein and Yisroel Natan Bruckstein, from Buština in the Czech Carpathians, is alive and going home."

By the time we got to Budapest, I found myself itching in the most private places, which then evolved into a rash that covered my entire body, even the skin between my fingers. My uncontrollable scratching produced bleeding welts. I remembered that, as a young child at home, Mother warned me not to go near a beggar who was scratching himself. As we entered Budapest, the address of my Aunt Vali and Uncle David popped into my mind. I remembered the name of their street, Sas utca, because it meant Eagle Street. I had been fascinated by the name as a child. I decided to make it my destination.

I found Aunt Vali (my mother's sister) still living there with her two daughters, Kitty and Erika (my city slicker cousins). They had survived the war and had reclaimed their apartment. My aunt was obviously thrilled to see that I had survived but, at first, she recoiled from me as she noticed my highly contagious condition. However, she quickly recognized the severity of my situation and took me to the Jewish hospital of Budapest. On the way, I told her that I had been with her husband, Uncle David, in Birkenau and that one day he had not come back from work. Aunt Vali told me that she already knew that Uncle David had perished in the camp. During the next few days my aunt managed to buy or barter hard-to-come-by milk, cheese, etc. and brought them to me on her daily visits. Her love and concern for me formed the first truly human contact I had felt since being separated from my mother and later from my father and brother in Birkenau.

My stay at the hospital began a completely new episode in my life. As a child, I spoke Yiddish, Ukrainian, Czech and Hungarian, and now had a passive understanding of German, Polish and Russian, and could speak them a little bit. Speaking both a Slavic language and Hungarian was highly unusual in Hungary, as they are completely different, without any words in common. The Hungarian language has a slight resemblance to Finnish, but is not close to either the Romance or the Slavic language families.

Russian soldiers would often come into the hospital bleeding from wounds as a result of brawls and knife fights. Some were ill and most were drunk. The soldiers would announce their presence by firing their machine guns at the ceiling or the walls. While bullets were ricocheting all over the place, the doctors and nurses would scatter, running in fear of their lives. The drunken soldiers would then proceed to search for a doctor or nurse. Inevitably, before the night was over, some nurses — and too many times, even patients in bed — would be raped. When the soldiers did find a doctor, they would sometimes demand treatment while holding a gun to the doctor's head. The doctors were terrified and could not understand the Russian. The dynamics often made it impossible for the doctors to render treatment, which inevitably resulted in the doctors being beaten, and sometimes even shot and killed.

To understand the Russian soldier in 1945, at the end of the war, is to understand that Hungarians were the enemy. Hungary was occupied and the Russians were the conquerors. By this time, the Russians were "crazed" by their experiences and suffering at the hands of the Germans and their allies, including Hungary. The Russians had seen their families brutally and indiscriminately killed and their villages burned. What the Russians did in Hungary was simply revenge; it was payback time, so to speak. Russian soldiers cruised around in their trucks, grabbing Hungarian girls and women off the streets. Some Hungarian women began wearing scarves over their heads and walking slightly stooped to give the impression that they were old. This ruse resulted in some truly old women being grabbed by soldiers who thought that they were in disguise. Unbeknownst to me at the time, my Aunt Manci, Father's youngest unmarried sister, who lived through the concentration camps, was killed in Budapest when a drunken Russian truck driver drove his military truck into her on the sidewalk. Nevertheless, as far as the Hungarians were concerned, I looked upon the Russian soldier as God's instrument of revenge.

Once the doctors and nurses discovered that I spoke a Slavic language as well as Hungarian, they made me their interpreter. I was assigned to a bed in the front room, the first room at the entrance to the hospital, and in exchange for good, otherwise unavailable, food, I was to intercept any commotion that I heard. The staff liked how I handled the situations with the marauding soldiers. As soon as there was a commotion, I would run out into the foyer and greet the soldiers in Russian with great fanfare. I would say to them, "I greet the flower of the Russian Red Army," and they would hug and kiss me. I would then translate their needs to the doctors. My interference, however, did not always prevent them from grabbing a nurse. Nevertheless, I provided a very useful service to the hospital, namely the ability to communicate, which made all the difference.

Two weeks passed and I was already better. My scabs were healing and I was reluctant to stay and waste more time in Budapest. I felt that I was well enough and wanted to resume my journey home. The doctors and the administration pleaded with me to stay, saying that I would be stronger if I stayed just a little longer. I was the *tolmács* (interpreter). They gave me unheard-of privileges. They acquiesced to any demand I could think of. I must admit that I felt important as I stood next to the doctors while they were treating the Russians. When Aunt Vali came to visit me, the hospital staff enlisted her help on their behalf. They asked her to encourage me to stay. They won her over and she too encouraged me to stay, emphasizing the importance for me to restore my strength. It was difficult to counter my aunt's wishes, so I decided to stay — but just a little while longer.

REUNION WITH FATHER AND TIBI

Once again, it was fate that intervened on my behalf and delayed my departure from the hospital. The decision to stay forever changed my life. Three weeks passed from when I first entered the hospital and I felt that I could no longer justify staying any longer. A Russian officer offered to give me a ride to Prague in a week and I informed the powers that be of my decision. I told them, "My parents and my brother must be waiting for me at home.

Andrew Burian listed on the *SS Washington*'s ship manifest from Southampton to New York, March 5, 1948.

Andrew Burian listed as a passenger on the *SS Washington* to be transferred to Ellis Island, March 14, 1948.

Tibor and Therese at their wedding,
Lille, France, 1950.

Andrew and his father, c. 1950.

Tibor (left) and Andrew, Atlantic City, 1952.

Andrew and Ruth Burian at their wedding,
New York, November 23, 1960.

Andrew (left) and Tibor
at Andrew's wedding,
November 23, 1960.

Giselle (Gizi) Burian
(Andrew's stepmother).

Left to right: Valerie Wieder (Matilda's sister), Ibi Bruckstein (Matilda's cousin), Rela Katz (Matilda's sister), Edith Stern (Matilda's sister). Front: Peter Stern (Edith's eldest son), c. 1960.

Bar Mitzvah of Ervin Brandstein's son, Yoav, Haifa, 1966.
Includes: Matilda, Ruth and Andrew Burian holding Saul (back row furthest left), Tibor Burian (back row furthest right) followed by Vicki and Ervin, Oti (middle row second from right) and members of their families; Lili and Cuna (Jeno's daughters), Alice and Mania (Izidor's daughters) and members of their families.

Burian family
at Saul's *bar mitzvah*, 1977.

Burian family at Lawrence's
bar mitzvah, 1982.

Ida and Irving Allerhand
(Ruth's parents), 1982.

Gizi and Ernest Burian,
1982.

The entrance to Buština, 1994.

Andrew with some local townspeople, Buština, 1994.

Andrew's first childhood home, which was later rented to the Czech police,
Buština, 1994.

Amalia and Eliezer Brandstein's home, now city hall,
Buština, 1994.

Tibor mourning the loss of his mother,
Birkenau, 1994.

Andrew being comforted by his son, Lawrence, as he mourns the loss of his mother,
Birkenau, 1994.

Andrew's daughter, Matilda (Burian) Anhalt, with her family, April 2015.
Front: Matilda; Middle (left to right): Kenny, Jordan, Arielle (Anhalt) Brenner, Daina;
Back: Marvin, Adam Brenner.

Andrew's son, Saul, with his family, October 2012.
Left to right: Jennifer Gross Burian, Saul, Jason, Michael,
Atara, Lauren Gross, Mathew Gross.

Andrew's son, Lawrence, with his family, May 2015.
Clockwise from left: Jonah, Adina, Lawrence, Ethan, Adam, Erin.

Andrew with his first great-grandchild,
Sydney Juliet Brenner, born March 2, 2015.

"Tragedy, Testimony…and Responsibility," Andrew Burian sharing his Holocaust story as the keynote speaker before a live audience of more than 13,000 students at a Liberty University Convocation, November 2014.

Ruth and Andrew Burian, May 2015.

Ruth and Andrew Burian surrounded by their children and grandchildren (with spouses) and great-grandchild, Mother's Day, May 10, 2015.

Andrew's three children – Saul (left), Matilda and Lawrence, August 2015.

Andrew celebrates his eighty-fifth birthday in his home, surrounded by family, Long Beach, NY, December 2015.

Andrew and his grandson, Jonah, with their new Tissot watches, on the occasion of Jonah's *bar mitzvah* and Andrew's second *bar mitzvah*, 2013.

They don't even know that I am alive. I must leave and go home." I had made up my mind that nothing would persuade me to stay another day.

On the day of my planned departure, the hospital administrator followed me to my room and again tried to persuade me to stay. I told him that there simply was no way I was going to miss my ride to Prague. I explained that I had already been to the Jewish Agency and acquired a suit. I got annoyed by his continued pressing. While we were debating, the door to my room burst open and a young man poked his head in and yelled in Hungarian, "Is there a doctor here?" Not getting an answer, he continued running down the hall bursting into rooms and shouting at the top of his lungs, "Is there a doctor? Does anybody know where there is a doctor?" He had no way of knowing that his shouting had driven any doctor within earshot into hiding. In front of my eyes the image of my brother was conjured up, and my mind shouted before I did, "Tibi! Tibi! My brother! It is my BROTHER! That's his voice!" I ripped the door open and ran out into the corridor attempting to follow the sound of the frantic panicky search for a doctor. In my single-minded haste I tripped and fell over the body of a man who was propped up outside my door and had slid down into a prone position. I fell and slid hard on the marble floor. As I got up and turned toward the obstruction, I recognized that it was my father! I fell upon him with screams of *"Tate Ziser!"* "Papa!" "Sweet dear Father!" and hugged and smothered him with tears and kisses. The whole emotional greeting was repeated when my brother and I saw each other. This is how Providence brought my father and brother to me after liberation.

Papa was sick with an inflamed lung. I gave Papa my bed and arranged for my brother to stay. My brother, Tibor, who himself had just recovered from a bout of typhus, literally carried Papa to the hospital on his back. He had propped Papa up at the entrance to the first door he came to, while he had run from room to room looking for a doctor. Of all the cities and hospitals in Europe, fate had somehow brought them to the hospital where I was the "chief cook and bottle-washer," where I literally had the run of the place and could help.

I believe that this fateful encounter saved our father's life. Being a *macher* (a person who can make things happen), I immediately found doctors to take good care of him. As in the Holy Scripture, I felt like ancient Joseph who had risen from the depths of despair to become Viceroy of Egypt. From that position, Joseph was able to pave the way for his father, Jacob, and his brothers, and to care for them when they later arrived in Egypt in need of help. Just as in the Joseph story when word spread throughout the kingdom that Joseph's family had come, so too the hospital was soon abuzz with "Andi's father and brother are here." Whenever I read in the Torah the part that describes Jacob's encounter with Joseph in Egypt, a shiver runs through my body and a vivid reenactment of my encounter with my father and brother takes place in my mind.

Now that we were together in the hospital, we were a family once again. We were, unfortunately, though, without our crown jewel. We were without the centerpiece of our very existence, the jewel that was our mother. However, God, in His good graces, had preserved our father. So now Papa and his two sons, Tibor and I, although decimated, were a family nevertheless. We hugged, kissed and cried.

While we were focused on taking care of our father, Tibi and I were also running from agency to agency, constantly inquiring about our mother. We spent our days hoping against hope that our inquiries and searches would result in finding her. We did manage to make contact with some other survivors of the transport on which we had arrived at Birkenau. We learned some more information about their loved ones who had gone with the elderly upon arrival, like our mother did, and that only reinforced the hopelessness of our search. As we acquired more and more information about their fate, we became convinced that our dear, darling mother had been one of the victims killed among the hundreds of thousands of Jews transported from Hungary between May and June 1944.

By the middle of June, the earliest that Papa could travel, we, now as a family, resumed our journey home. Order was being restored. Papa told us when, what, where and why. We had family consultations, but Papa was in charge once again. We decided to resume our journey and travel to Prague, the capital of Czechoslovakia, as our next destination.

No sooner had we arrived in Prague, than Papa's medical condition got dangerously worse. He was terribly sick. Based on Papa's and Tibi's previous experience, we thought that Papa had come down with typhus. My brother and I checked him into the Masarykovy Domovy hospital, which was also a sanatorium. Papa was diagnosed with the recurrence of his previous infection in one of the lobes of his lungs, as well as sunstroke and dehydration. We were assured that it was not the prevalent, dreaded, tuberculosis and that with proper long-term care and good nutrition, he would be all right. After the initial hospitalization, Papa was transferred to the sanatorium for an extended recuperation. My brother and I were left to fend for ourselves in Prague, intending to wait for the day when Papa would be well enough to resume our journey home.

I spent a lot of time at the hospital with Papa. There, he told me the story of their survival. Papa and Tibi had been together throughout their incarceration. They were mostly in the service of the Todt Organization (a German construction firm) as slave laborers. Their first destination had been Dachau, where they were imprisoned for a month and were known as numbers 948 and 949, respectively. They had been in Birkenau, Dachau, Rothschweige and Allach, where they had been part of the Kommando Knoll, working with over 1,000 slave laborers at building an underground BMW factory, which was being bombed every night by the British. In Karlsfeld, they worked at the Munich rail station replacing rails damaged by Allied bombing. In Mittergars (Muldorf), they unloaded coal from railcars. Their final camp was Waldlager V, which was known as *"Besondere Strafkompanie im Osten"* (Special Punitive Unit in the East).[2]

Papa and Tibi worked as slave laborers, which, at least, meant there were no systematic killings. Many times an SS group would show up at the site where they were working and demand that the Todt Organization give up the Jews, with the clear intent of killing them. The Todt engineer in command would then argue with the SS. In one incident, the Todt engineer said, "Okay, you sign for them and have the SS and your soldiers build the bridge." The SS, of course, would not sign and would walk off, disappointed that their thirst for blood had not been satisfied. That is just one story of

2   Waldlager (forest camps) V and VI, located near the town of Ampfing, were part of the Mühldorf camp complex, established by the SS in mid-1944. The inmates were housed in earthen barracks partially submerged in the ground with soil-covered roofs designed to camouflage the structures from Allied aerial reconnaissance. Prisoners frequently worked ten-twelve hours per day, hauling heavy bags of cement and carrying out other arduous construction tasks. Most of the prisoners were Hungarian Jews, but there were also Jews from Greece, France, Czechoslovakia, Yugoslavia, Poland, Lithuania, Italy and the Netherlands. In late April 1945, as the US Army approached this and other nearby camps, the Third Reich SS guards evacuated and forced some 3,600 prisoners on death marches.

Papa's and Tibi's survival. They were both ultimately liberated by American forces on May 2, 1945. Papa was forty-four years old and Tibi was fifteen. My brother was unaware of his liberation, which came just in time to save his life. He was unconscious from typhus and was nurtured and cared for by Papa. Throughout their incarceration, they sustained each other with love and care.

Papa's recuperation in Prague was steady but excruciatingly slow, at least not as rapid as we wished it to be, to say the least. The doctors advised against his resumption of our journey home, especially given that there would be very little, if any, medical help available along the way, which they insisted he would need. There were, at the time, rampant and contradictory rumors concerning the Russian political intentions towards the Carpathian section of Czechoslovakia. We determined that at least someone should travel to our hometown of Buština both to assess the situation and perhaps to meet up with other extended family members and friends who may have survived and returned. Tibi was the natural choice to go. This was to be an exploratory trip and we did not know what Tibi would encounter, so Papa decided to keep me safe with him.

This reminds me of a different biblical story involving our forefather Jacob (described in my *Bar Mitzvah* portion) when he, too, held back his youngest son, Benjamin, from travelling with his brothers to the unknown land of Egypt. Papa instructed Tibi to seek out the possibility of selling some property or possessions in order to gain some funds. He further instructed Tibi that safety should be his paramount concern and not to tarry longer than absolutely necessary. Within a few days of our arrival in Prague, in July 1945, three and a half months short of his seventeenth birthday, Tibi left for Buština.

While Papa was recuperating and Tibi was away, I lived on the streets of Prague. I stayed in various refugee shelters. Most nights, I stayed in shelters that were set up by the American Jewish philanthropic organizations such as the famous and very effective Joint Distribution Committee, which was known as "the Joint." There were other transient places to stay where a refugee could get some money, clothing and food. Prague was a liberated city in the center of Europe. It had a history of civil liberty and freedom and a benevolent, compassionate government beloved by its constituents. Prague was a city full of refugees who were milling all around the town, which was pulsating with energy as people tried to restore their lives. At one point, I somehow made contact with Aunt Judith (my mother's next-to-youngest sister), who had survived the war, and her new husband, Andrew Valenta.

Czechoslovakia and even the capital city of Prague, although no longer occupied, had all kinds of scarcities. Anything American was at a premium and I soon noticed that some people were willing to pay much more for scarce American cigarettes than I was able to buy them for. This realization afforded me an opportunity to become a small-scale entrepreneur. I first attempted to buy a pack of cigarettes from other vendors in order to find out the going price, then I plunged in with my big investment — I somehow managed to buy a pack of Lucky Strike cigarettes for less than the typical asking price. When I offered my merchandise for sale, I found that many buyers were just as smart as I was and made lower offers, beating the price down to near cost, instead of buying at the profitable quoted price. However, I did have opportunities to make sales if I was willing to break a pack. There seemed to be a market for more-affordable loose cigarettes. I further noticed that men who were going into restaurants were likely customers for cigarettes, especially if they were with female company. I took advantage of the situation and positioned myself at the entrance of middle-class restaurants.

This strategy worked until I became too successful. My success substantially cut into the entrepreneurship of the head waiters who made very good money supplying cigarettes, at inflated prices, to their clients. At first, the waiters tried to shoo me away and when that was unsuccessful, they reverted to threats of bodily harm. The proprietors noticed the commotion created by the waiters in front of their restaurants and ordered them to stop. Finally, I offered a solution to the problem, which was accepted by the head waiter of my most successful spot. The deal was that I would stop selling in front of his restaurant if he would buy his supplies from me at wholesale. While this deal was not as profitable as the previous per-unit sales, the overall profit was made up in volume. In addition, my overall costs of the cigarettes were now cheaper because I could now afford to buy them by the carton. The waiter had the additional advantage of having access to me as a supplier, and I was willing to run to get a special brand if requested by a customer. My entrepreneurship made it possible for me to eat better and to purchase better clothing. Most of all, it made it possible for me to buy nourishing commodities such as milk, butter, cheese, vegetables and fruit, which I took to Papa on my daily visits. These commodities were scarce and expensive, but essential to Papa's recuperation.

While in Prague, I had the opportunity to meet the chief rabbi of the city, Rabbi Forehand. Although he was a young man and short in height, he was a giant in his wisdom, dedication and deeds. Rabbi Forehand had a ministerial standing in the Czech government and yet he personally dedicated himself to, and involved himself in, the welfare of all who were in need of his services, which was almost everybody. The door to his office was open and all were welcome. He was everything to anyone in need, whether the need was monetary, good advice, or perhaps a recommendation to the authorities for a passport or a copy of something to file for citizenship. Rabbi Forehand was ultimately instrumental in procuring the necessary documents for my immigration to the United States. A few months later, after the Communist takeover, his situation and status became untenable, so he and his family immigrated to the United States.

Tibi stayed in Buština for three weeks. He slept on the floor at his friend Imre Schwartz's house along with five other Jewish boys from surrounding villages. Among the five boys were: Schmilku Blat; Shimonovitch, one of grandpa's salesmen; and Shlamtchu Bruckstein, our mother's cousin. Imre had returned earlier and successfully reclaimed his house.

Tibi was astute and highly motivated to correctly observe and absorb the prevailing situation. On the first day, he noticed that the notary's son was wearing a suit that had once belonged to him. He made nothing of it. A local approached Tibi with the proposition of Tibi selling him the slates of our lumberyard shed, and Tibi agreed. This action immediately fulfilled our desperate need for some funds. Unbeknownst to Tibi, however, the result of this sale provoked a local NKVD (Communist secret police) official, who had previously befriended him. The NKVD claimed that this was a "bourgeois" act and that the tiles were not Tibi's to sell. The official added that all possessions belong to the State and that the transaction, therefore, constituted stealing from the State. Tibi was afraid of being arrested.

Tibi lingered in Buština just long enough to explore some of the hiding places that were now accessible to him; places where he, Papa and Grandfather Bruckstein had hidden valuables and important papers before deportation. Tibi found one of the caches, which contained some jewelry and papers. He went to look in Grandfather Bruckstein's house, where they had hidden all kinds of bank records and insurance policies, but he found nothing. In a third hiding place he found some photographs, which we considered our treasures. The local authorities, who were part of or complicit with the confiscators and squatters in the various homes, were not cooperating in the restoration of properties to their rightful, legal owners. In any case, my brother quickly got the drift that the situation in Buština was unsafe for him and he abruptly left for the safety of Prague.

We greeted Tibi's return with great anticipation. We were eager to hear what he had found in Buština and about the situation concerning our home as well as those of the extended family. We quickly became disappointed when he related that he had barely managed to slip out of Buština a step ahead of the NKVD. He reported that the old house of my grandfather Brandstein had been razed and a church now occupied the site. Our synagogue had also been destroyed and turned into a lumberyard. He explained that the new house of Grandfather Brandstein, the only multistory home located in the center of town, had become the City Hall, and that our house, the house in which I was born, had become a school (it had first been taken over and turned into a police station before deportation). Tibi went on to tell us that Grandfather Bruckstein's house now had a cannon ball hole right through it and that our last home, where we had been living just before we were taken away, was occupied by the sister of our former maid, Ilona. Her sister had always been somewhat of a rebel, a hothead, and had never been too well disposed towards us. Tibi also described the desperate, sorry state of the town in general. We also heard numerous unsavory stories of efforts by others to reclaim confiscated properties from squatters. In fact, one of Father's former superintendents sent an explicit threat: "If Mordche is thinking of coming back to town to reclaim his property, come on, I'm waiting for him with an axe." The idea of repossession was simply inadvisable, at least for the time being.

My brother and I registered at the State Agency and applied for Czechoslovak citizenship, which was duly granted and we received our identity papers. Unlike in Hungary and Buština, which the Russians occupied, we were dealing with a legitimate Czechoslovak government. The Russian Army had liberated Czechoslovakia and, unlike in Hungary, they did not carry guns in the street nor did they wield any authority other than over their own armed forces. The liberating Russian soldiers in Czechoslovakia were under Czech civil authority when dealing with civil matters. They behaved themselves.

We learned that, in addition to our Aunt Vali who lived in Budapest, Aunt Fanny and her husband, Zoli Simsovic, together with their daughter, Juliana (who had been spirited out of Buština prior to our deportation), and their newly born son, Peter, were living in Debrecen in Hungary. Our father arranged our itinerary and sent us to stay with Aunt Fanny for a few days to have a taste of home. Papa's instructions were for Tibi then to continue on to the city of Nyíregyháza where he was to visit our Great-Uncle Joseph, the youngest brother of our mother's father who had survived. From there, Tibi was to go to Mátészalka, to the site of the ghetto in an attempt to dig up a metal pail that had been hidden under the brick shed by Papa and Tibi the day we were evacuated to Auschwitz. Tibi was then to return to Debrecen and pick me up for our return to Prague.

I find it difficult to describe the few days of joy I experienced in Debrecen. There were moments when I had the feeling that all was well. The days went by quickly, as is always the case when they are joyful. One day, though, I took Peter for a stroll in the park. This wonderful serene scene should have been a tonic. Instead, it caused me to play out the scene in my head of my awful experience in Mauthausen, where I had observed a woman pushing a baby carriage just beyond the wall of the concentration camp. That contrast had been devastating to me. The proximity to my aunt, and even the fact that she tucked me into bed at night, also triggered for me horrendous nightmares concerning my mother. I would cry out in my sleep screaming, "Mama!" When awake, I could not get out of my mind the episode during the first night of our arrival in Birkenau when the kapo had grabbed my head, turned it toward the chimney flames and said: "There! Your mama, there, there is Mama!" And, when asleep, I could vividly see the whole episode with a grotesque twist. I could see the lovely, graceful, beautiful face of my mother swirling and rising in the flames while keeping an eye on me. Finally, she would stretch out her arms towards me as she rose towards the heavens, out of sight. It was a terrifying and, unfortunately, very realistic dream. When I cried out, Aunt Fanny would come running to hug me and soothe me back to sleep. The dream reoccurred every night of my stay with my aunt.

Mercifully, my brother came for me and we returned to Prague where my dreams were placated by the daily visits with my father. Tibi had visited

Uncle Joseph and Aunt Annush in Nyíregyháza, who showed great interest in our family.[3] He had then proceeded to Mátészalka, where he was promptly arrested by the Russian authorities. He was held by them for two days until he persuaded the Russians that he had come to revisit the ghetto where he and his family had been incarcerated. Tibi successfully found the stash of some precious old photographs as well as a very large sum of Hungarian pengő. In 1944, when the money had been hidden, it was worth approximately five years' salary for a skilled white-collar worker. However, postwar inflation under the authority of the Russian Army had turned the precious Hungarian pengő into nothing. A half-hour game of ping-pong could cost six million pengő!

Then, in 1945, the government of Czechoslovakia passed a law affecting the Sudetenland section, confiscating as many German properties — and deporting their owners — as was needed to satisfy the need of house-returning to political prisoners who were not necessarily the previous owners. The law affected only those ethnic German inhabitants who had voted for Hitler's plebiscite. I believe that Czechoslovakia was the only, or certainly the first country, to enact this law. Meanwhile, Russia had effectively annexed the Carpathian section of Czechoslovakia that the Russian Army had liberated, claiming it as part of the Ukraine. Once again, Czechoslovakia was in no position to object, especially since there was at this time a large Communist representation in the Czech government. Russia called upon all former Carpathian residents to return home. Since we had no wish to live in the Ukraine, a country that had amassed an awful antisemitic record prior to and certainly during the war, the call to return frightened us.

Papa concluded that there was no future for us in Buština, and to that end he was inclined to take advantage of the new Sudetenland law of repatriation. He chose the city of Liberec (called Reichenberg by the Germans) for us to live. Liberec was a beautiful city, striving to develop itself, with good schools and commerce, and surrounded by industrious towns such as Jablonec, which was (and still is) famous for its jewelry industry. It was about sixty-five miles away from Prague.

Unfortunately, Papa was still stuck in the hospital. Once again, Tibi — at sixteen years old, looking like nineteen and with the maturity of a

---

3   Joseph and Annush Bruckstein later made *Aliyah* and established their lives in Jerusalem.

thirty-year-old — was sent on an important mission. He was to go to Liberec and register us as political prisoners and secure an apartment. I was to wait for his return. It was important that everything be accomplished without delay so that both of us could register as students in the Real Gymnasium of Liberec. It was now late August and Papa was anxious for us not to miss the school year.

The German owners or tenants of the apartments and homes in Liberec had already been ordered to leave with their personal possessions, not exceeding fifty kilos per person. The short notice, as well as the weight limit, was the same as what the Germans had given the evicted Czechs in 1938. It was payback. The Germans were told to register with their possessions in the yard of the textile factory that was situated near the Gymnasium for the purpose of deportation. The evicted German families were transported by truck to the nearby German border and ordered to cross.

When my brother arrived in Liberec, he made contact with our family members, Jacob and Leibi Bruckstein, our mother's two cousins, who had survived and now lived in a home provided by the Czech Government. My uncle and aunt, Adolf and Margit Brandstein, as well as their children, Oti, Ervin and Vicki, also all managed to survive and were similarly reunited after the war in Liberec.[4] Tibi stayed with Jacob and Leibi for the three days that it took him to accomplish his task. Upon registering with the Czechoslovak repatriation office as a returning political prisoner, Tibi was given a choice of apartments available under the law. He chose an apartment on the main street of Liberec, number 16, Ulica 5 Května (May 5 Street). It consisted of two bedrooms, a living room and a dining room. After checking it out and judging it to be more than suitable for our needs, Tibi took legal possession of the apartment and received the keys. He then made haste to return to Prague to inform Papa of all that had transpired.

---

4   Adolph was in Budapest on business when the Hungarians deported the Jews of Buština. He survived there by obtaining a fake Swiss passport. Margit survived many months in Birkenau, and was later liberated from the Zitau concentration camp in Germany. Ervin and Vicki survived the war together, first in Birkenau and were later liberated by the US Army in the small town of Ludwiglust. Oti was deported from Auschwitz at the same time as Andrew's father and Tibi, and was with them for some time in Munich and Allach. He was ultimately liberated by American soldiers from a German transport train in southern Germany.

Within a few days, my brother and I left Prague for Liberec to live in our new home.

My brother and I arrived in Liberec in October 1945. Due to Tibi's description of the apartment and his enthusiasm, my expectations were high and I was not disappointed. Like a child with a new toy, I could not believe that this elegant and spacious apartment was ours. I could not wait to see how pleased Papa would be.

Tibi and I ran from room to room examining every nook and cranny. We looked in every drawer, which were filled with clothing and things. We admired the crystal chandelier in the dining room and the down comforters with damask duvets in the bedrooms. The kitchen pantry was well stocked; there were dirty dishes in the sink. It was late in the afternoon and we were hungry, so Tibi suggested that we go to a café and get something to eat. There was ample food in the apartment, so I suggested that we eat at home and go to bed early. I fancied myself as having the skills of a short-order cook, so I went to the pantry with an eye to finding something to prepare. I soon announced that I had found a bag of powdered eggs and some dry crackers. I cleared the dishes out of the sink and proceeded to mix the eggs with a little water and poured the mixture into a greased frying pan. The rest is something that Tibi and I would talk about for more than the next sixty-five years. Tibi would never fail to remind me that the first "meal" I ever served him was yellow powdered paint mixed with a little water and fried to cement. Civility will not permit me to convey his reaction to the eggs. For years, it was a regular refrain: Whenever he was served a meal and was asked how it was, his standard response was, "Better than eggs."

On August 31, 1945, I registered with the Czech repatriation office under my Czech birth name, Ondrej Brandstein. As a returning political prisoner, I had the privilege of not having to wait in line when dealing with official agencies. I was always guaranteed a seat, as well as a 50-percent discount on all government-owned transportation (trains, buses and trolleys). Shortly thereafter, according to Papa's instruction, Tibi and I registered at the State Real Gymnasium of Liberec. Tibi was admitted to the seventh year, while I was admitted to the fifth year of the 1945-1946 semesters, with my student identity card issued on October 13, 1945. An admission test was administered to assess for eligibility, which was difficult for me. Prior to the war, I had first gone to a Czech public school and then, for a short time, to a Ukrainian school. Following the short episode of being in the Ukrainian school, we were occupied by Hungary and I therefore went to a Hungarian high school. Now, after having been in the fourth year of the Hungarian high school, I had to qualify for the fifth year of the Gymnasium, a much higher level grade where Russian was a required course.

Our total "wealth" consisted of the money from the sale that Tibi had made in Buština as well as money saved from my "entrepreneurship." After turning over all our funds to Papa, he gave us enough to live on while we were alone in Liberec. While in school, Tibi obtained a part-time job, stringing tennis racquets in a sporting goods store. Given his good looks and self-confidence, he also managed to become a part-time actor. Soon, Father became sufficiently well enough to leave the hospital for short trips to the city. The first thing he did was to look up some of his customers from before the war. These customers were owners of large firms and officials of the state forestry. Papa found that they were now well entrenched in the affairs of government and that some of them were holding important positions. Papa had no difficulty getting an appointment to see them and was warmly welcomed. Each official warned him about the upcoming call for all skilled businessmen to return to the city, town or village of their origin, which, for us, was Buština, which was now in the Ukraine. They further indicated that if Papa was clear of this "problem," they would be prepared to offer him the directorship of a state lumber mill near the city of Mariánské Lázně (which the Germans called Marienbad).

FROM BRANDSTEIN TO BURIAN

Fearing reprisals for not returning to our hometown, Papa decided to ensure our safety by changing our family name from Brandstein to Burian, a common action at the time for those who were in danger of being arrested by the Communist agents of Russia. He changed and duly registered our name as Burian (keeping the same initial), a name that was on billboards advertising the performances of the Czech actor Vlasta Burian. Following the official name change, I secured a new student identity and certification. The change was originally intended to be temporary, but over the years, as fate took each of us to different countries where we established ourselves at different times, we all wound up sticking with "Burian" so as not to have conflicting names.

With his newly acquired name properly documented, Papa secured his Czechoslovak citizenship papers and registered with the necessary agencies. Armed with his new identity, he met with the same officials, who, true to their word, issued him an official invitation to the position of director at the state lumber mill near Mariánské Lázně. He was to assume the post as rapidly as possible, and while it was all right for Papa to make short excursions to the city, traveling to Liberec was another matter, which, in his weakened condition, he was afraid to undertake alone. He therefore asked Tibi to come for him, which he did.

Papa's arrival in our home in Liberec was a cause for celebration. We made the apartment spotless for his arrival and stocked the pantry with food. The only thing wrong was a sour smell emanating from my attempt to make wine by fermenting bread, yeast and sugar. The concoction was bubbling and releasing an objectionable odor, but there was no need to get rid of it, as the process was in its final days. Before the weekend, I strained the murky liquid and gained a very tasty brownish liquid, which we called "bread wine." It was better than eggs!

EPILOGUE

s I described earlier, after the war, when Tibi went to visit our Great-Uncle Joseph in Nyíregyháza, I was left in Debrecen for a few days, in the care of Aunt Fanny. While there, Aunt Fanny mothered me through some very rough days and nights. I was, and still am, very fragile on the subject of my mother. Reality aside, I was still looking for my mother after the war; I hallucinated — at subway stations, as the train pulled away — that I saw my mother through the window. I was forever looking for her.

I was now fifteen and a half, and Aunt Fanny's proximity to me, as well as her mannerisms, triggered the worst nightmares I had ever experienced in my life. When Tibi returned to Debrecen, he conferred with Aunt Fanny, who described my state and insisted that I should stay with her. But when they told me of Aunt Fanny's invitation, I would not hear of it. I did not convey that I believed my nightmares were triggered by her; however, my opposition was so vehement that they accepted my contention that we were a family and that we belonged together.

While Tibi and I were living in Liberec, Aunt Vali told my mother's cousin, Giselle Goldberger, that Mordchele had survived the war with his two sons. Giselle was born in the same year as my mother, but was orphaned at a young age. As I previously explained, when her mother passed away, her father, my grandmother's brother and a very learned scholar, was not equipped to raise Giselle and her siblings on his own. Therefore, Gizi went to live with my Bruckstein grandparents in Buština and grew to become best friends with my mother.

Giselle had been deported in 1941 to Ukraine, but had managed to make her way back to Budapest, and survived the war in a refuge house provided by Raoul Wallenberg. Her father and younger sister were deported and did not survive (her older brother had moved out before the war to become a skier and did not survive either). As soon as Giselle learned that my father, my brother and I had survived the war, she immediately asked Aunt Vali to arrange to have Tibi and me sent to her. Instead, my father decided to visit her in Budapest. While there, Aunt Vali presented Papa with compelling arguments for him to marry Giselle — he already knew her well, she was a good person and she would be a good mother to Tibi and me. They quickly married in Budapest but they could not return to Czechoslovakia, as the Czechs would certainly not issue a visa to a Hungarian citizen. Therefore, Giselle took on my mother's identity and arrived in Liberec as Matilda Burian. Since she was the nearest thing to my mother as possible, it was as if an angel had come into our lives.

Sometime later, I began to attend the *yeshiva* (a Jewish institution that focuses on the study of traditional religious texts) in Marienbad, where I supplemented the allowance sent by my father with money I earned doing small repairs. I had always been extremely skillful with my hands, and would take things apart in order to learn how to put them back together — toys, typewriters, phonographs and even a motorcycle. However, the political situation was rapidly changing in Czechoslovakia, and when Tibi received his draft notice to join the security forces, my father, as a former political prisoner, insisted that he leave the country. Thus, through various and complicated ways, Father sent Tibi to Belgium, where he was promptly arrested. Father managed to buy his freedom, and Tibi then made his way over the border from Belgium to France. There, he married a wonderful Jewish girl named Therese Komar, and they settled in Lille, near her family.

One week before the Communist regime took power in Czechoslovakia, Father took me to Prague. As I previously described, the Chief Rabbi of Prague, Rabbi Forehand, who knew that his official power would be suspended by the Communists within a few days, was arranging exit papers for as many Jews as possible. Papers were arranged for me to immigrate to the United States.[1]

In early 1948, Father put me on the Orient Express, which went from Zagreb to Constantinople. One English pound was placed into the lining of my jacket, and I traveled with a single bag containing underwear and a prayer book. I was to leave the train at Ostend, Belgium, cross the Channel to England, and then try to make my way to the USA. My cousins, Oti, Ervin and Vicki, took a different path. As members of the Zionist youth movement, Hashomer Hatzair, they were determined to establish their lives in the Jewish homeland. In 1946, via a British displaced persons camp, they immigrated to the Land of Israel.[2] I was not attracted to the secular, somewhat anti-religious, dynamics of the Zionist group and was determined to return "home" and to re-establish my previous family life.

Since I was travelling without a ticket, I used an old trick: When a conductor came up and spoke to me in Russian, I would answer in German; if he asked me anything in German, I would answer in Russian. Father informed Tibi of my journey, and he and an uncle were supposed to meet me to say goodbye at a train station along the way. Instead, they got delayed due to a flat tire and wound up racing the train all the way to Ostend, with Tibi driving

---

1   Years later, my son Lawrence informed me that Rabbi Forehand was living on the Upper West Side of Manhattan and he had a *shtiebel* (a small synagogue, typically in a room of a private home) in the basement of his building. One evening, Lawrence and I stopped by and inquired as to whether I could meet Rabbi Forehand. When I explained the reason, his son immediately escorted us up to the rabbi's private living quarters where I was able to thank him personally for all that he had done for me. I was extremely happy to have had the opportunity to illuminate and praise his good deeds in front of his children, who were obviously and rightfully very proud of their father. It was a special moment.

2   After arriving in the Land of Israel, Oti, Ervin and Vicki joined the Jewish fighting forces and served in the 1948 War of Independence, during which Ervin was shot and permanently lost the use of his left arm. Their parents, Adolf and Margit, joined their sons a year later, and they all settled in Haifa. While serving in the Israeli Army reserves in 1956, Oti permanently injured his leg when his command vehicle rode over a land mine. Vicki went on to become an Israeli naval submarine officer (Chief Engineer). Adolf and Margit passed away on January 14, 1966 and February 18, 1967, respectively. Vicki passed away in 1966. All three brothers had successful careers, got married and had children. Among them, they have twenty-three grandchildren and one great-grandchild (with more on the way), most of whom live in Israel.

like a maniac. They arrived in time, but I was cordoned off with the other passengers. Tibi was only able to wave to me but he somehow also managed to throw me a bag containing a salami. It was so dramatic, like a scene from a movie!

I embarked on the SS *Prince Albert* bound for England, and I was thrilled to see the White Cliffs of Dover, about which I had read. A fellow passenger paid for my train ticket to London when it became clear to him that I had no ticket and insufficient funds. I headed to the London refugee office of the *jüdische Gemeinde*, the Jewish community, where they would give me a few shillings. The office was trying to encourage the refugees to go back to their home countries, but I knew I had to continue onward. I vividly remember how bombed out London was after the war. Also, I was unable to buy even a pair of socks because I didn't have any kind of rationing coupon. At one point, a taxi driver tried to take advantage of me and called the police when I refused to pay the fare. The policeman found a translator at a local travel agency and then paid the fare for me when he realized my background and saw the tattoo on my arm. Within a few days of being in London, I learned that I needed to make my way to Southampton if I wanted to find ship passage to America.

When I went to the train station for my trip south, I humorously thought I needed to avoid the carriages that had a "Smoking" sign, as I thought this meant I was not allowed to board without a smoking jacket. I finally found some "No Smoking" cars and boarded the train to Southampton, where I subsequently found a ship travelling to the United States. I was seventeen years old and alone on the SS *Washington*. After about a week, we finally sailed past the Statue of Liberty, which I remembered learning about in school, and came into the port of New York. However, when I tried to disembark from the ship, I was not allowed to do so. I had a passport and a visa, but as of March 1, my Czech passport was no longer valid.

Three uniformed men in leather jackets took several of us in a car. We didn't know where we were headed. Then, suddenly, the car got a flat tire, and as the men were changing it, we sat on a bench in what I now know was Battery Park, watching the people milling around. It was a brilliant sunny day. Once the tire was changed, we were driven to the ferry station and put on a boat to a refugee center on Ellis Island. I got very nervous when we sailed past the Statue of Liberty, as I thought I was being sent back to Europe. At the refugee center, we were given soap and a towel and told to rest on metal bunks. There were signs in many languages cautioning people about diseases and giving information on medical matters. I exchanged my single English pound and received six dollars! At a fruit and vegetable cart, I took an apple, bit into it, and was then told it cost ten cents. I could have lived for a week in Czechoslovakia on that amount of money! I had learned an important lesson: Don't bite into anything before knowing the cost.

Since I requested kosher food at the refugee center, I was put in touch with the group Jewish Women Lawyers for New Americans, which had some connection with HIAS — the Hebrew Immigrant Aid Society. I had a referral to the Mesivtah Torah Veda'as *yeshiva* in Brooklyn, as well as the name and address of my mother's first cousin, Sam Brochenstein.[3] However, in order to be released from the refugee center, I had to go before a judge. The organization of lawyers found me an interpreter, and he took care of everything. Instead of translating for me what the judge was actually saying, he just told me to say anything and he would "translate" back to the judge whatever needed to be said. It was funny but effective. I believe my cousin, Sam, also posted some sort of bond for me. I was finally released and I made my way back to Battery Park, where I had to deal with taking the subway and finding my way to the *yeshiva* in Brooklyn. I remember buying a token for the subway, dropping it in the slot, and then pushing the turnstile forward until it clicked. I didn't realize that I needed to walk through and I was forced to buy another token. That was my second economics lesson. The word "Brooklyn" on a piece of paper was insufficient directions, but with some help from a friendly passerby and a few wrong turns, wrong trains and several hours later, I finally arrived at the *yeshiva* on South Third Street. The staff there pointed me to a bulletin board with signs for rooms to let and I found a room, which was more like a closet, on South Second Street. The landlady, Mrs. Kleiner, was charging sixteen dollars a month for a small room and a *glaizele tey* (glass of tea) whenever I wanted.

---

3   Sam was the US-born son of Miriam Bruckstein, the sister of the author's maternal grandfather, Yisroel Natan Bruckstein. Miriam married Joseph Bruchenstein. It was considered at the time a family scandal that Joseph did not wear a beard and that the couple decided to move to the US in the late 1800s. Miriam and Joseph returned from the US to visit Buština in 1925 for a family reconciliation. The author has in his possession several cherished photographs from that family reunion.

I did not stay more than a day at the *yeshiva*, and instead decided to enquire about finding a job. For my first job, I was paid forty-five cents an hour tying bundles in a factory that manufactured bras and girdles. I was a cutter's helper but I had no interest in trying to join the union and become a cutter. Soon thereafter, I landed a job fixing machines. The owner of the establishment asked me where and for whom I had apprenticed in Europe. It turned out that he had known well my former boss in Europe and therefore hired me immediately. Since I was skilled in fixing European machines even without the available parts, for which there was a great demand, I made what seemed like a lot of money. Thus, I lived very well for a kid — I bought a used jeep, then a new car and clothing, but I did not spend freely or wildly. I sent money to my parents and brother and bought my first stock. I worked long hours and was paid for every machine that I fixed; there were always more to fix.

I remember from that time that I had a very good Italian friend who drove a delivery truck and would take me home to his family. Since I ate only kosher food, his mother would go out of her way to find food that I could eat. Sometimes we would go to a bar where I would drink a beer and eat free peanuts. Other than him, my friendships were superficial.

The separation from my father and brother was very difficult. Today, I still have a beautiful postcard sent to me by my father from Czechoslovakia. On the front, it has a photograph of the beautiful Czech mountainside with my father's then home underlined by him with a pen. On the back, it reads: "I'm sitting in the room, thinking of, imagining my life. I could enjoy the place, if you, "My Life," were here. But I will not lose hope and I believe that the good God will help us, that somehow we will be together. The building underlined (in the picture) is where I live. With warm love. Sending kisses and hugs, Your Daddy." We were not apart for long.

Meanwhile, back in Europe, my father was offered an extremely attractive opportunity to become the head of multiple lumber mills. The only condition was that he would be required to join the Communist Party. Instead, he picked up and left everything. He left the key to the apartment with a letter of appreciation, deposited sufficient funds to pay all taxes, recommended a foreman to take over the mills and wrote a note to the government explaining that he needed to rejoin his children. He and Gizi traveled as displaced persons and wound up in a DP camp in Salzburg, Austria.

In the meantime, I myself received a government notice that my visa had expired and that I was required to leave the United States. With the help of the Jewish Women Lawyers group, I pleaded my case at hearing after hearing. I did much of my own research in the public library and built the argument that it was too dangerous for me to return to Czechoslovakia. Finally, a postcard arrived assigning me as "DP #82" and the deportation notices stopped coming.

In 1950, I came up with the "brilliant" idea that I should join the American Army. I figured that I could volunteer to be sent to Austria where I could try to assist my father and Gizi. I started the paperwork, and when the Korean war broke out a sergeant came looking for me at my apartment. Thankfully, both Mrs. Kleiner and the sergeant convinced me not to enlist.

Three years after my arrival in the US, in 1951, Father and Giselle obtained the correct papers and arrived in New York. I was proud to be able to pick them up at the port in my own car, and I took them to a two-bedroom apartment I had found for the three of us in the Bronx, where I had filled the refrigerator for them. It was as if I had been reborn after they arrived. Father pressed me to return to school, but I wanted to work, so we compromised on night school. I attended the Theodore Roosevelt High School at night and won many prizes for excellence. I was even accepted for admission at both The Cooper Union and Rensselaer Polytechnic Institute (with a scholarship). But I felt (probably mistakenly) that I needed to work, and despite my father's and Gizi's encouragement, turned down the opportunities.

One day, a young man came up to me on the streetcar and greeted me enthusiastically. It took me a few seconds to recognize him. It was my friend, Michael Ruvel, who was about six months older than me. His tattooed number was four or five numbers higher than mine, meaning that towards the end of 1944 when we were tattooed, he was behind me by just a few men. Since the last time we had met, he had lost his entire family and had arrived in the US as the adopted son of an American soldier. I was thrilled to meet Michael again, whom I regarded as a brother, but I still missed Tibi.

In 1959, while I was living in the Bronx, I was set up on a blind date with a young woman from Brooklyn, which was a rarity in those days for an immigrant like me. I fell in love with Ruth at first sight, and still remember her standing in front of me in her salmon-colored dress with a big bow and introducing herself. She saw me as a dashing European man (all her other dates were boys) and I saw her as a smart, beautiful, innocent, fun-loving girl from a wonderful family. I married my sweetheart, Ruth Yellen Allerhand, who completed my life. We were married on Thanksgiving weekend in 1960 and we have a wonderful life, very much like the one I would have had if I were "home" — a life lived with morals, standards, beliefs and love.

POSTSCRIPT

I have been married to the beautiful Ruth Yellen Allerhand for more than fifty years. We raised three wonderful children who are each married and have children of their own. Our eldest and only daughter, Matilda, is married to Marvin Anhalt; our son, Saul, is married to Jennifer Gross; and our youngest son, Lawrence, is married to Adina Schainker. I am blessed with fifteen fabulous grandchildren: Arielle, Adam, Daina, Kenny, Yael, Atara, Jordan, Michael, Matthew, Lauren, Jason, Jonah, Ethan, Adam and Erin. Just writing their names brings me great pleasure! I include in my list of grandchildren the spouse of my eldest grandchild, Arielle, the fiancée of my grandson, Kenny, and the two children of Saul's wife, Jennifer. I love each of them like my natural grandchildren. We were recently blessed with a great-granddaughter, Sydney. My heart is overflowing with joy and gratitude. Please God, I look forward to welcoming more grandchildren into the family through marriage and to many more great-grandchildren. My *machatonim* (my children's in-laws), the Anhalts and the Schainkers, have become both family and friends. My entire family is a precious gift and a miracle. They embrace me with their love and we support and sustain each other. There is nothing more important or more valuable to me than my family.

We have done well in the United States. While I value the impressive personal and professional accomplishments of each of my children and grandchildren, I am most proud that each of them embodies the words of my father, spoken to me as we were separated in Birkenau: "No matter what," he said, "be a *mensch*, and come home to the family." My children and grandchildren continue my parents' legacy. They are wonderful, good people who care deeply for each other and for their heritage. My father and Gizi loved and were very proud of each one who was born during their lifetimes and our additions would have further enriched their lives.

When I married Ruthie on November 23, 1960, I not only got the girl of my dreams but I also entered into an extended American family that had not experienced the Holocaust and was not haunted by destructive recurring visions of unimaginable horror. Laughter, optimism and religious commitment reentered my life. The embrace of a large and confident family accelerated my healing process, reduced my flashbacks and helped ease my longing and mourning for my mother.

After Ruthie and I were married, we lived in Brooklyn, round the corner from Ruthie's parents and siblings, Hershel, Judie and Joseph, and close to my father and stepmother. My in-laws, Ida and Irving Allerhand, were warm and loving as well as pillars of their community, who treated me like a son, and I loved and respected both of them. Matilda was born a year after our marriage and Saul two years later. We fell into a rhythm that centered on family and holidays, creating new traditions and making new friends. We had fun and I began to relax. I still kept a gun at home, just in case, but it was hidden away. My friend Michael Ruvel often ate with us on Friday nights. Our discussions were disturbing but necessary.

In 1969, we moved to Long Beach, a relatively small seaside community where the air is clean and our kids could enjoy grass, trees and a gorgeous boardwalk and beach. I like consistency and Ruthie cannot believe that we still live in the same house after more than forty-five years. Lawrence was born after our move to Long Beach and our nuclear family became complete. Long Beach was, and still is, a wonderful place to raise children and Ruthie and I made lifelong friends there. We divided our time between the synagogues of Young Israel and Bachurei Chemed and I was active in various types of communal affairs. I also became an avid sailor. I love the calm of sailing, the beauty of the ocean and the harmony with nature that fills the sails. Sailing also draws upon my natural resourcefulness.

We live a wonderful, American, modern Orthodox Jewish life. We have a home in Jerusalem, which brings us both practical and ideological pleasure (probably more the latter) and a home in Florida where we now spend our winters. We continue to celebrate most holidays together with Ruthie's extended family and watch our children, grandchildren and now great-grandchild grow up together. On Passover, I love how Ruthie, together with her sister, feeds *matzoh brie* (the way I remember it from home) to armies of children, nieces, nephews, in-laws and cousins, and *matzoh* pizza (the way nobody in Buština could have ever imagined!). I love playing with the new babies and watching the extended families of Hershel and Liz, Judie and Eddie and Joseph and Randi all mix with our immediate families, as the kids forge bonds that will hold forever.

I used to love our long family drives down to Florida (yes, we used to drive), together with our neighbors, the Schwartzsteins, for vacation. I've always enjoyed experiencing the open road, including passing through the Georgia cotton fields, and then, on arrival, playing with our children in the pool. There is nothing quite like the hilarious family memories that come from spending quality time together, and we have some terrific stories. Ruthie and I have taken fabulous vacations together all over the world and when we're home, we enjoy participating in various social and charitable events. I do not think I can ever adequately thank Ruthie for the beautiful and joyous life she created for us.

My family, the Brucksteins and the Brandsteins, were decimated by the Holocaust.[4] I was only thirteen when we were separated; those who survived and their descendants are scattered around the world. Recently, we had a gathering of some of my Bruckstein cousins and their families. It was an emotional and heartwarming experience.

I lived with my father and stepmother in an apartment in the Bronx from

---

4   The author described in detail the separation and loss of his mother, grandfather and great-uncle in Auschwitz-Birkenau. In addition to his many aunts and uncles who also perished during the Holocaust (see the family tree on pp. 14-15), the author lost many of his first cousins. The Bruckstein family lost Aunt Rela's daughter, Kathy (her two sons, Geza and Mutzu, survived). The Brandstein family lost Uncle Jeno's son, Imre (his daughters, Lilly, Vera and Cuna, survived); Uncle Izidor's daughter, Kato (his daughters, Aliza and Mania, survived); Uncle Jozsi's daughter, Marta (his daughter, Agnus, survived); Aunt Helen's son, Laci; and Aunt Margit's daughter, Edith, and son, Ervin (her son, Yankush, survived). The author tragically lost many more members of his extended family. May this memoir forever provide to those who perished a 'memorial and a name' (*yad vashem*; Isaiah 56:5).

the time they arrived in America until I got married. In 1952, Tibor and his wife, Therese, came to live in America. Tibi and I even purchased and operated together a gas station and auto repair shop for a time. Unfortunately, Tibi and Therese needed to return to France when Therese's mother became critically ill. They have two children, Mathilde and Marc. Mathilde has three children: Tal (married to Marie-Charlotte), Ouri (married to Karine) and Tamar; and six grandchildren: Leonore, Jean-Baptiste, Edouard, Mina, Lison and Lola. Marc and his spouse, Laurence Wallach, are blessed with three children: David, Charlie and Elliott. Both Tibi's Mathilde and my Matilda are named after our saintly mother. I am not able to express the deep and conflicted feelings of love, gratitude and, sometimes, sadness, that their names evoke.

It was difficult for my father and Gizi to adjust to America. However, with inner strength and courage, they made a life for themselves, first in the Bronx and then in Brooklyn. Our kids loved to visit them and my parents often joined us for weekends and holidays in Long Beach. Gizi was the perfect grandmother — baking the kids' favorite cookies, teaching them silly Hungarian songs and cooking elaborate meals. She never had children of her own and showered all her love and energy into her "adorable" and "perfect" grandchildren. A lasting memory for my children is Gizi talking to all her plants and flowers while watering them, and explaining that all living things deserve respect, have feelings and want to be loved. My father had deep pride and satisfaction at what we all created out of the dust of the Holocaust. He and Gizi lived their final years in Long Beach. For several months, my father lived with Tibi and Therese in France, which was a great opportunity to spend meaningful time with them. My father passed away on September 27, 1989, just shy of his ninetieth birthday. Gizi passed away on October 23, 2006, at the age of 100.

All his life, my brother called me almost daily and visited frequently. Although we were separated by an ocean, no two brothers could have been closer, and Ruthie was a true sister to Tibi and Therese. Tibi became a leading and extremely successful manufacturer of textiles in Europe. He would frequently tell me how he was determined to restore the reputation and stature of our family. He both built a *mikvah* (ritual bath) in memory of our mother and commissioned a Torah scroll in memory of our father, both for the Jewish community of Lille. Tibi also traveled to Buština and paid for the upkeep of the abandoned cemetery. Three years before his death on January 23, 2012 (at the age of eighty-three), Tibi became a citizen of the State of Israel. Tibi cherished his Israeli passport. He finally found his home.

I am very proud that all three of my children and all of my grandchildren attended, or attend, modern Orthodox *yeshiva* day schools. The quality Jewish and secular education that they receive, or received, emphasizes the responsibility and beauty of Jewish life, American citizenship, constructive engagement with the world and love and respect for all people. In both school and at summer camp, our children made great friends and developed pride in their Judaism and love for the State of Israel. I am very proud that all three of my children have graduate degrees and that Ruthie and I were able to fund their full educations. Our grandchildren are similarly achieving terrific academic success. Educating our children was always of primary importance to us. I am grateful that my in-laws, in their quiet and modest manner, helped us along the way.

I can never repay what the United States of America has done for me. Her sons liberated me from hell, her institutions opened their doors to me and her government and citizens provided a level playing field where anyone willing to work hard could succeed. Where else could a homeless immigrant teenager, who did not speak the language, grow to live, thrive and prosper with a successful career and have his children and grandchildren educated in the country's finest institutions and succeed professionally? Even my dad became successful at investing in the stock market. I am living proof of the "American dream," and I am proud to be an American.

As my family, thank God, continues to grow, it is very meaningful to me that I have children and grandchildren who carry Hebrew names in memory of my mother, grandfather or great-uncle, who walked arm-in-arm to the gas chambers, or in memory of my father or Gizi. I try to do my part to help educate the younger generations about the Holocaust and regularly speak publicly about my experiences. This book, I hope, will contribute to that effort. My children and grandchildren are engaged on many fronts in their communities, and are actively committed to the cause of Holocaust education and the passionate continuity of the Jewish people. It warms my heart to feel the respect and love I receive from each of them and I cherish the ability to share with them my life story personally.

Today, I wear a brand-new Tissot watch that was gifted to me by my son, Lawrence, at the same time that he gifted one to his eldest son on the joint occasion of my grandson's *bar mitzvah* and my second *bar mitzvah* (at the age of eighty-three). The Nazis confiscated my first Tissot *bar mitzvah* watch…but seventy years later the Nazis are gone and my grandson and I wear our watches with pride.

I look back at the indescribable horrors and devastation of the Holocaust. Notwithstanding the years, the pain remains real and present. However, the beauty and success of the life Ruthie and I were able to create in the United States of America, the miracle of the creation of the State of Israel and the love and pride I feel from and for the family that we have created together are a remarkable consolation for all that I have suffered.

On December 12, 2015, my eighty-fifth birthday fell on a unique day that was the Sabbath of the festival of *Hanukkah* as well as *Rosh Chodesh* (a new month). The following day, Ruthie and I celebrated in our home, surrounded by our extended families — the Burians, Allerhands, Boims, Anhalts, Brenners and Schainkers. Who could have imagined this back in 1944? It is a miracle. I am supremely blessed.

* * *

I am no longer young. At some point in the future, I will stand next to my mother in heaven and look down on what Ruthie and I have accomplished. We will hug, kiss and cry. My father, Gizi and Tibi will join us. The tears may start as tears of sadness and loss, but will quickly change to tears of joy and satisfaction. With love and perseverance, we have flourished and succeeded. We have raised a new generation of committed, successful and responsible Jews living in freedom and security. My mother will be proud of me.

Speech by Andrew's children to their father on the occasion of his eighty-fifth birthday, December 13, 2015

Dad,

Growing up we used to have a poster hanging in the kitchen. It read "Children Learn What They Live." In thinking about your eighty-fifth birthday, that poster came to mind. We learned these, things from you:

Because you treated your father and Gizi with true *kibud av v'em*, love and respect, you gave us both a grandfather and a grandmother to cherish and adore;

Because you treated Mom's parents, Ida and Irving, much the same way, you taught us what it means to care for and respect both our own parents and our in-laws;

Because you cherished your brother, Tibi, and loved Therese, you kept the family ties close despite the miles that divide us. You taught us what it means to appreciate, value and protect family without excuses of language barriers or distance;

Because of your commitment to Judaism, you taught us what it means to hold on to tradition despite any and all logical reason to abandon faith;

Because you pursued your love of sailing, you taught us the value of finding what you love and finding peace in doing what you love;

We are not sure what vegetarian *chulent*, raw herring or dipping *challah* into scotch taught us, but we are sure we are the beneficiaries of a somewhat eclectic palate;

Because you have a special way of doing things, and can fix literally anything, we learned many "old Czechoslovakian tricks" to pass on to our children;

Because you built a new life after losing everything and yet were able to bring your old life alive for us, you taught us the value of appreciating our roots while looking forward to the future;

Because you stand strong and relive your story over and over for the benefit of an unknown audience, you, again and again, teach us strength. The simple knowledge that you stand behind us gave us strength when we needed it and continues to give us confidence everyday that there is strength within each of us if we ever should need to be strong again;

Because you value hard work and education, deal honestly, and live a clean, moral life, you taught us the simple value of being a *mensch*;

Mostly because you and Mommy are the most wonderful, loving, generous parents, grandparents and great-grandparents, you taught us how to love and raise our own families.

You did everything your father asked of you.

You valued home, you lived a clean life and you stayed a *mensch*.

Your parents would both be very proud.

Moreover, we are very proud.

Happy eighty-fifth birthday Daddy.

We love you,

— Matilda, Saul, and Lawrence